# INTRANETS

# INTRANETS

Steven J. Vaughan-Nichols

AP PROFESSIONAL

*AP PROFESSIONAL is a Division of Academic Press, Inc.*

Boston    San Diego    New York
London    Sydney    Tokyo    Toronto

# AP PROFESSIONAL

*An Imprint of ACADEMIC PRESS, INC.*
*A Division of HARCOURT BRACE & COMPANY*

ORDERS (USA and Canada): 1-800-3131-APP or APP@ACAD.COM
AP PROFESSIONAL Orders: 6277 Sea Harbor Dr., Orlando, FL 32821-9816

Europe/Middle East/Africa: 0-11-44 (0) 181-300-3322
Orders: AP PROFESSIONAL 24-28 Oval Rd., London NW1 7DX

Japan/Korea: 03-3234-3911-5
Orders: Harcourt Brace Japan, Inc., Ichibancho Central Building 22-1, Ichibancho Chiyoda-Ku, Tokyo 102

Australia: 02-517-8999
Orders: Harcourt Brace & Co. Australia, Locked Bag 16, Marrickville, NSW 2204 Australia

Other International: (407) 345-3800
AP PROFESSIONAL Orders: 6277 Sea Harbor Dr., Orlando FL 32821-9816

Editorial: 1300 Boylston St., Chestnut Hill, MA 02167 (617)232-0500

Web: http://www.apnet.com/approfessional

*United Kingdom Edition published by*
ACADEMIC PRESS LIMITED
24–28 Oval Road, London NW1 7DX

ISBN: 0-12-518045-4

Printed in the United States of America
96 97 98 99 IP 9 8 7 6 5 4 3 2 1

*To Betty Jean Richards, Promises Made, Promises Kept*

# CONTENTS

## Contents

# Preface

## In the Beginning

New ideas don't spring forth like Athena from Zeus' forehead. The idea for this book had been running through my mind for years. Indeed, long before anyone knew what an intranet was, I was writing lines like: "The WEB is potentially the most powerful automated information-gathering tool in existence" in the Web's first mention in a mainstream publication (*Computer Shopper*, April 1993) and, years earlier, in *Byte* magazine: "Interoperability is the golden grail of computing." But intranetting itself? Nah. I was nibbling around the edges; but I didn't get the idea itself until everyone else did.

What I know now, and some people are still missing, is that the intranet concept is the most important technical development that business has stumbled across in the last decade. The Internet and the Web, both of which are vital parts of intranetting, are on the front pages of *The New York Times*, *The Washington Post*, and the *Wall Street Journal* almost every day. Microsoft and NBC, in one of the most perverse marriages of media and advertising ever, have launched a combined television and Internet/Web news network, MSNBC. All these changes will be dwarfed by what happens when intranets turn the separate blows of Internet and Web into a powerful, one-two combination. Don't believe me? Skip ahead to the meatier chapters and you'll see why.

Books also don't simply spring from a writer's fingers. Mind you, we wish that they did, but they don't. Instead, we depend on the help of others to get the work done. So, without further adieu, here's to my inhouse editor, fellow writer at Vaughan-Nichols & Associates and one of my best friends, Rachel Schmutter. Without her, my work would be far the poorer. I'd also like to thank Esther Schindler, who convinced me that there was gold in them there books; Mark Van Name, for showing me the ropes of the writing game; Barbara Jackson-Jewell, for keeping the Vaughan-Nichols & Associates paperwork from burying Vaughan-Nichols & Associates; and Heidi Petty, my part-time partner, who showed me that you can change your life with enough grit and determination.

Finally, I also must thank my seven-year old daughter Alicia. I'm not just doing so because she's the light of my life, although she is. I'm doing so because without her, I would have remained a blaze of talent and potential without focus. Because she's in my life, I went from being a brilliant dilettante to that rarest of creatures, a full-time writer. Thanks, kid; I couldn't have done it without you.

# Introduction

## Everything Old is New Again: Intranets

Intranets are hotter than hot, newer than tomorrow, the greatest thing since sliced bread. Sound familiar? You've read the hype, now here's the reality. First, intranets are indeed wildly popular and they're only going to get more so. As you read on, you'll find out why intranets are white-hot. Believe it or not, no business that aspires beyond the neighborhood grocery store level will be able to finish out the '90s without an intranet. As for the rest of it, forget it: Intranets are old news. Heck, they're the original news of networking.

I've been in this biz for a long, long time; but even when I started back in the mid-'70s, Transmission Control Protocol and Internet Protocol (TCP/IP) was binding networks together. Not much has changed. An intranet is simply a local area network (LAN) that uses TCP/IP as its networking protocols. The first network—ARPAnet, the Internet's progenitor—was using this and Ethernet, TCP/IP's medium of choice, since 1969. That's years before Novell's intranet-oriented IPX/SPX stalked the network wire, and decades before Microsoft came up with NetBEUI.

Why is it only now that intranets are becoming exciting? There are several reasons. First, TCP/IP vendors didn't have clue one about marketing. NetWare was everyone's NOS of choice not because it was inherently better than TCP/IP, but because Novell made you want to buy the product. While Novell was making billions in the '80s, TCP/IP was sitting unused in dusty corners of many a stockroom.

Next, until the Internet became popular—which I will explain momentarily—no one saw the potential of using TCP/IP to build an intranet. Once it became clear how versatile a tool the Internet could be, people everywhere woke up and smelled the TCP/IP coffee. Then, they realized how much more useful the intranet model was than proprietary networking systems; and the intranet stampede was on.

## No Miracles

A lot of business books will tell you how being a 30-second manager or adopting Windows for Plumbing will transform your business: Bullshit. Businesses change because you and your people grab a new idea and put the time and effort into making it work for you.

It's the same thing with intranets. Simply sticking the hardware and software in and switching it on won't help your business one darn bit. If that's your approach, the only change you'll see is that your out-of-pocket expenses will have jumped like a jackrabbit with a coyote on its tail. To make an intranet work, everyone in the company is going to have to learn not just how to cruise the net or how to send a memo, but how to use these techniques to do their job better.

Some changes will come easily. If you've been riding the technology wave at all, you already know how to use e-mail. The differences between proprietary systems like Microsoft Mail or Lotus' cc:Mail and Internet-based mail are significant, but no one's going to get heartburn over them. Learning from groupware programs like Netscape's Collabra is another matter entirely. Also, wasting time on the Web can be an almost incurable disease. Before you dismiss intranets as another excuse for employees to be wasting time, though, consider that the former VP of marketing for Netscape Communications, Mike Homer, said "we get more than 70% of our revenue from internal corporate networks." That's a lot of money that your competitors are shelling out, and it's not just for letting their employees play Doom.

To benefit from an intranet requires hard work, education, time, and last but far from least, a commitment from the top down, that you're going to fundamentally change how your company works. If you're willing to pay these costs, then you can reap the benefits of an intranet. If you expect to find magic, forget about intranets—try J.R.R. Tolkien instead.

So how did TCP/IP, which any LAN expert in the '80s would have told you was as likely to win the networking races as a half-dead horse, suddenly become the backbone of the hottest networking trend around? Here's the story. It won't help you a bit with the technical side of setting up an intranet; but there is a moral to this story that today's intranet business planner should take to heart: Always keep an eye on the big political and business pictures. In the end, these are more important than TCP/IP standards and who's signed a deal with Netscape today.

# The AT&T Breakup

On the stroke of midnight back on January 1, 1974, telecommunications changed forever when the government broke up AT&T into the seven Baby Bells. The immediate result was that AT&T was left with long-distance, and the Regional Bell Operation Companies (RBOCs) got local services. That was only the beginning.

No one was shocked with AT&T's breakup. A changing marketplace and increasing government deregulation had been hammering at AT&T with various legal challenges and failed attempts at federal strictures for decades. Finally, in 1974, the Department of Justice filed a successful antitrust suit against AT&T. As a regulated monopoly, AT&T argued that it had to partake in actions which would otherwise be subject to antitrust law. In 1978, Judge Harold Greene of the US District Court for the District of Columbia took over the case. Little did anyone know what Greene would do when the case came into his hands. By January 8, 1982, AT&T and the Justice Department finally reached a revolutionary settlement; and on August 24, 1982, Judge Greene approved the settlement, known as the Modification of Final Judgment (MFJ).

With the MFJ, Justice Department agreed to drop the 1974 antitrust suit. AT&T was required to divest itself of local telephone operations, retaining only long-distance service, with each step to be approved by the court. Notice the stinger on the end? In effect, what the MFJ did was to make all of AT&T's plans subject to the court's—specifically,

Judge Greene's— approval. Greene had become the czar of telecommunications deregulation and would have more influence over telecommunications in the United States than any AT&T or RBOC president.

Under Greene's guidance, AT&T was slowly melted down from what was once the largest monopoly this country had ever seen. We all know the immediate results. A small amount of competition sprang up between the RBOCs; but for the most part, they were content to reap the profits from their individual territories. On the long-distance side, AT&T, which had once supplied long distance for everyone in the country, now found itself beset on all sides by aggressive, fast-moving companies like MCI and Sprint.

Less obvious to all was that throughout this period, the TCP/IP-based Internet was allowed to grow without interference in its academic, military, and research hothouses. So it was that Greene's dictatorship over the telephone industry enabled the Internet to flourish rather than be stomped out as potential competition by the telephone monopoly.

## The Internet & The Businessman

In 1991, the Commercial Internet Exchange (CIX) consortium was formed to make some business sense out of the then wild, woolly, and effectively unregulated Internet. The CIX was created by the Internet service providers behind AlterNet, CERFnet, and PSInet, three major Internet providers who were more than happy to supply business services. Their goal was to create a system by which commercial traffic could flow freely through the Internet.

In that, they were successful. After their intervention, a business in Pasadena, California, could use ftp to get to its accounting records in Bangor, Maine. This inadvertently created the expectation that other Internet/Usenet services could also be used for such commercial purposes as selling goods or services.

CIX enabled people to run commercial connections over the Internet without worrying about the Acceptable Use Policies (AUPs) that had thus far made the Internet a pain in the net for business networking. AUPs, which had been established by the government, military, and academic communities, made it almost impossible to run any sort of business enterprise over the Internet. If you set up an Internet site that had pricing lists for your goods, you'd soon find that the people who were in control of all the connections to your site had made it impossible for anyone to get there. With CIX, however, any enterprise could use the Internet for commercial traffic and rest assured that their business mail wouldn't be frozen out by a section of the Internet which wouldn't pass their mail along simply because their site's name ended in ".com."

Suddenly, businesses could send mail and files around the world without dealing with the major financial obligations of wide area networks (WANs) based on dedicated T1 or X.25 lines. That was only the first step.

The vast majority of Windows-based computers still had trouble hooking up with the Internet. For Unix workstation users and university users content with their X-terminals hooked up to minicomputers, this wasn't a problem at all. In fact, they rather liked it that way, since it kept the Internet firmly in the hands of people to whom, instead of French, German, and Greek, grep, sed, and awk were the foreign languages of choice.

# Desktop Connection

Of course, by that time, the 10-year-old PC standard had won over the desktops of most businesses and home users. These folks, who may well have included you, made up more than 80% of the single-user computer audience. Most of them had as much chance of hooking onto the Internet as you would hitching a ride on the space shuttle.

Part of the problem was that there were more flavors of TCP/IP than Baskin-Robbins had flavors of ice cream, each of which got along as well with the other types as pistachio goes with strawberry. Worse, there was no standard for connecting applications to the network. So it was that you had to have just the right application for just the right TCP/IP stack, or your Windows program would just blithely sit there and flash error messages at you till the sun went down. For most people, the answer to this was the WinSock standard.

WinSock, an open standard created by the industry consortium, used Unix's Berkeley Standard Distribution (BSD) sockets as a quick, easy way to let WinSock-compliant applications speak with WinSock-compliant TCP/IP successfully.

This problem wasn't just limited to PC fans. Macintosh users were also stuck. Because the Macintosh operating system makes it impossible to build unsupported applications, Mac users struggled to make the connection between their LocalTalk networks and the Internet. Apple saw the problem and introduced MacTCP. This TCP/IP network stack was sold as an extra to early versions of the MacOS. System 7.5 and up have MacTCP as an Apple-supplied option to the operating system. So for Mac users, getting net connectivity is little more than a matter of shoving the MacTCP icon into the control panel and filling out the appropriate Internet information.

The stage was set. The Internet was growing in popularity like a Kennedy in the '60s. WinSock and MacTCP made it possible to build applications that would work with the appropriate TCP/IP stack.

# Days of Change: The Web and Mosaic

The tinder was all in place; but the fire didn't really start until Tim Berners-Lee, a British computer programmer working at the European Nuclear Physics Lab—CERN, to give it its better known European abbreviation—combined hypermedia with the Internet's vast information resources to create what we now know as the World Wide Web. Berners-Lee was trying to find a way for scientists to share information across the Internet in an easy, accessible manner. His first proposal dates back to March 1989; but the first character-based browser, the not very inspiringly named www, didn't make it on to the net until January 1992; and no one was really using it until late that year.

Before the Web, you could do a thousand interesting things on the Internet, but none of them easily. In essence, the Web was the prototype for a worldwide string of computer databases using a common information retrieval architecture. With the Web, it didn't matter whether the information you needed was next door or in the next country. The Web gave you a way to find that information no matter where it was hidden.

Say, for instance, that you wanted to see if a copy of this book was in the Library of Congress. For a net expert, that didn't pose much of a problem: He would just set his gopher client to connect with the gopher server at rs5.loc.gov. For anyone else, of course, the job was almost hopeless. Not only did you need to know how to run gopher—which, by Internet program standards, was a very simple program—but you also needed to know the Internet address for the Library of Congress' gopher. It was enough to make users tear out their hair.

Furthermore, before the Web, to use the Internet's information resources, you had to be a Unix wizard. Unix is the operating system that underlies the Internet. That was fine, if you were a Unix wizard; but most people weren't and still aren't.

In 1989, working at CERN in Geneva, Switzerland, Berners-Lee faced the eternal problem of getting people the information they needed to work together effectively on many projects in real time. His solution was to use hypertext technology to form a web of documents. Unlike books or many databases, there was no hierarchical structure to this information web. Instead, there were many possible connections between documents without a beginning or an end. The messy details of how this information was linked was hidden by a character-based hypertext interface. With the Web, a physicist could jump from an article on quantum physics in Geneva to a biography of Richard Feynman, the famous American physicist, on a system at Cal State with less trouble than you would have paging to this book's index and then back to its first reference to the Web.

Of course, in order for the Web to work, documents had to be written in a special format that enabled the hypertext links to work. This format is called Hypertext Markup Language (HTML). HTML is a subset—some would say a bastard subset—of Standard Generalized Markup

Language (SGML). SGML is an International Standards Organization (ISO) standard for defining formatting in text documents. Primarily, SGML is meant for desktop publishing. Berners-Lee and friends seized upon its hyperlink capacity to form the basis of the first Web documents.

To access these first strands of the Web, people used a line-based Web browser. This interface was so simple that it couldn't even use a full-screen character interface. To get to it, you would telnet to either of the first two WEB servers: info.cern.ch or nxo01.cern.ch. This first version, which you ran with the login "www," had only two commands: "start a search" and "follow a link." Not much for the start of the new information revolution!

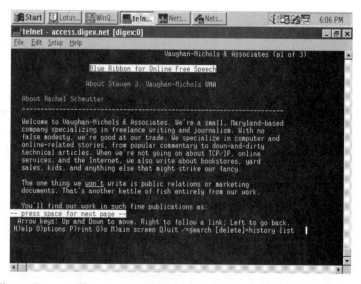

**Figure Intro.1**: The newest version of www is more sophisticated than its ancestor, but not by much. At first glance, this view of the Web doesn't look very interesting at all. But, if you take a look at Figure Intro.2...

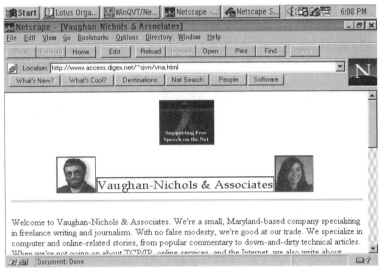

**Figure Intro.2:** ...you'll see how Netscape gives an entirely different and more exciting view of the same resource.

That may not sound like much; but the difference was phenomenal. For the first time, users could seek information without worrying about its location, or what key to use to unlock the information. At first, since much of the data that the Web dealt with wasn't in hypertext format, the advantage was clear. Then, the Web often came across as simply another Internet data hunting tool with a more consistent interface.

The result was that while the Web did grow, it grew very slowly. In those days, if you asked Internet information jockeys what was hot in net information retrieval, chances are most of them would have mentioned Wide Area Information Servers (WAIS). What changed the Web from being an interesting but neglected part of the Internet to being the hottest news in the net ever was Mosaic.

No one set out with a plan to build an interface that would free the power of the Web. Instead, Mosaic began as a project by Marc Andreessen, a graduate student at the University of Illinois at Urbana-Champaign (UIUC). In 1993, Andreessen faced the same problems at his part-time job at the National Center for Supercomputing Applications (NCSA) that Berners-Lee had dealt with at CERN—many people working on many projects at once who needed to share information. Specifically, Andreessen was working on tools for scientific visualization.

In the course of working towards that goal, Andreessen began building Mosaic. At first, Andreessen didn't even know of the Web's existence. Not being one to reinvent the wheel, Andreessen searched for existing solutions, and found the Web. Once he discovered the Web's power, he began turning Mosaic into a Web browser.

Even using the existing Web, building Mosaic was not an easy task. Fortunately, Andreessen was joined by Eric Bina, who helped develop the prototype. In April of 1993—yes, that recently—the first version of Mosaic, Mosaic 1.0 for the X Window System, appeared. The program took off like a Concord jet, and the Web's popularity flourished with it. Why? Because, while Mosaic didn't really bring anything new in functionality to Web interfaces, it did bring together the best ideas of existing programs and give them an attractive, easy-to-use interface.

If Andreessen and the NCSA had been Microsoft, you would have heard of Mosaic months in advance of its actual arrival. Instead, what happened was that Mosaic's popularity boomed within the confines of the Internet. The NCSA, a nonprofit government agency, was stuck in the odd position of having an extremely popular product without any intention of marketing it. Programs made at NCSA were freeware programs "for academic, research, and internal business purposes only." Despite the lack of marketing, the new look and feel which Mosaic gave the Web caused the program to spread like wildfire. (The fact that it was free didn't hurt, either.)

It didn't take long for the NCSA to realize that, part of its mission or not, Mosaic was fantastically popular and needed some support. As a result, NCSA set student workers to developing Windows and Macintosh versions of Mosaic. These programs were released in the early autumn of 1993—just in time for Mosaic to ride the wave of Internet interest to the beaches of broad popular acceptance.

NCSA was in a quandary by this point. Their resources were meant for providing supercomputer resources to researchers, not helping Microsoft Windows users navigate the difficulties of setting up Mosaic. Their first solution was to grant several companies, such as Spry, Quarterdeck, and Mosaic Communications (later to become Netscape Communications), the right to commercially develop Mosaic.

This proved only a short-term solution, as the NCSA found itself in a commercial world that it was ill-suited to deal with. Finally, in August 1994, the NCSA came to an agreement with Spyglass Inc. Spyglass was given the right to commercially develop and license Mosaic. This doesn't mean that the free version of Mosaic has come to an end. There will continue to be a freeware Mosaic, which will include some Spyglass improvements.

While the Spyglass decision may have washed NCSA's hands of the dirty difficulties of commercializing Mosaic, it also muddied the Mosaic marketplace. Today, there are companies developing Mosaic from older versions of

Mosaic, while others are using Spyglass' Enhanced Mosaic as their base. As it turned out, more importantly than all of this, Marc left academia behind and got together with Jim Clark, former head of Silicon Graphics. They formed a new company. At first, it was called Mosaic Communications; but to avoid trademark troubles, they quickly changed it to Netscape. Before it even came up with its new name, however, Andreesen and company had come up with a new, improved version of Mosaic—the program we now know as Netscape Navigator. Netscape quickly became the ruling power of Web companies. These days, Netscape Navigator is the standard by which all other browsers are judged.

Other companies, like computer giants Microsoft and IBM, have weighed in with their own browsers—Internet Explorer and WebExplorer, respectively. Though they'd be the last to admit it, even Microsoft, which ran pell-mell over all competitors in the '80s and early '90s, has run up against a brick wall in trying to compete with Netscape. For now, the commercial future of the look and feel of the Web seems to be firmly in the hands of Netscape, with Microsoft, IBM, and SunSoft alternatively supporting Netscape's initiatives or—without notable success— proposing alternatives to the Netscape way of the Web.

For all Netscape Navigatorís stunning success, Mosaic was where it all began. With the introduction of Mosaic, the World Wide Web became not just a text-bound research program but the first new medium to hit the market since television in the 1940s—and one that anyone at all could publish on.

You know what happened next. The Internet became *the* cover story on television, the mainstream press, and magazines. Businesses charged on to the Internet like lemmings over cliffs. Sadly, I'm not using that analogy to be funny.

While there are many expert TCP/IP administrators out there, most of them cut their teeth on Unix and not Windows. Worse, network administrators who couldn't tell a Cisco Router from an Adtran Codex, much less a network address from a broadcast address, were set to bringing their companies' LANs onto the net. It hasn't been a pretty sight (or site).

# Pulling it Together: Groupware

Even as everyone is scrabbling to understand the Internet well enough to run it, new applications are coming to the Internet—and from there to your intranet—that promise even more radical changes. You may never have heard of it (although Lotus will be greatly annoyed if you haven't); but a big factor in the growth of intranets will be groupware. Groupware programs allow groups of people to work together over the network on one or more common projects. It may sound too simple to be much of an idea, but its still waters run deep. The Gartner Group, a major industry analyst group, has predicted that the groupware market will top 50 million users in the next four years. If you haven't heard of groupware yet, you will. As for how this connects with intranets, intranets are an ideal and largely untouched platform for groupware applications. That's going to change.

There are two basic kinds of groupware. Both are based on the fancy academic theory of computer-supported cooperative work. It sounds complex, but the practical ideas that spring from the theory are fairly basic. The first is that by enabling everyone in a company to have integrated communications and information, key business procedures like order processing, product development, and technical support can be handled by workflow support programs.

The main difference between workflow groupware and, say, a combination of e-mail and database management (DBMS) programs is interoperability and interactivity. With a true groupware program, like Lotus Notes, one doesn't simply send a message saying "this should be changed." The message can actually cause the change to be made, and inform everyone in the loop of the change.

This is a real difference in how most companies work; and therein lies groupware's big weakness. To get the most out of groupware, your company must be willing to abandon its old way of doing internal business and wholeheartedly embrace the new. For most businesses, that's a lot easier said than done.

Another hurdle for workflow technology on an intranet is that all the major groupware products to date—Notes, the watered-down Microsoft Exchange, and Novell's unheralded but powerful Groupwise—are proprietary platforms. That's in the process of changing. Lotus, still the field's leader, has introduced the InterNotes server, which enables Notes databases to be published as HTML Web pages. Notes clients, attached to an InterNotes server, can also act as Web browsers.

Other companies, notably the undisputed champion of the Web browser, Netscape, are working on groupware solutions that rely on already existing Usenet standards like Simple Mail Transfer Protocol (SMTP), Post Office Protocol (POP), and Network News Transport Protocol (NNTP). These programs, which should be on the market by the time you read this, will give workflow groupware a rocket boost on intranets.

Even so, many groupware products can automatically synchronize shared information. These programs also have built-in security that's more robust than current Internet standards. With the rise of net security standards like Secure HyperText Transfer Protocol (S-HTTP) and Secure Socket Layer (SSL), the Internet will gradually lose its inherent insecurity.

Groupware's other half is meeting support software. Thanks to programs like Netscape's Collabra Share, you can meet over your intranet instead of in person.

There are many advantages to this approach. No longer must you play mix-and-match scheduling with conference rooms and individuals. No longer will you need to fly 1,000 miles for a one-hour discussion. These programs even break the time and space barrier, since you can join a virtual meeting at your convenience from your home PC or your office machine. By recording all the conversation and decisions, tardy members can quickly get up to speed; and there can be little question about what was said and decided. With all these advantages, what's not to like?

Well, meeting programs are no panacea. They take the traditional meeting and put it into an electronic venue. This is a much more radical change than that of replacing the interoffice memo with interoffice e-mail. For people to use these new meeting metaphors efficiently, training is essential. When you buy an electronic meeting support program, you're not just buying software, you're buying a new way of running your business. Unless you treat it that way, you're likely to be disappointed by a program's results.

What exactly do these programs provide? On the surface, they're very similar. Each provides you with a specialized front-end to a client-server database engine. Don't worry about Structured Query Language (SQL) and the like: It's business approach. The key to groupware success isn't in the software, it's in how people use it.

## The Completed Puzzle: Intranets

Does all this sound incredibly difficult? Here I am, not only asking you to consider adding in all this high technology; but on top of all that, I'm asking you to change the very nature of your business dynamic.

After a comment like that, you might be wondering if it's worth going to the extra trouble of an intranet when individual users can simply be given a modem on their desktop for their Internet needs. Unfortunately, that's a lot like getting a bicycle when the rest of the world is moving on to the Model-T Ford. The business world is undergoing a massive transformation. You can either jump on the bandwagon or get run over by it.

Still not sure? The final answer depends on how you conduct your business. If you can deal with slow connections, minimal interoffice communications, and only a feeble attempt at cooperative work, you really don't need an intranet. If your business can benefit from fast e-mail, true groupware, Web advertising, and getting up-to-the-minute software and news updates, then stop waiting! The Internet awaits your intranet; and the 21st century awaits your enterprise.

# Web Introductions

## Welcome to the Web

Before there was the Web, before the Internet, there was Ted Nelson's dream of Xanadu. In Xanadu, all of human knowledge, all documents, images, sounds, and videos, would be instantly accessible to anyone with a computer, anywhere, anytime.

Nelson, a true computer visionary, foresaw a world where all information could be linked together in a worldwide web of hypertext and hypermedia; a world where the constant Babel of incompatible data formats and protocols would be replaced by a universal library of information. It would be a world transformed, one that has as much in common with our world as ours does with the one before Gutenberg invented the printing press. It would be a world where everyone could be empowered by information.

That was the dream; today we have a reality—the World Wide Web. It's not Nelson's vision. To get to the Web requires more resources and expertise than a working Joe and Jane with two kids and a mortgage are likely to be able to spend. But, while the Web may not be Nelson's dream, it attempts the same grand unification theory of information; and for well-off individuals and companies, it is that same information dream come true.

Sound crazy? Think again. The Web links together information from anywhere and makes it available to anyone with the price of admission. My second grader can jump from a story about Cookie Monster to a piece on the history of Sesame Street to the life story of Jim Henson without ever leaving her desk. Now, think about what having all the online information in the world at your fingertips could mean for your business.

It's not just the information, but the hands-on nature of that information which make the Web so special. You can find static facts in any book. Books take months to update, but Web pages take minutes to update. Finding something in a book can take hours, if you have access to the right volume. Finding something online can also take hours, but there's a decent chance it will take mere seconds; and every volume that's online is available for your search.

With the combination of databases and the Web, manually updated pages will become the rarity rather than the norm. Today, we have a Web made up mostly of static, unchanging information. Oh, it moves in hours and days instead of weeks and months; but still, most of its information stays untouched by an editor's hand for months. Not anymore. With the one-two punch of DBMSs and the Web, we're quickly moving toward the day when the Web is as live as television broadcasting, if not more so.

Before being carried away by the potential, remember that old computing phrase: garbage in, garbage out (GIGO). Just because something is on the Web doesn't make it accurate. Always, always consider your sources. Yes, a one-person newsletter might give you more accurate and up-to-date information on a narrow topic than the *Wall Street Journal*, `http://update.wsj.com/`; but the *Journal* earned its reputation for excellence by always doing its damnedest to have current, in-depth information on many subjects.

You should also remember that when you put your trust in Web information, you're putting your faith in editors and webweavers who just might change the official dicta on a subject on a whim or based on the political climate of the day. In Stalin's Soviet Union, encyclopedias were changed from year to year to reflect the communist state's viewpoint. On the Web, this kind of disinformation can be written, edited, and published in less time than it will take you to read this chapter. Am I telling you not to use the Web? Of course not. I'm just warning you not to blindly trust of its information.

The Web also dynamically links information into a seamless whole. You may start your information hunt next door and finally track down your quarry somewhere in Taipei.

From where you sit, however, there's no difference between the two. The Web gives you the most powerful information research tool in history, and you can use it with a swish and click of a mouse. The Web manages this feat by employing the twin concepts of hypertext and hypermedia. Both concepts date back to—no surprise—Ted Nelson.

## Hypermedia

In hypertext, related information is linked together. Instead of being forced to move in a linear fashion from page one to page two and so on, a hypertext document lets you leap from word to word, page, or document using what are called links.

For example, on the Web, you could be reading about the NBA's Chicago Bulls from the Chicago Tribune's Bulls HomePage, `http://www.chicago.tribune.com/sports/bulls.htm`, and decide you want to know more about Michael Jordan. In an ordinary book, you'd find the information, but it would take you time. You'd either have to go to the index, or continue reading through the book searching for the right information. In hypertext, the author can set up a Web page so that a quick click on the phrase "Air Jordan Collection", `http://www.chicago.tribune.com/sports/jordan/jordan.htm`, takes you to a collection of still graphics, videos, and more than 40 stories about pro basketball's best player of all time.

Now, take this concept one step further. With hypermedia, we can link pictures, sounds, and so-called movies to form multimedia documents. In the example above, you don't have to click on the phrase—there's also a constantly changing photo of Michael. You can get to the Air Jordan page simply by clicking on it. Words?! We don't need *words* to depict Jordan's mastery!

In hypermedia, not only words are joined, but images, video, and sounds are bound together as well. For example, you can click your way from a review of "Star Wars" on the Internet Movie Database, `http://us.imdb.com/`, to a collection of Star Wars stills housed in Sweden.

Hypermedia, in short, tries to make computers work the way people think—that is, it jumps rather than always moving straight forward or backward. It's not perfect, of course. A hyperdocument author's links may lead you far astray from the destination you have in mind. Still, hypermedia can be a great help in chasing down elusive information.

# Hypermedia History Lessons

The first important popular use of hypertext was in the Apple Macintosh and Apple IIGS' application development system, HyperCard. HyperCard, created in 1987, was also the first noteworthy use of hypermedia.

HyperCard deserves more than a passing mention because some of its strengths and weaknesses mirror those of the Web. For example, people have trouble wrapping their minds around the hypertext and hypermedia concepts within both. HyperCard has been called an application prototyping package, a software construction kit, system software, and a multimedia authoring system. Like the Web, it's all these and more. No matter what you called it, HyperCard was a new way at looking at information, a way that the Web would follow.

For several years, few followed HyperCard's lead. The concept of multimedia was too tricky for many people to grasp and the hypertext's hardware demands too high. Times have changed. Now, you'd have to try hard to buy a computer that can't handle multimedia!

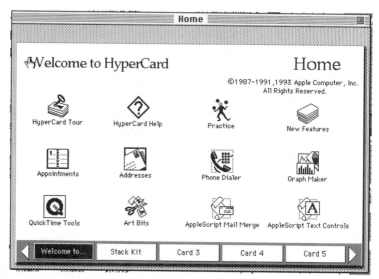

**Figure 1.1**: It sure doesn't look like the Web, but HyperCard led the way to the Web.

The Web has, of course, far outdistanced HyperCard. Still, there are multimedia CD-ROMs that do a better job of unifying information than does even the best of Web sites. For years, CD-ROMs have been created by artists, authors, and editors all working together to form complete hypermedia works of art and information. The Web, on the other hand, comes from the efforts of thousands of people each going their own way with little cooperation and no management at all.

Even so, ten years from now, CD-ROMs will have all but died out. The Web's connection speeds ramp-up and more skilled site production will inevitably lead to the day when the only real difference between Web publication and a CD-ROM publication is that the Web work will always be more timely. When that day comes, only specialized CD-ROM vendors will remain.

# Looking at the Web Today

Today, there are dozens of different versions of multimedia Web browsers. Some, like Netscape and Microsoft's Internet Explorer, seek to define the market. Others, such as America Online's (AOL's) proprietary model, struggle desperately to keep up with the constantly evolving edge of Web browser development.

Right now, deciding between Web browsers is a matter of looking at your operating system, performance, and features, and who supports the standards you'll need for your intranet. This situation isn't going to last long. Today, with any graphical Web browser, you can pretty much get data from any Web server. In the future, which we'll look at more closely in a bit, that will no longer be the case.

A current problem, but one that is likely to disappear soon, is that most Web browsers are not universal front-ends to all Internet services. While any Web client can use gopher, the also-rans can't read newsgroup messages or read or write e-mail. By the time you read this, however, any Web browser worth its salt will be able to act as a universal client for all the most common Internet and Usenet applications.

One problem that's specific to PC and Macintosh browsers is the inability to use WAIS databases directly. This headache is being worked on at this very moment; but with the decline of WAIS' importance, particularly in light of how almost every DBMS company in the biz is working on directly integrating their databases with existing Web standards, this is not likely going to be a problem for anyone except those companies that have already made a commitment to WAIS.

While the state-of-the-art Web browsers of 1996 are all very easy to use, they're also alike in a less favorable way: They're all a pain in the neck to set up. If you're a TCP/IP network administrator, you'll find setting up a Web browser no trouble at all. For everyone else, be ready to earn your power user stripes, because setting up a Web browser can be a real job. Don't get me wrong, they're getting easier by the day; but some things, like finding and installing the right "plug-in" application that will let you listen to x-wav audio, is a tough task for someone who already knows the Internet, let alone someone who's just getting on board for the first time.

As for the Web itself, it's continuing to expand at a remarkable rate. If you keep an eye on the Usenet newsgroup devoted to Web servers, at **news://comp.infosystems.www.providers**, on your Web browser dial, you'll see that new public Web servers are springing up at a rate of more than one an hour. This surge in Web servers has several causes. A large part of it is that Web servers are relatively easy to set up. As more and better HTML editors and text converters emerge, new Web servers will flood the Web. Equally important, however, is that more Web servers enable more businesses to enter the Internet.

Another problem that any Web user should know is that the Internet and the Web are getting very crowded. Many popular Web sites are being mobbed by your counterparts; and as a result, they are often unavailable or their performance is very poor. This trouble is not going to pass quickly. Whether your company connects to the Internet by a 56 kilobits per second (Kbps) frame-relay/Integrated Services Digital Network (ISDN) line or a T3's zippy 44.736 Megabit per second (Mbps) line, there are times you're going to feel like you're stuck in an online traffic jam.

That's a useful analogy, because that's exactly what's happening. I'll save the technical details for later; but essentially, there's simply too many people trying to use the Internet at once. Would you be surprised, for instance, if I told you that standard business hours are some of the busiest hours on the net? I didn't think so. Conversely, if you can schedule updating your Web page so that a lot of the grunt work—such as getting mostly static pages from the West Coast offices to a site on the east coast for distribution to your company's eastern branches— is done at four in the morning, the work will get done quicker. This will also increase your daytime throughput, because that online equivalent of a convoy of tanker trucks will no longer be jamming the Internet at large, and the local lanes of your intranet in particular.

Ultimately, the only way out of this jam will be an increase in the Internet's data throughput capacity. Everyone in the Internet provider business knows this, and they're all working on it. For now, the bandwidth—the total amount of data that can pass through a network at a given time-- isn't catching up with the demand. This will change. Between the tiny Internet Service Provider (ISP) down the road and the huge data communication giants on the Internet's equivalent of interstate highways, hundreds of millions of dollars are being spent on broadening the roads.

For the time being, the Web can often be a hassle for both consumers and would-be business users. Within the next two or three years, all these problems should be dealt with. Of course, by then, we'll have a whole new set of troubles.

## Tomorrow and Tomorrow and Tomorrow

Over the next few years, we'll see many Web developments. By the turn of the century, we'll look back at today's Web and think it as antique as we now see an Osborne "portable" computer. If you didn't catch that reference, consider my point made. The Osborne was the first portable computer using a popular operating system, albeit only for those of us with a strong arm: The now-obsolete CP/M-80 portable weighed about 27 lbs.

**Figure 1.2**: Clearly, we were all a lot stronger back in 1981 if this was portable!

The biggest change will be ease of software installation. The Web browser of the year 2000 will be as easy to install as a simple word processor is today, except you're probably not even going to have install it. Either the browser will be part of your operating system, or your PC's vendor will already have bundled it with your hardware package. We may not even be calling them browsers by then. These programs will combine all network services into a single graphical user interface (GUI) that will be keyboard, mouse, and voice-activated. If you're brand new to computing in 2001, you probably won't think of the browser as being any more separate from the computer than today's new users think of the graphical user interface (GUI) as being something apart from the operating system.

What won't change, alas, is that the Web will still make some kinds of information retrieval difficult. While there are efforts afoot to standardize and catalog Web data, there's no consensus on how this should be done. Even if rules on how to catalog the Web's data existed, it wouldn't matter. The Web is just too bloody huge for anyone to catalog, index, or organize in any kind of complete and effective matter. There will be great attempts made, probably by today's leaders at making Web information manageable—such as Yahoo, **http://www.yahoo.com**, and Digital Equipment Company's AltaVista , **http://www. altavista.digital.com**—but they won't be enough.

Instead, we'll be relying more on agents, programs that go out and use existing catalogs and search engines to track down information for you. The first of these, such as Quarterdeck's WebCompass, **http://www.qdeck.com**, have already arrived; but there will be many more to follow. No matter how expert these programs get, I suspect that human professionals—call them cyberlibrarians—will be utilized by companies who want the best possible information rather than the quickest information.

Overall, we'll also see faster performance from our software and the Internet itself. In particular, ISDN will increase the throughput speed of individual "modem users" from a top of 28.8 Kbps to 64Kbps. Even the smallest companies will be using either Bonded ISDN (BISDN) or frame-relay technology for speeds of 128Kbps.

In the near future, we'll also see the end of most Web browsers. The market is already shaking out the non-contenders. There will doubtlessly still be free browsers, but the odds are that your choice is going to be Netscape or Microsoft. Even though some products may be technically superior—though in this particular software category, I haven't seen any--the browser field is reaching the point where marketing expertise is more important than technological expertise.

We'll also see greater incompatibility problems between browsers and Web servers. Netscape has already gone its own way with extensions to hypertext markup language (HTML), the language that most Web pages are written in, which other browsers don't include.

A more serious problem is that HTML is being challenged by Adobe Acrobat. Acrobat produces documents in the Portable Data Format (PDF). While PDF has advantages for document designers over HTML, users must have an Acrobat reader integrated with their Web browser to read PDF documents. This makes PDF less portable, but PDF also has the advantage of giving authors more control over the look and feel of their documents than HTML will ever be able to.

The commercial online services, like AOL, CompuServe Information Service (CIS), and Prodigy, are moving onto the Internet. In order to survive, these services will have to transform themselves into Web-based services. To date, their progress in that direction—with incomplete translations of their content, look, and feel to the Web, not to mention downright lousy Web browsers—gives little hope that all three will survive to the 21st century. Some small services, like Delphi and BIX, will survive for a time by catering to their small, specialized audiences. Boutique Web services, however, will ensure that the smaller online services will be short-lived.

Commerce will boom on the Internet. The science-fiction concept of using a computer to order everything from groceries to your wardrobe is already becoming a reality. In the next year alone, we'll see the current handful of online stores grow to the tens of thousands.

Some refuse to believe that there is money to be made on the Web with online stores. I suspect those are the same people who refused to believe that specialized catalog marketers, like LL Bean and Victoria's Secret, could make a go of it, or that companies like Dell or Gateway 2000 could ever make money from selling computers via 800 numbers instead of stores.

Let's put it this way. Every demographic study of Web users shows that: 1) their numbers are increasing; and 2) they're likely to be young adults with high incomes and not much free time. I don't know what your marketing forecast people are telling you; but to me, that's practically a rallying call to the millions in sales to be made on the Internet.

Other resources are pouring onto the Web. If you're from a big city, chances are you're already able to read your hometown newspaper, access neighborhood event information, visit virtual museums, look through the local want ads, and arrange to meet that special someone through a Web dating service. I know that's already the case in Washington, DC, and I have every expectation that will be true for every city with over a million population by the year 2000. In each and every case, there's a profit to be found by supplying these needs.

Within your company, it will become easier and easier for you to use the same techniques to achieve the same results. Company newsletter? Put it on your internal Web. Coordinating meetings and events—that's what group-ware was made for. Does the L.A. office want a new human resources manager? Advertise it within the company first, or put it on the company's world-accessible, help wanted Web page.

Quite simply, the Web's potential is as unlimited as human communications. So let's get things started here by taking a closer look at what underlies the Web—the Internet; and beneath that, the networking protocols that enable you to have your very own controllable version of the Internet—an intranet.

# Welcome to the Internet

## Come On In, the Water's Fine

There's a line in an old Eagles' song, "Hotel California," that says: "You can check out any time you like, but you can never leave." That's not a bad way of thinking about the Internet. Once your enterprise has made a commitment to the Internet, brother, you're committed. In sickness and in health, for richer or for poorer, once your company is on the Internet, you're there to stay, no matter what second thoughts you might have. Oh, you can get off of it, of course; but it would probably have been easier to get a divorce in Henry VIII's time—and we all know how much trouble he had!

If you're confused as to what exactly the Internet is, you're in good company. There's no neat answer. A noninclusive definition, but one which most experts can live with, is that it's one immense network that connects innumerable smaller networks and their individual resources via the Transmission Control Protocol/Internet Protocol (TCP/IP).

So, where does the Web fit into the picture? The World Wide Web is actually a subset of the Internet. It carries hypermedia information around the globe using Hypertext Transfer Protocol (HTTP) and hypermedia languages like HTML.

Usenet is another term often confused with the Internet. It's actually a superset of the Internet. Usenet isn't a network at all, but a distributed peer-to-peer message distribution system. These messages consist of e-mail (using the Internet's RFC-822 addressing standard) and publicly available messages bundled by topic, called the Usenet newsgroups. Usenet information travels on everything from lightning-fast T3 (45 Mbps) lines to floppy disks carried from node to node by hand. The Internet's traffic, in contrast, always travels via a network connection.

Beyond even the Internet and Usenet is what Internet expert John Quartermain calls the Matrix. The Matrix is the sum of all networks that can communicate with each other, not just those joined by TCP/IP. While your current LAN may be no intranet, if it can do as little as send e-mail to the outside world, it's part of the Matrix.

An important thing to understand about all three of these is that there is no one in charge. You won't find any federal agency or grand committee of scientists regulating the Internet. There are groups like the Internet Society (ISOC), the Internet Engineering Task Force (IETF), and the

Internet Architecture Board (IAB) that try to direct, design, and approve Internet changes. But these groups lead the way by the worldwide Internet community's consensus rather than by any legal authority.

Of course, you can expect that to change, but it's not going to be a pleasant experience. The Internet truly is global; and anyone who thinks that the world has any sort of universal government hasn't been to a United Nations meeting in the last 50 years. Each country will try to regulate first content then other elements of the Internet. In the US, we've already seen politicians trying to run over the First Amendment with the Communication Decency Act of 1995 in search of votes for the '96 elections. That parochial piece of paranoia has, for now, been knocked on its head by the courts. Like the villain in any bad horror movie, though, you can expect to see it rise from the dead again.

Regardless of what happens with that piece of US legislation, governmental agencies around the world are going to start controlling the Internet. In the US, my best guess is that the Federal Communications Commission (FCC) will end up with the job. They might not want it, mind you, but logically, it's the agency that's most likely to get stuck with it. When that day comes, you can count on having, at the very least, additional paperwork for your intranet. At the most, you might need to deal with government teams coming in and checking your network for compliancy with federal standards. This isn't something to worry about for today, but don't say that I didn't warn you!

In the meantime, even the technical rules are subject to change. The Request for Comments (RFCs) that make up the Internet technical standards are working notes, not hard and fast standards. Whether you're a net administrator or an information systems manager, you'll need to accept that when you've made a commitment to the Internet way of doing things, you've agreed to work in an extremely fluid and fast-moving network environment. Neither job is for someone who expects to learn a system once and then live off of that knowledge for a decade or two. You need someone who's always willing—and able—to learn.

## Packets of History

The Internet was born during the Cold War. The US Department of Defense's Advanced Research Projects Agency (DARPA) set about developing a network that tied together geographically distant computers using a new technology that shared data lines by packet switching.

That was DARPA—according to the Defense Department's bureaucrats, anyway. The scientists who were actually building the first networks were actually far more interested in seeing how packet networking really worked than building a network that could literally have huge holes blown in it by atomic bombs and keep working.

Like many Defense projects of the 1960s, the academics took the research money for their purposes, the military took the results for theirs, and everyone was happy. Both sides were fortunate that violent revolutionaries like the Weathermen either had no clue what DARPA was up to, or if they did, they didn't have the technical expertise to recognize the power inherent in the networking concept.

To leave history behind and get back to technology, in such a network, your data is divided into small blocks called packets. Each packet contains a header. These header bytes carry the packet's identification number and information about its destination and point of origin. Once split up, the packets are sent to their destination over a web of possible connections. No particular route or data line is laid out.

Instead, each packet trundles along to exchange nodes, which today we call routers.

At each node, the headers are examined for the packet's destination; and the node sends it along on whatever happens to be the best possible route at the time. That optimal road may change from moment to moment, and the packets will split up along several different routes. Once the packets arrive, their headers enable the receiving system to reassemble the data into its original form.

Packet switching has several advantages. First, packets can be sent successfully even when large sections of the network fail. We never—thank God—got the chance to see how it would work under a full-scale nuclear attack; but in 1993, the Internet kept going even after a construction firm in Virginia inadvertently took out a major fiber-optic link.

Another plus for packet-switching is that if you keep the packet sizes small, the effect of data errors is mitigated. When a packet does become corrupted, only that packet needs to be re-sent, not the entire message. So, even when errors do occur, throughput speed is not significantly slowed.

All this theory was turned into practice in the fall of 1969, when four Honeywell 516 minicomputers located on various West Coast university campuses connected together to form ARPAnet, the Internet's predecessor. This first network was built around the now-obsolete Network Control Protocol (NCP). However, NCP wasn't robust enough to connect with ARPA's other experimental packet-switching networks.

# TCP/IP Rules

In the early '70s, work progressed on a network protocol that could handle interconnecting heterogeneous packet networks. The resulting protocol was TCP/IP. Today, long after these first packet networks became history, TCP/IP's flexibility enables it to continue on.

The great strength of TCP/IP is that it enables computers of different architectures and operating systems to communicate easily with each other. The resulting network of networks is known as a catenet. The largest catenet is the Internet. TCP/IP enables network designers to build these communications structures by encapsulating IPs inside lower-level, system-native network packets.

Packets, or IP datagrams, are made up of four separate levels. From top to bottom, these are: application, host-to-host transport, Internet, and network access. Each level of the packet contains not only data, but a header with directions to ensure that the packet gets to its destination. When a packet arrives at a router, the layers are peeled off and the headers read to guarantee proper delivery. To translate IPs into and out of packets, the routers combine packet-examination and packet-translation functions with packet-switching technology.

Of course, for the systems to make any sense of where a datagram should go, an addressing scheme is needed. In the Internet, each Internet host has a domain name. In English, a domain name consists of labels separated by periods. For example, vna1.com is the name of my Internet domain.

Computers don't understand English. What the Internet hosts use as addresses are called IP addresses. These consist of 32-bit integers represented by four 8-bit numbers written in base 10 separated by periods. Confused? Don't worry about it. The important thing to know is that you can use these numbers with some commands—ftp and telnet, usually—to contact a remote system. For instance, one of my own domains, vna.digex.net, has the IP address 164.109.213.7.

If everything goes right, neither you as an administrator nor your users will have to deal with IP addresses. That's because a distributed name/address directory, the Domain Name System (DNS), takes care of translating from domain names to IP addresses and, using a technique called reverse look-up, vice-versa. Sometimes, however, either your DNS server will be down or its address list will be incorrect. In that case, your network administrator will need to take things into her own hands and use IP addresses.

Another TCP/IP plus is that it's not bound in any way to one specific physical medium. Whether it's wireless, token-ring, ordinary phone lines, an X.25 packet-switching network, or smoke signals, if you can transmit data through it, you can use TCP/IP on it.

While there have been many attempts to replace the TCP/IP design, TCP/IP remains interoperability's shining success story. Most experts agree that the switchover of ARPAnet and the Defense Data Network (DDN) from NCP to TCP/IP on January 1, 1983, marked the true birth of the Internet.

# Internet Evolution

As TCP/IP was becoming popular, one of its first ports of protocol was to a DEC PDP-11 minicomputer running Unix. Later, this would prove to be a technology marriage made in heaven. TCP/IP would be incorporated into the "free" academic version of Unix, the Berkeley Standard Distribution (BSD). BSD Unix, together with TCP/IP, became popular throughout the computing world; and with their growth, the Internet expanded at an explosive rate. Today, Unix, TCP/IP, and the Internet are permanently bound together in the public's view. In reality, with all the connectivity services now available to patch you through to the Internet, all you need is phone access from just about any old PC.

For a very long time, the TCP/IP sinews of the Internet were limited to 56K main lines or backbones. By 1987, it was time for an upgrade. The National Science Foundation (NSF) began developing a backbone system fast enough to meet the needs of Internet users accessing supercomputers.

Simultaneously, the NSF decided that rather than having small Internet networks plug directly into the NSFnet, these LANs should go through regional, mid-level networks. Companies and organizations known as network service providers sprang up to create and maintain these mid-level networks. Without realizing it, the NSF started the process that would lead to our current Internet market. Today, there are Internet providers for everyone from major corporations needing T3 speeds to Joe User with a 1,200 baud per second (bps) modem.

The immediate effects were first seen at higher levels. Advanced Network & Services (a.k.a. ANS, formed by

IBM, MCI, and Merit) first connected with NSFnet, and then began developing its own high-speed backbone. At the same time, other government agencies began building their own backbones. In an attempt to combine efforts and leapfrog over existing data communications technology, the federal government began working on what became known as the information superhighway—the National Research and Education Network (NREN).

This was all well and good; but as more companies and private individuals got on the Internet (thanks to ANS and customer-oriented network service providers), usage problems became more prominent. Until then, the Internet had been meant solely for research and educational purposes; commercial Internet use was expressly forbidden.

Some "business" parts of the Internet, like UUnet's Alternet, did exist, but these were islands surrounded by packet seas that their information could not cross. The solution was clear: There needed to be a commercial Internet backbone. In 1991, the major commercial Internet providers created the Commercial Internet Exchange (CIX, pronounced "kicks").

# The People's Internet

Thanks to CIX, we now have an Internet that can be used for any purpose and is available to anyone with a PC and a modem. There are three different end-user Internet connection levels: shell, Unix to Unix Copy Protocol (UUCP), and IP. All of these come from Internet points of presence (POPs), which, in turn, are maintained by Internet Service Providers (ISPs).

An Internet POP is simply a place with modems and terminal servers that allows outside users to call in to connect to the Internet. When you call a POP, you first connect with a modem. Your signal is then relayed to a terminal server via one of its RS-232 serial interfaces. A terminal server is an asynchronous multiplexing device that takes your call and translates it from an asynchronous data stream into TCP/IP packets. The terminal server then sends your transformed data to the local Internet host computer. In return, the terminal server translates the Internet's computer responses into signals that your modem can understand and use.

What happens next depends on whether you have a shell account or a UUCP account. With a UUCP account, your PC and the Internet system copy e-mail and newsgroup messages between the systems. In this case, you read and write your messages offline, and only connect with the Usenet long enough to transfer messages. Once a popular low-end technology, UUCP is slowly withering on the vine as it's surpassed by the growing availability of direct TCP/IP connections over telephone wiring.

A shell account is an entirely different animal. Here, your system becomes a terminal of an Internet host system. Therefore, you can run such TCP/IP-borne utilities as ftp and telnet. You don't run these programs on your PC. For instance, if you ftp a file from a remote site, the file appears on your host Internet system, not your PC. What's happening is that your Internet host is "ftping" the file to its system while simultaneously copying the file to your PC by an asynchronous data transfer protocol such as Zmodem.

Both of these methods are all well and good for teeny-tiny businesses and individuals; but neither cuts it for someone who wants an intranet. For an intranet, you must use the third kind of link: an IP connection.

With an actual IP connection, your network—or at least the gateway system—becomes an actual part of the Internet. When you're part of the net, like it or not, you're opening at least one system in your LAN to everyone in the world. I'll talk about ways of minimizing the security risks from this; but even if you put Doberman pinschers, barbed wire, and machine guns around the gateway (or their virtual equivalents), your system is still part of the worldwide Internet. Since that gives you access to all the benefits of the net, most people consider it a deal well worth making. But it's not a deal you should make without being aware of the risks that come with it.

As you'll recall, one of TCP/IP's strong points is that it will run on just about anything that can carry data, including normal phone lines. There are several advantages to the IP approach. For instance, you can run multiple programs at once. In one telnet window, you can be chatting with someone using Internet Relay Chat (IRC), while simultaneously ftping a file directly to your computer in another window.

The oldest modem method of IP connection with the Internet is SLIP: Serial Line Internet Protocol. SLIP, while still popular, is slowly being overtaken by Point-to-Point Protocol (PPP). One advantage that PPP has over SLIP is that PPP can assign IP addresses automatically, which makes it a boon to laptop Internet argonauts. PPP can also encapsulate other network layer protocols, like NetWare's IPX, instead of just IP. This makes PPP useful for hooking into non-TCP/IP networks that are connected to the Internet by a router.

With either protocol, even with just a modem, your machine becomes an actual part of the Internet. Of course, to do this, you'll also need TCP/IP programs such as telnet, ftp, or Mosaic resident on your computer.

What you won't have with either SLIP or PPP is a connection that's fast enough for intranet purposes. Again, for one person, either one is fine. But let's face the facts: You're going to need at least 56Kbps speeds to make serious business use of the Internet.

# Intranets

So, other than using TCP/IP straight, no chaser, what's the difference between the Internet and an intranet? Here's a little secret: practically nothing.

An intranet is simply a LAN using TCP/IP and Internet programs to connect employees. On an intranet, instead of using Lotus' cc:Mail for e-mail, you'd use a mail server like Alta Vista's Mail Server, and Pegasus Mail for the client. For document sharing, instead of using groupware programs like Lotus Notes or Novell's GroupWise, you'd use Web servers and browsers.

If you want to take your intranet one step further, you can also connect it to the Internet. In this case, the crucial difference between your intranet and the Internet is that you must have security measures in place to keep your corporate traffic and data separate from the Internet.

Since you could already do most of these things—except contacting the Internet—with the tools that you already have, your next question might be: "Why should I bother?" The answer's right there on your bottom line. Intranet programs and their upkeep are more efficient and cheaper—a lot cheaper—than proprietary e-mail systems, groupware, and the like.

Notes, for example, is a fine program that I've used for years. Even so, while its latest version is much better behaved than earlier versions, it is one cranky program that gobbles up system resources like there's no limit on what one poor little client can handle. That's just at the user end. Installing Notes, especially across a network using different operating systems and computer architectures, can be a nightmare. Once up, you're still going to need a team at every site that can program, support, and maintain your Notes installation. You can get by with less people; but if you do that, you're short-changing yourself of all of Notes' document and workflow management properties.

An intranet, on the other hand, is downright cheap to install and administer. No, running an intranet is not a cakewalk. If you already have expert Unix or NT administrators around, though, it'll take a lot less effort to keep your intranet up and running and in good health.

Top-quality intranet programs are available either at inexpensive rates or, believe it or not, for free. With cc:Mail, my own personal pick for the best LAN e-mail client around, the starting price for a client is $99.95. With site licenses you can drop that down considerably; but no matter how far Lotus drops its price, it can't compete with the price tag of Pegasus Mail, **http://www.pegasus.usa.com/**: $0.00.

Pegasus can pull this trick off because they have no marketing budget to speak of, a development group of one, and because the manuals do cost you money: $195 per copy. That's not the shell game you may think it is. Pegasus

Mail is perfectly usable as is, sans manuals, for anyone who knows how Internet mail works.

The same is true of other programs. A GroupWise, Microsoft Exchange, or Notes client will cost you some sort of up-front fee. The Netscape browser, **http://www. netscape.com**, on the other hand, is free.

How can companies like Netscape do this? Well, in Netscape's case, it's very simple. The plan is that by making Netscape the browser standard of the world, everyone who wants to publish on the Web will naturally want to use Netscape's servers for the best possible results. And, you guessed it, the servers aren't free.

The servers, however, aren't that expensive either. Since prices change faster than the weather, I'm not going to bother to give you exact numbers, but suffice it to say that currently, a Netscape server with all the trimmings costs about one-fifth the amount of an equivalent proprietary network groupware system. That's not likely to change.

There's also a hidden cost-saver. Because both the Internet and your intranet will let people use the same friendly interface for almost all network functionality, you don't have to worry about the end-user training and support costs that frequently drive the prices of older groupware systems into the stratosphere. Your people are also going to be a lot happier because once they've learned how to use a browser for e-mail, workflow jobs, and document tracking, they don't need to learn anything else. They can concentrate on their jobs, instead of learning how to do their job anew with each new trend in technological fashion.

As an example , let's look at Mosaic. This freeware program was the first graphical Web browser. By Web standards,

Mosaic 1.0 is prehistoric. Nevertheless, you can take some-one who's used to Mosaic and plop them down in front of the latest version of Netscape Navigator or IBM's Web Explorer, and they'll be up and browsing by the end of the day. Try that with any proprietary system, and you're talk-ing weeks or months of relearning before your disgruntled employee can get back up to speed.

It's really rather funny in a way. For decades, creating the universal interface was the ultimate goal for client-server companies. Of course, it never happened, because every-one wanted their interface to be the one that everyone else used. Now, all those failed attempts are being swept away by Web browsers. It wasn't the intent of the browser cre-ators—at first—to change the face of not merely network computing, but computing as a whole into a single, easy-to-use front-end, but that's exactly what's happening.

# TANSTAAFL

Don't know the term? Head over to a bookstore and pick up a copy of Robert A. Heinlein's finest novel, *The Moon is a Harsh Mistress*. TANSTAAFL stands for: "There Ain't No Such Thing As A Free Lunch." With intranets, the price of lunch is shifting your LAN and WAN to TCP/IP.

If you're already running a TCP/IP-based LAN, congratu-lations. You probably didn't know it when you installed it, but you were way ahead of the curve. As for the rest of you, you're facing a big job.

First, to run TCP/IP effectively, your systems almost cer-tainly need more memory. If you're already running Windows95, Windows NT, OS/2, Macintosh OS System 7.5 and up, or Unix, that's not likely to be a problem. If you're still wedded to older systems, now's a good time to think about upgrading; because TCP/IP software can eat up a lot of memory.

Your network administrators are going to be in for a steep learning curve—or more aptly, a learning cliff. On the hardware side, you're also likely to need more capable routers. If you don't have routers, get ready to buy some.

On the other hand, you don't have to give up your old LAN equipment and software for an intranet. Products like Firefox Communications' NOV*IX for Internet, **http://www.firefox.com/**, provides NetWare administrators with a NetWare Loadable Module (NLM) that enables users to access the Internet via their existing NetWare connection. Similarly, the latest version of Artisoft's network operating system (NOS), **http://www.artisoft.com**, enables you to connect using the NetBIOS protocol to the Internet via a Windows95 gateway machine.

You can, of course, add TCP/IP to your existing network. You still get all the administrative headaches, but you don't lose any of your existing network-specific resources. Of course, getting two network protocols to live happily together on the same wire and on the same PCs is a whole other headache. In this case, since everyone and their brother knows just how important intranets are becoming, almost all NOS vendors and operating system vendors are making it easier for their default network protocols to peacefully coexist with TCP/IP.

Another problem you may face is keeping your intranet traffic from overloading your existing network hardware. If the sudden flood of Web traffic gives your network a case of the slows—or better still, if you can see this coming beforehand—there are two different approaches to take.

The first is to upgrade your network infrastructure. In particular, you'll want to look into either Fast Ethernet or 100VG Ethernet. These technologies both give standard Ethernet traffic a kick in the pants, going from a maximum throughput of 10Mbps to a peppy 100Mbps. It is pricey; but many Ethernet vendors are also selling 10/100 network interface cards (NICs). With these, you can upgrade only your crucial machines without shutting the slower systems out of the network conversation.

Another approach would be to create a subnet that would hold all the intranet servers. This way, most of the intranet traffic is kept to its own network segment where it can't slow down other network activities. These are matters to take up with your own network administrators, so I won't go any further with these thoughts. Suffice it to say that there are real-world solutions to any network traffic bottlenecks that an intranet can cause.

## Intranets and Webs

At the same time you're bringing up your intranet, you'll also be bringing up your internal and external Web servers. The main difference between the two is, again, a matter of security. Your external Web server should be set up to make it nigh onto impossible to break into your main systems from it. You don't have to be quite as careful with your internal-use-only servers, but it couldn't hurt.

In any case, you'll want to avoid one error that companies are always making with Web design. Almost everyone believes that the same person who administers the intranet should also be the one to handle creating and maintaining Web pages: Wrong! Don't even consider it. Yes, it made sense when the Web was first starting out; but we're a long way past that stage. Your intranet administrator is going to have more than enough to keep him busy. Some of those duties will involve the care and feeding of your Web server; and for that reason, one of your network administrators should get the additional title of webmaster.

The work, and title that goes along with it, that he should not get is webweaver. A webweaver doesn't sweat about whether the DNS is having fits or if there's a cracker knocking on the corporate financials. Her job is to create, maintain, and manage your Web pages. Think of it this way: a webmaster is like a carpenter. He built your house, and when a joist springs out of true, he hammers it back. A webweaver, though, is an interior designer. She doesn't care about the walls, floor, and ceiling so much as she cares about what can be done with the space within. If you think of it that way, you can see that they're two very different jobs calling upon two very different sets of skills. Besides, to be frank, just because someone can count in octal doesn't mean that they can write in English, or that the reverse holds true. Now, there are a few of us around (Hi!); but I'd venture to guess that we number at the most in the hundreds.

Back in those long ago days of two years gone by—scary, isn't it?—the jobs often went together; because to write Web documents, you had to master raw HTML. With today's power editing programs, writers and editors can focus on creating well-written, well-designed Web pages. Some nitty-gritty knowledge of HTML still helps, but it's no longer an absolute requirement. It's far more important that your webweaver knows her English than her HTML.

# Beyond Words

By the time you read this, most people will be wrestling with the next stages of Web evolution: the integration of groupware workflow software and live data from corporate databases into your Web sites. To cope with these changes, you're going to need to get your management, database administrators, webmasters, and webweavers all together.

Don't even think about putting these meetings off. No one from any of these groups will want to be there; but for the sake of your company's future, you have to collectively choose and implement a solution to these questions as soon as possible. That's because the Internet is rapidly shifting over to a new, dynamic mode. Even as I write this, it's already happening.

This isn't just a matter for groups that have the kind of programmers that can make great-tasting Java or are hyper about ActiveX. Many of today's DBMSs are rapidly shifting over to new versions that include Web compatibility as a standard feature.

Today, when I visit the Open Text search engine, `http://search.opentext.com`, and do any search containing the word "advertising," I know that at least one of my search results (called "hits" in the information biz) is going to be an advertisement. Let's try looking at some examples which go beyond text to show you what I mean.

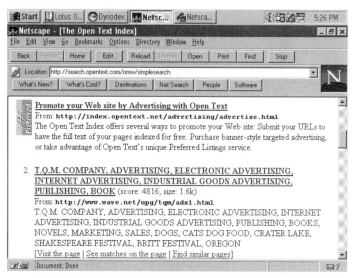

**Figure 2.1**: Just what I needed—an advertisement, when I'm working on a research project.

In this particular case, I think this is just annoying.

There's a lesson here for people who make their living from researching the net: you can't trust your tools. OpenText at least makes it clear when they're manipulating your results. With other search engines, there's a chance you may only find *registered* sites. Or, perhaps, you'll find such sites at the top of a list. In any case, let the searcher beware.

Other businesses, however, are being far more clever in their use of intranet Webs. Take, for example, Zima, **http://www.zima.com**. Zima entices me with promises of real stuff and assures me that I'll get cool virtual stuff like JPEG graphic files and access to exclusive areas on Zima com. Well, gag me with a phone, but this isn't going to work with me. But then, I'm a cynical writer by trade. If the Earth were invaded by Martians, my first question would be: Will they be here in

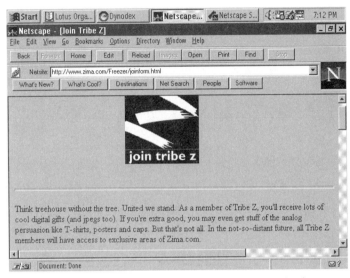

**Figure 2.2**: Zima's Web site sparkles with both style and substance.

time for me to make the morning deadline?

Most of the time, though, Zima gets people who are more than willing to tell them everything and anything about their lifestyles—which Zima faithfully records in its databases. At the same time, Zima is recording every page you visit and how long you're spending time on that page. This is pure, unadulterated, marketing information gold. Zima uses this information to craft their page so that when you come visiting again, the first page you'll see is one that's been crafted to your known likes and dislikes.

Zima's on the cutting edge—for now. By tomorrow, everyone will be able to get that level of user information and more from every visitor. With that information in hand, you can then apply it to your groupware and databases so that when users visit you, they'll find pages that are customized to the last detail for that user. Narrow-cast advertising will have reached its peak.

That's only outside the company. However, the same techniques can be used to make internal Web page use more productive. A proper mix of groupware, DBMSs, and the Web will enable you to supply every user with a customized page that can contain an automatically generated to-do list, complete with links to the particular jobs, and the latest company news tailored to a particular employee's interests. And none of this is going to require anyone to manually write a line of HTML.

So much for the bright side of the coming intranets. The dark side is that companies can use the same techniques to spy on employees in a way that George Orwell would have recognized in a moment, and that Joseph Stalin would have used it in a nanosecond.

This is not a sin of the intranet. All that computing, networking, and now the Internet and intranets have done is to put more powerful tools in our hands. For the most part, we look to the positive benefits of these tools. We should never forget, though, that this power is a double-edged sword. If your company uses it to snoop on its own employees, whether you just work at the firm or you're its president, you owe it to everyone to stop the abuse.

Like it or not, that's the world we're heading to; and there's no gear shift. We're stuck in high gear, and you can forget about pushing in the brakes—they were never built into this model. Your best choice is to use this power responsibly and with the full awareness of just how strong this technology can make you. Otherwise, you can ruin yourself by abusing this power and, quite likely, taking your entire enterprise down with you.

# 3

## All for One & One for All

### Connectivity

Be warned: I pull out a lot of technical stops in this chapter. The theories of intranetworking and interoperability are not lightweight subjects. Like it or lump it, though, this is an area that you'll need to know, if for no other reason than to explain to upper management why such a seemingly simple matter as transferring a MacWrite file from a Mac to a PC so that it can be read with WinWord can be fairly complex. In later chapters, I go more into the practice; but without a good, solid theoretical background, you'll eventually end up utterly confused as to why "quick" jobs of transferring information can end up taking weeks.

# Intranetworking

If you're not a LAN expert, it all sounds so easy. You want to hook all your computers into a network? Simple, just hook them up to the same wire and away you go. By this time, your network administrator is either laughing or crying hysterically.

TCP/IP, the network protocol core of any intranet, does offer a one network protocol solution. Unfortunately, if you're working with a preexisting network, you almost certainly won't enjoy the luxury of just turning off the old and turning on the new. Instead, for a while at least, you're going to have to deal with the joys of running multiple network operating systems, protocols, and system architectures: Oy!

At least, in the age of the intranet, you're going to avoid many of the problems of the past. It used to be that whenever the idea of connecting, say, Macs and PCs, together into one network came up, you'd proceed immediately to religious wars over which network standards would be used. Should you go with 10Base-T wiring or 10Base2? Should you try to run NetWare, at least the NetWare IPX stack on the Macs, or should you stick with LocalTalk?

**Table 3.1 Common LAN Protocols.**

| Name | Description |
| --- | --- |
| **AppleTalk** | Apple Macintosh network protocols based on OSI's seven-layer model. |
| **DECnet** | Digital Equipment Corporation's proprietary network protocols based on the OSI model. Formerly used on VAX/VMS minicomputers, it's being swiftly superseded by TCP/IP. |
| **IPX/SPX** | Internet Packet Exchange and Sequenced Packet Exchange protocols used by Novell NetWare. Despite the name, IPX doesn't have a thing to do with the Internet. |
| **NetBEUI** | NetBIOS Extended User Interface used by IBM LAN Server, Microsoft LAN Manager, and Windows NT. |
| **NetBIOS** | Network Basic Input Output System. While left behind by its creators, IBM and Microsoft, NetBIOS is still popular with small network vendors and is still found at the heart of Artisoft's LANtastic. |
| **OSI** | Open Systems Interconnect protocols based on a seven-layer model was made as an interna tional standard. While a very useful model for understanding networking, it has little direct utility in North America. |

| | |
|---|---|
| **SNA** | System Network Architecture used on IBM mainframes and AS/400 minicomputers. |
| **TCP/IP** | Transmission Control Protocol/Internet Protocol is used by most UNIX systems and is practically synonymous with the Internet and intranets. |

Those questions are still going to get asked, but there's an overriding answer: We'll use whatever it takes to get every box to speak TCP/IP. Fortunately, almost every NOS on the planet now makes TCP/IP an option; so as you upgrade your software, the problems of running multiple protocols on a single NIC are disappearing. In other words, the first stop on your way to an intranet is upgrading your operating system and your NOS. For example, the latest versions of Windows NT, Windows 95, Mac OS, and Unix all come with TCP/IP as one of their default protocols. By making sure you have these, you'll save yourself many painful hours of network tweaking.

If you're stuck with running multiple protocols, you need operating systems or add-on programs that can deal with more than one protocol at a time. I've already mentioned two such products in the previous chapters; but some others to consider, for people using the popular NetWare NOS, are Cisco's IPeXchange gateway, **http://www.cisco. com/**, for converting Novell's proprietary IPX networking protocol to IP, and Performance Technology's Instant Internet, **http://www.perftech.com/**.

Using something a bit more exotic? Check with your NOS vendor. If your NOS value-added reseller (VAR) or system integrator (SI) can't help you, dump them and the NOS they rode in on. Sticking with a contrary NOS today makes as little sense in the '90s as sticking with the CP/M-80 operating system in the '80s. All you'd be doing is dooming yourself to obsolete technology that will pull you down like an anchor in the buoyant, modern competitive world.

# Network Models

Before jumping into the details, it won't hurt you and it may very well help you to know something about the OSI and TCP/IP networking models. You may never have to work with either one directly, but some basic understanding of the concepts can be very helpful in figuring out why a properly setup intranet will occasionally not act properly at all.

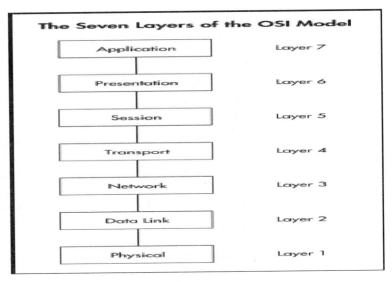

**Figure 3.1**: The OSI model at a glance.

One useful way of looking at a network is as a layer cake. At the bottom of this cake, according to the OSI Reference Model, is the physical layer. Moving up from there we find the data link, network, transport, session, presentation, and finally the application level. The actual contact between layers is called the Service Access Point (SAP).

Each level is independent of the other, but at the same time dependent on the lower levels supporting the weight of the upper levels. In the OSI Model, a data link protocol like Novell's sequenced packet exchange (SPX) should be able to do its work so long as the physical layer does its part. What that physical layer is made up of should be totally irrelevant to the data link protocol. It could be Ethernet, it could be FDDI; heck, it could be someone flashing a flash-light. With the OSI model, it doesn't matter so long as each layer does its job without requiring anything of other layers except that they do their jobs.

The physical layer defines the actual hardware. It covers all the electrical, mechanical, and procedural issues involved in transmitting data bits. A concrete example of the hardware level is an NIC (network interface card) and its cable. Next up, we find the data link level. This level is responsible for organizing data into packets and insuring error detection and correction. At the network level, the task is to insure packet delivery by dealing with routing procedures and flow-control functions. At the network level, issues like how connections are established, terminated, and maintained are dealt with. The network layer also takes care of internetworking.

From here we go to the transport layer. This level takes care of end-to-end data transmissions by defining higher levels of error recovery and flow control. This is the bridge level between the network itself and a user's system. Another step up, and we arrive at the session level. The session level of a NOS controls communications between applications. In one view of OSI, when we move to the session level, we've moved from the "network" levels to the "application" levels.

A crude way of looking at it is that the lower layers are like the engine of a car. When you're driving, you don't need to know what each piston is doing, as long as the engine runs. The session level describes the actual mechanisms that transmit your commands to the network "engine." Next, we come to the presentation level. In presentation, you're dealing with issues like data formatting and application interfacing. Finally, at the top, we arrive at the application level. The name says it all. Network applications like groupware, network schedulers, and electronic mail (commonly referred to as e-mail) are all examples of products with application-level interfaces.

Each layer of this cake is important; but it's easy to get tangled up in the theory and not enjoy the cake. The OSI model is just that—a model. While some vendors make a big deal about their applications fitting the model, many more NOSs don't. Some, like systems built around TCP/IP, can't be OSI compliant. The Internet's design includes features on a single level which OSI would place on separate levels. After years of trying, the OSI camp is finally conceding that while their model would make for cleaner and easier to administer Internet, TCP/IP rules.

That said, the OSI model is still useful for understanding networking basics. The idea of OSI, to make each layer each independent of each other, is laudable. OSI networks should be very easy to maintain and make intersystem networking much easier. In reality, TCP/IP rules the intranet; but the model is still a useful one to have at hand.

# Hard Contact

With that out of the way, your next problem will be getting all of your hardware to physically talk to each other, even if they're all using TCP/IP. While the problems are literally right there in front of you, wiring differences can be just as tough to handle as hashing out the clashes between various networking protocols.

**Table 3.2: Wiring Varieties**

These are the main Ethernet cabling types. You must be certain to have compatible wiring and/or connectivity equipment, or your LAN will be dead in the water.

| Name | Description |
|------|-------------|
| **10Base2** | 10MHz Ethernet running over thin, 50 Ohm baseband coaxial cable. 10Base2 is also commonly referred to as thin Ethernet, or "Cheapernet." |
| **10Base5** | 10MHz Ethernet running over standard (thick) 50 Ohm baseband coaxial cabling. Now obsolete. |
| **10BaseF** | 10MHz Ethernet running over fiber-optic cabling. |
| **10BaseT** | 10MHz Ethernet running over unshielded, twisted-pair (UTP) cabling. |

| | |
|---|---|
| **10Broad36** | 10MHz Ethernet running through a broadband cable. |
| **100BaseT** | 100Mhz Ethernet running over shielded twisted-pair (STP cabling). Also known as Fast Ethernet. |
| **100BaseT4** | 100MHz Fast Ethernet that can run over lower quality Category 3 UTP. |
| **100BaseVG** | 100Mhz Ethernet that's incompatible with Fast Ethernet. |

Again, the easiest solution is to pick one wiring solution and dump the rest. Of course, this is also the expensive solution; but now may be the time to make such a radical shift. The rise of Fast Ethernet, **http://www.alumni.caltech.edu/~dank/fe/**, and 100VG AnyLAN, **http://www.io.com/ ~richardr/vg/**, makes shifting over to 100Mbps LAN speeds as affordable as switching over to old-fashioned, and far slower, Ethernet or token-ring NICs. If you make the change now, you not only take care of the compatibility problem, you also get a tenfold speed increase over typical Ethernet, and almost as big a gain over run-of-the-mill token-ring networks. If you can afford it, this is a real bargain. If you can't afford that kind of network plant investment, then it's time for you to start looking into the world of bridges, gateways, hubs, and routers.

Bridges work exactly like their names imply. These devices provide a pathway between two or more network segments. Bridges are useful for many different networking jobs; but for intranetworking, a bridge's primary importance lies in its ability to bring together dissimilar networks, like Ethernet and token-ring, and pass messages back and forth between them—so long as they're running the same network protocol. In short, you'll want a bridge in situations like where the Mac folks are running MacTCP over LocalTalk wiring, and you need them to have a common ground with your PC people who are all running Win95 TCP/IP on 10Base2.

Gateways go one step beyond bridges. Before the confusion begins, let me just say that there are at least five different device types out there that are called gateways. Give people a useful word and they'll use it to death. A LAN gateway, which is the one we're concerned with at the moment, doesn't merely bridge the gap between dissimilar architectures, but actively translates dissimilar protocols from one network to another.

A gateway can also connect different types of wiring. One common use for a gateway is to hook up an Ethernet to the much faster WAN technology called Fiber Distributed Data Interface (FDDI). A LAN gateway's real job, however, is to take a protocol like AppleTalk and convert it to TCP/IP and vice versa. As you might guess from that job description, LAN gateways have this one little problem: This equipment tends to be slloooowwww.

Hub is yet another device name that's been used half to death. For our purposes, there are two kinds of hubs. The first, passive hubs, simply act as bridges. At Vaughan-Nichols & Associates, for instance, we use passive hubs to connect our Macs to the rest of the network. An easy way of thinking of a passive hub is to see it as a train switching station. Many inputs go in from—in our case—10BaseT and 10Base2, and then use TCP/IP to find the right exit, without the hub doing anything but providing the virtual train tracks.

Active hubs, however, can do much more. An active hub will almost certainly act as a repeater, which allows you to build bigger networks by amplifying LAN signals. The newest versions of hubs, often called third or, for the really fancy ones, fourth generation hubs, also provide back-plane, a.k.a. internal high-speed connection buses, for multiple network wiring and protocols at once. In short, a top-quality hub combines all the features of bridges and gateways into a single, easy-to-manage and fast package. So why doesn't everyone have one? Well, let me put it this way: Where in my description did I say anything about their being cheap?

Routers are the last type of network equipment you need to consider for internetworking, and also one of the more important. If you have a permanent connection to the Internet, you will need a router. Working the net without one is like tightrope walking without a net—or a rope, for that matter.

A router acts as a packet switcher. These devices keep track of the best routes to other network devices on your intranet and the Internet. If your local router can't figure out the best route, it will forward the packets along to what it believes will be the best router to figure out the exact route. In the process, routers can handle either a single protocol or multiple protocols. Before buying a router, check and make sure that it can do the job you have in mind. A router that doesn't understand AppleTalk isn't likely to do a whole lot of good with a network full of Macs.

Some protocols don't route worth a hill of beans. Even these stubborn protocols can be hauled across an intranet by a technique called encapsulation, or tunneling. No matter which name you use, the results are the same. A router capable of encapsulating IPX packets can load the IPX packets onto an IP datastream so that the IPX message can get from one NetWare system to another over an otherwise uncrossable TCP/IP network.

Another router advantage is that when your LAN gets big and messy—and what LAN doesn't?—the router can handle information bridging far more efficiently than multiple bridges or gateways. Too many bridges or gateways can lead to a slow network. Too many bridges can lead to network congestion; and gateways have inherently tortoise-like speeds.

Routers don't have to exist as independent hardware. There are programs that let servers work as routers. Usually, this requires that the server has at least two NICs. Besides the cost of this technique, routing can really slow down a server's performance. If you have a server with power to spare, then a software router makes good sense. Me, I'd stick to a standalone router from one of the major router vendors: Cisco, Livingston, `http://www.livingston.com/`, or Bay Networks, `http://www.baynetworks.com/`.

For internetworking, what you really want is a multiprotocol router. This type of router can handle all the jobs that ordinary bridges, gateways, and routers cope with in a single box. Better still, unlike all the other devices, you can switch off support for the other protocols as you move towards a single TCP/IP standard while at the same time increasing the router's ability to deal with TCP/IP traffic.

Before going out and buying any of this equipment, stop, take a deep breath, and consider exactly what you need for your network. Having a top of the line router is great, but its also going to set you back in excess of 20 grand—and network vendors don't tend to take returns.

Your best move is to consult with your network vendors and ISP to determine what the best equipment is for your intranet. After that, get a second opinion. Most network VARs and ISPs are as honest as the day is long; but there are some who won't hesitate for a moment to sell you overpriced, overly powerful hardware just to fatten their profits.

Having taken that paranoid pill, you should, nevertheless, pay attention to your ISP's opinions. Even when you're convinced to the bottom of your socks that Livingston routers are just what you need, if your ISP works with nothing but Cisco routers, you're going to be better off with Cisco routers, or switching to an ISP that does work with Livingston equipment.

## Interoperability

One of intranet's golden promises is interoperability. With true interoperability, you not only don't have to know where information is, you also don't need to know its format. Excel spreadsheet, dBase database file, or WordStar document—it doesn't matter. The browser will let you read them all without any effort on your part. For years, interoperability and its twin, open systems, have hovered like a mirage on the computing horizon. Now, interoperability's dream of liberating data from the bonds of a single architecture or operating system so that data can be used throughout a heterogeneous network is coming within reach.

By the early 1990s, we've struck off many of the chains shackling the interoperability dream. Standards, like Sun's, **http://www.sun.com**, Network File System (NFS), the

Object Management Group's (OMG), `http://www.omg.org`, Common Object Request Broker Architecture (CORBA), and IBM's Systems Network Architecture (SNA) Advanced-Program-to-Program Communications (APPC) LU 6.2 are in place.

These standards enable application programmers to pour data from its current location to wherever it is needed. NFS, in particular, once only Unix's darling, has been ported to many environments and stands an excellent chance of becoming the rock-solid foundation upon which interoperability will be built. On intranets, SunSoft's WebNFS holds the promise of making distant Web sites deliver data to you ten times faster then the current Web data transfer protocol, HTTP. With WebNFS, you'll be able to access data thousands of miles away just as if it were a network drive already set on your system.

NFS is not the only one of these interoperability standard sets that are being retrofitted for the intranet. OMG is porting its technology to the Web in an initiative called CORBAnet, `http://corbanet.dstc.edu.au`.

Unfortunately, these approaches don't go far enough. The problem is not simply that these standards mix as well as oil and water, which is indeed the case. Mere access to files located on systems with different architectures isn't enough. What users really need is the ability to use data no matter where it's located or in what format it's stored.

## Look and Feel

A false start in this direction are the host of programs that carry the same look and feel across differing operating platforms and systems. There are some small advantages, primarily in training costs, to being able to move from Lotus 1-2-3 under MS-DOS to 1-2-3 under VAX-VMS or Unix. This saving masks a far more important benefit: the ability to move data, regardless of its origin, to the user who needs to work with it. A Lotus maven, for example, could pull in needed information for his Unix-based spreadsheet from MS-DOS based spreadsheets as easily as he could from a local spreadsheet.

As useful as this ability is, the restricted scope of these applications limit their usefulness. For instance, while a dBase user with an MS-DOS system can gather information from a Unix-powered dBase system, this doesn't do much good if most of the needed data is kept in Oracle databases.

Of course, one could point out that it's not the application designers' fault that there are so many incompatible data formats. This situation seems unlikely to change. So long as vendors must distinguish their products from one another, their support in creating universal data standards will be more hype than actual work.

There are exceptions. Adobe fully intends on making Portable Document Format (PDF) the new document standard for the Web over HTML. Of course, while Adobe is being more successful than most in this attempt, everyone has always wanted to make their standards the world's standard.

## Let the Protocol Do It

Another popular idea is to use data transfer protocols to handle the translation jobs. In this case, vendors aren't asking that everyone use their particular file format. Instead, they're asking for everyone to use a common protocol that numerous applications, especially database clients and servers, can use to transfer information to end-users, regardless of what format the data is actually kept in.

The most popular of these approaches is Open DataBase Connection (ODBC). Programs that are ODBC-compliant can, in theory, share data over any network. While ODBC has become the data transfer standard of choice for databases, there's enough looseness in its definition for applications to be ODBC-compliant and still be unable to communicate with each other. The moral for intranetworkers here is to test out ODBC programs before putting them into a production environment.

## Scissors and Paste-Pot

Until the day when data formats are standardized, if ever, programmers have several methods at their disposal to make piping data from one application to another easier. The first procedure, most often seen in graphical user interfaces (GUIs), is cut and paste. This method allows character and numeric values to be transferred from one application to another. Familiar GUIs that provide virtual scissors and paste are the Macintosh interface, Windows95, and Unix Inter-national's Open Look. While workable, cutting and pasting is both crude and slow, since it requires user action for all data exchanges.

Historically, the next approach has been to build interprocess message protocols. The most well known of these is Microsoft Windows' Dynamic Data Exchange (DDE). DDE falls short because it's a Windows-only solution and, in any case, its abilities are too limited. In a way, DDE is like the transport and session layers of the OSI networking model: It establishes connections between processes, but it doesn't concern itself with the way data is represented or encoded. Making sense of the data sent is the responsibility of the sending and receiving applications. Thus, while data transparency could be achieved with DDE, it could only be done by programming each application to recognize other applications' data formats. In other words, DDE simply masks the complexity of moving data from one application to another. DDE is not a data transparency solution itself.

No one is more aware of this lack than Microsoft. To better enable Windows programs to work together, Microsoft, along with other software vendors, is developing the Object Linking and Embedding (OLE) protocol. OLE presents an interesting approach to the problem of dealing with data in a multiple application environment. In OLE, data is associated with the application that created it in the first place. In many ways, this is taking a page from the Macintosh's book.

More specifically, in OLE, if I took an illustration made by Zsoft's Publisher Paintbrush and imported it to an Adobe PageMaker document, the illustration could still be modified by Paintbrush's tools from Page-Maker. As a user, I don't have to invoke Paintbrush. Pointers associated with the illustration notify OLE-aware applications of what I'm trying to do and take care of that for me. While the illustration is virtually within my document, physically, unless directed otherwise, the illustration remains a PaintBrush file. All I'm actually working with in PageMaker is a hotlink directly to the illustration and its application.

OLE manages data by dividing information into two classes. The first, objects, will be immediately recognizable to object-oriented programmers. Objects are instances of a user-defined data type that contains data, its structure, and the actions that can be performed on and with the data. Those actions that can be conducted with the data are called the object's appearance.

To manipulate and link objects to applications, Microsoft provides the container concept. Containers serve as the controls for objects. A foreign application doesn't have to worry about the exact properties of an object imported from another program. All a programmer who wishes to use OLE needs to know is how to use the container. If the container's simple controls aren't sufficient for the job, the object's original application is called on to get the work done.

OLE makes everyone's life a lot easier. Programmers don't have to slug it out with DDE and fine-tune their application's format for every other Windows application. Users can use the same old import and export data commands, but their control over the data is far more powerful.

Like everything else, OLE has a few problems. OLE relies upon the somewhat rickety structure of DDE to support data communications. Of more immediate concern to would-be OLE users is that documents made up from OLE objects are not easily transportable. In my example above, were I to move my PageMaker document to a system without Paint-Brush, my illustration would vanish like the morning dew. OLE has the dubious distinction of being a data transportability tool that can make thoroughly unportable files.

Of course, Microsoft wasn't going to put up with this level of failure. After fumbling around with object linking and embedding (OLE) custom controls, or OCXs, Microsoft has both rechristened OCXs as a standard for linking

Component Object Model (COM), Microsoft's universal data type, and given it a new name—ActiveX—to gather more publicity. For now, I'm going to leave ActiveX and save it for a discussion of active data links across the net. The important thing to remember is that beneath ActiveX's hype is an old and fairly well-established technology. Now, if only it would work more reliably, it would be worth more consideration.

## The Opposition

Apple and IBM are the main parties behind plans for a meta-datatype that would serve as a universal translator (shades of Star Trek) for data: OpenDoc. OMG has adopted OpenDoc as part of their CORBA strategy; and if Microsoft didn't have such an iron grip on the desktop market, OpenDoc might have a prayer of becoming a universal standard.

As it is, while OpenDoc is popular on Macs, OS/2 systems, and some Unix variants—notably IBM's own AIX—it's been hard pressed to progress beyond these markets. OpenDoc is, in my opinion, the better technology; but its failure to gain much market share leaves me convinced that it's as unlikely to rule the intranet of tomorrow as it has the networks of today.

## Active Solutions

Once, the Web was a relatively passive medium. When all was said and done, all you used to do on the Web was send and receive ASCII or binary files. Translating those binary files, as we've seen, has been a nightmare of clashing standards in the night.

With the advent of Sun Microsystems' Java, the Web changed. Now, developers could use this interpreted, object-oriented language to deliver actual working programs, or applets, over the Internet. Java, still wet behind the ears, became the new rage of Web publishers. Microsoft, although slow to recognize the importance of the Internet, quickly realized remote Internet computing's popularity and announced the release of their ActiveX application programming interface—a product that simultaneously both competes with, and conceivably complements, Java.

Some of these changes are still happening. For today, ActiveX isn't much more than "veneerware"—that is, software that may look good in demos but has little substance behind it. Nonetheless, ActiveX must be taken seriously. While it's really just a repackaging of what Microsoft was already doing, that already puts it years ahead of Java. Of course, in the past, under the guise of OLE, it was a Windows-only standard; so that advantage may not be as big as it seems.

Beginning with Internet Explorer 3.0, Microsoft's Web browser, and Internet Information Server 2.0, Microsoft's Web server, ActiveX is theoretically available to provide a common, distributed object-oriented way of transferring active data from one site to another. ActiveX's API will, of course, also be used to make Microsoft BackOffice products capable of running data updates and programs across the Internet.

If you take out the word Internet, all of this will sound very familiar to the interoperability community. With ActiveX, nothing has changed except the name: It's still COM and OLE. OMG's CORBA and its Object Request Brokers (ORBs) are the multi-platform equivalent of Microsoft's COM and ActiveX. Unlike ActiveX, however, ORBs are already alive and well in such systems as DEC's ObjectBroker, Hewlett-Packard's ORB+, and IBM's System Object Model (SOM). Beyond this, of course, are such open desktop information systems as Apple and IBM's OpenDoc. ActiveX may end up integrating with CORBA; but CORBA and OpenDoc are about fully distributed, platform-independent objects. Microsoft's ActiveX is all about running distributed programs across the intranet.

CORBA standard applications will soon be appearing on the Internet. Besides the CORBAnet project, SunSoft and OMG have come up with a standard for Java applets to connect with CORBA applications: Java Objects Everywhere (JOE). Java applets that can work with a CORBA object request broker (ORBlets) will eventually be compiled with the OMG's Interface Definition Language compiler. SunSoft, Postmodern Computing, and Iona Technologies are all working on JOE compilers.

This development might be just the boost Java needs to move from an overly complex toy language to a major tool in the Web page developers' toolbox. Despite the attraction of applications that actually run on the net instead of over it, Java has its own woes. Until recently, Java's learning curve was not for humans. Products like Symantec's Caffeine, **http:www.symantec.com**, a free Java plug-in for its C++ development environment, however, are finally making Java somewhat easier to program. Still, even when you understand the programming, Java's attractiveness is marred by its dog-slow interpreted nature.

Both Java and ActiveX have problems in common. Besides their speed troubles, many Internet security authorities are wary of active network applications' potential for security holes. In fact, one group, the NASA Automated System Incident Response team (NASRIC), has already gone on record as stating that by its very nature, Java is insecure. NASRIC has a point. Simply by running online programs, like Java and ActiveX enabled programs, client systems cannot check for those programs' compliance with local security requirements.

That's in the short run. In the long run, CORBA's use of proxies and other security features should make JOE applets safe. Microsoft, of course, believes that its security measures will also make ActiveX safe for all users. For now, though, Java and JOE, security risks and all, are the only real, interactive, distributed object Web languages.

## Today's Problems, Today's Solutions

In the meantime, Java just makes cute graphics and ActiveX is merely a neat idea, and users still need to share information. Fortunately, there are several tools that make moving data from application to application, while not entirely transparent, certainly more practical than waiting for the resolution of the aforementioned conflicts.

For Web browser users, these applications are called helper applications and viewers. Helper applications are external programs that enable a browser to handle a data type that the browser itself can't cope with alone. Plug-ins are programs that don't come fully integrated with your browser, but once you've installed them, you can use them as if they were part of your browser. For example, the Adobe PDF helper application launches itself and then, outside of the browser, lets you read the document. The plug-in, though, lets you view the document on wire within the browser. From a user's point of view, a plug-in appears to be just another part of the browser. From an administration viewpoint, this works really well, because it decreases the temptation for users to play around with their settings.

**Table 3.2: Plug-In Ports of Call**

Here are some of the best places on the Web to get the most up-to-date plug-ins and helper applications.

| Site | URL |
| --- | --- |
| Explorer | `http://www.microsoft.com/msdownload/` |
| Macintosh | `http://browserwatch.iworld.com/plug-in-mac.html` |
| Netscape | `http://home.netscape.com/comprod/mirror/navcomponents_download.html` |
| OS/2 | `http://www.utirc.utoronto.ca/HTMLdocs/OS2TOOLS/os2_helpers.html` |
| Windows | `http://www.stroud.com/` |
| Unix | `http://browserwatch.iworld.com/plug-in-unix.html` |

Many users don't need to worry about importing exotic MPEG movies. They might want to, mind you; but as a businessperson, you might have a rather low opinion of an employee burning up hours watching "Debbie Does Dallas" clips. The far more mundane but important problem is how to transfer data between meat and potatoes, like Lotus 1-2-3 and WordPro.

For this, you need programs like Adobe's Word for Word, **http://www.adobe.com**, or Dataviz's MacLink Plus, **http://www.dataviz.com/**. Both programs are a godsend. Each one automatically recognizes file types and then converts them to a file type that you'll find useful. Despite its name, Word for Word also works with graphics, spreadsheets, and databases. The process isn't transparent with either program, but as manual methods go, it is easy. There are other programs that work with a particular type of file. Quarterdeck's HiJaack, **http://www.qdeck. com**, for example, specializes in graphic files.

One thing you won't want to do is to trust your own programs' import and export capabilities. Oh, chances are they'll be fine for basic information. But a colleague of mine, Esther Schindler, has just finished going over every word processor that anyone buys these days, and—horrors—when it came to complex documents, none of them were able to do a good job of translating the nuisances between document types.

Before buying any of these programs, if at all possible, get a sampling of file types that your company will be using internally and make sure the software at hand can translate them properly. Better still, you could get everyone in the company to agree on one standard for word processing, one for spreadsheets, and so on... Nah, some things really are impossible dreams!

# Clear As Mud

I'd love to be able to say that we can look forward to seeing data transparency sometime soon. I can't. It's not the state of the art that's the hitch. No, the real trouble is that there's no vendor consensus on how to handle interoperability. Until that day arrives, we must content ourselves with restricted access to our data, and be glad of what data transparency tools we do have at hand. Still, with the advent of the Internet, millions of users now know that they want fast access to any data, anywhere, anytime; so we can look forward to developers slowly but surely coming up with true interoperability answers to all our "Unknown Format Error" sorrows.

# From PCs to LANs

## The PCs

Someday soon, transforming your LAN into an intranet and catching a ride onto the Internet will be easy. Today is not that day.

Today, the newest version of everyone's operating system includes Internet connectivity and a Web browser. That's a good start, but it's not enough. For now, you must have just the right mix of hardware and software to explore the Web. If that was all there was to it, putting together an intranet would be as simple as following a recipe. Alas, we're a long way from there.

# Finding the Right Hardware

Most modern PCs are capable of running the software you need for the Web. At a minimum, you'll need systems with the resources of those listed below.

**Table 4.1: Bare-bones Hardware Requirements**

|  | PC | Macintosh |
| --- | --- | --- |
| Processor | 80386SX | 68030 |
| Speed | 25MHz | 25MHz |
| RAM | 4MB | 5MB |
| Disk Space | 8MB | 8MB |
| Graphics | VGA | Color |
| NIC | Ethernet | Ethernet |

You could get by with less powerful equipment, but you don't want to, since your performance would be marginal at best. The above is the very least you'll need for acceptable performance. If you're content to use only character-based applications, then you could get by with using almost any computer that can talk to a modem and a character-based browser like www or Lynx. Most users demand more; and an intranet absolutely requires more.

If you want better than the rock-bottom minimum, consider the requirements listed in Table 4.2.

## Table 4.2: Practical Minimum Hardware Requirements

|  | PC | Macintosh |
|---|---|---|
| Processor | 80486SX | 68030 |
| Speed | 25MHz | 40MHz |
| RAM | 8MB | 8MB |
| Disk Space | 8MB | 8MB |
| Graphics | SVGA | 8-bit, 256-color |
| NIC | Ethernet | Ethernet |

If you have the cash, you may wish to consider getting some of the seriously high-quality machines that are available, such as the ones outlined in Table 4.3.

## Table 4.3: Optimal Hardware Requirements

|  | PC | Macintosh |
|---|---|---|
| Processor | Pentium | PowerPC-601 |
| Speed | 75MHz | 75MHz |
| RAM | 16MB | 6MB |
| Disk Space | 8MB | 8MB |
| Graphics | Super-VGA | 8-bit, 256-color |

Network Card    Ethernet                Ethernet

Finally, let's pretend that the company has given you a blank check for upgrading an entire department's system base for kick-ass and take-name performance. Hey, we can dream!

**Table 4.4: Best Hardware Requirements**

|              | PC                  | Macintosh     |
|--------------|---------------------|---------------|
| Processor    | Pentium             | PowerPC-604   |
| Speed        | 166MHz+             | 150MHz+       |
| RAM          | 32MB                | 32MB          |
| Disk Space   | 16MB                | 16MB          |
| Graphics     | 24-bit true color   |               |
| Network Card | Fast Ethernet/100VG |               |

If you love computer hardware, one thing will strike your eye immediately. There's really nothing top of the line about these requirements. To run intranet programs, like a Web browser, you don't need a fast Pentium or PowerPC chip. Compared to the demands of most modern programs, intranets don't ask for much from PCs.

A fast hard drive is important, but not vital, for decent Web browser performance. Any modern drive with an access speed of 28 milliseconds or less should serve you well. Where CPU speed does get important is in translating graphic and PostScript files into viewable formats. If you think that you're going to be dealing extensively with these file types, go ahead and get a faster processor.

Another thing you won't need to be concerned about is the drive interface. Whether you're using small computer system interface (SCSI), integrated drive electronics (IDE), extended IDE (EIDE), or an older technology doesn't matter a fig to your intranet.

# Graphics

Graphics is another area where speed is nice but not essential. The critical factors you should look at in a graphics card are its graphics processor, its onboard memory, and its interface to the motherboard.

A graphics processor, like ATI's Mach128, speeds up your graphics in two ways. First, it takes the burden of displaying graphics off your main processor. Second, these chips specialize in speeding up the graphic routines that all programs use to display their images. No graphics processor, however, will do you any good unless you have the specific software driver for that specific processor. For instance, it doesn't matter how fast a graphics processor is supposed to be if you're an OS/2 Warp user and the card doesn't have a Warp driver. For Warp users, such a video adapter would be about as useful as the cheapest VGA card—which is to say, not at all.

Sad to say, you'll also need to make sure that the driver works properly. A number of graphics vendors have a nasty habit of releasing video cards with new hardware long before the software is ready to make use of the new equipment.

One thing that you won't need is a card that specializes in rendering 24-bit color images: 99% of all Web images are in 8-bit color.

For video memory, you can still get by with only 1 MB of video memory. That's because most color images on the Web have only 256 colors and 640 by 480 pixel resolution. As images with 16.7 million colors and 1024 by 768 resolution become more common, not to mention realtime video, you're going to want a system with 2 MB of video memory, and more would be nice. If you see videoconferencing in your intranet's future, you'll want to check with your software vendor for what built-in hardware for realtime video works best with their program.

Generally speaking, cards with video RAM (VRAM) are faster then their sisters with dynamic RAM (DRAM). Graphic board designers are constantly testing the limits of memory technology; and having VRAM no longer guarantees that a board will be faster then its DRAM twin. When in doubt, check reputable computer magazines like *Byte*, *PC Magazine*, and *Computer Shopper* for the latest hard numbers. Keep in mind that without the appropriate driver, a particular card is not worth an extra premium.

The card's connection to the system is the one place where, driver or no driver, your video card's performance can be choked off. Systems with industry standard architecture (ISA), extended industry standard architecture (EISA), and NuBus graphics cards will lag behind otherwise identical cards that connect with VL-Bus or PCI slots.

If you have a machine without these standards, don't rush out for a new one just to have a local bus video connection for the Web alone. While the faster slots will make a large difference to most applications, what's really going to be determining your browser speed is your connection speed to the Internet.

Let me make this last point very clear. The most critical part of any system you'll be exploring the Web on is your Internet connection. Whether you have a 56Kbps network connection or a T3 of your very own, that component's speed, more than any other, determines how quickly your overall system will run. For more on that side of networking, see chapter 5.

If you do have some funds available for upgrading preexisting systems, there are only two areas that are really worth spending the money on: memory and an Ethernet connection. With today's RAM-starved operating systems, More memory is worth more than a higher-end processor any day of the week. Similarly, a 100MB Ethernet LAN will give you more bang for the buck than any other network expenditure you could possibly make.

More memory can also help you because you'll be able to cache more Web pages on your local system. This, in turn, means that you'll need to access the Web site less frequently and take up intranet bandwidth less often. This will cause a local PC and your network to respond more quickly when you need to move back to a document you were looking at a moment ago.

# Modems

For intranets, you really should forget about high-speed modems. Even the best of them, with both data compression and error correction, aren't fast enough for business Web connectivity at the network level. If you're using your intranet only as a means of expanding your local e-mail system to the world, then a modem connection is worth considering. Just don't even think for a moment that it's going to be good for anything else.

A V.34 modem, with its 28,800 BPS, is the bottom line for an intranet modem. There are faster technologies, like V.34bis, which can supposedly push a modem to 33,600 BPS, but that's under factory test conditions. The honest truth is that with plain old telephone service (POTS), you can expect to see no more than a top throughput of 24,400 BPS. No technology advance is likely to change this. There's only so much you can ask of ordinary copper telephone wiring, and we're already asking it.

You don't want to use a modem without V.42 error correcting and V.42bis data compression. Modem TCP/IP connections, like Serial Line Internet Protocol (SLIP), don't include any error correction; and the least bit of line noise can knock your network connection for a loop. You'll need data compression because SLIP has a high latency. In English, this means that SLIP takes its own sweet time transferring information. Anything that improves SLIP, or its bigger, better brother, Point to Point Protocol (PPP) throughput—which is where data compression comes in—is well worth a try.

Before you go out modem shopping, you'll also want to check with your Internet provider to see what kind of modems they're using. While most modems will work with most other modems, the odds are you'll get more consistent connections if you have all the same brand. This also makes troubleshooting easier.

It also won't do you a bit of good to get a high-speed 33,600 BPS modem if your ISP uses modems that can only talk to your modem at a slow crawl of 21,600 BPS. Even if you don't elect to get a twin of your provider's modems, the company can advise you of what modems to avoid. People may be created equal, but modems certainly aren't.

You'll also want to get a dedicated phone line for your modem connection. An intranet needs 24-hours-a-day, seven days a week connectivity. Auntie Em calling in on your network line to let you know that Dorothy has just gone tornado hopping is a no-win situation for any data that dear old auntie has just knocked into the ether.

# Modem Standards

If you're going to go ahead with modems, you'll need to know something about the arcane standards which govern modern modems.

Some of you might find modem standards mind-numbing; but you must never buy a modem that doesn't conform to them. Yes, there are nonstandard modems out there that can fire data at unheard-of speeds; but they're using proprietary solutions. In the modem biz, proprietary means they can only talk to other modems using the exact same scheme. Even if it sounds so good that you think everyone should use it, don't bother. Proprietary solutions lock you in. If your Internet provider changes modems, or the modem manufacturer goes under, you're sunk.

This problem isn't just for new modems. Every now and again, you'll run across a deal for an older high-speed modem that sounds too good to be true. Chances are, it is. Older, nonstandard modems, even from such top vendors as Hayes, are of little use to the end-user or computer guru.

The most important modem standards are made by the International Telecommunications Union-Telecommunic ations Standards Sector (ITU-TSS), or informally, just TSS. You might also have heard of them by their older name: Consultative Committee for International Telephony and Telegraphy (CCITT). This international standards group sets the V-series of standards. Unlike some standards, TSS' rules are recognized and obeyed by almost every modem and fax manufacturer in the world. The reason is quite simple: Even on the datacom autobahn, there must be rules. Without the TSS' laws, data and fax traffic would slow to an inchworm's pace.

Other standards, such as Microcom's Microcom Networking Protocols (MNP), are de facto rather than de jure. While no standard-setting organization stands behind MNP, almost all modem and communication vendors recognize the MNP standards.

Before launching into communications standards, let's spell out some telecommunication basics. First, I'll deal with the difference between baud and bits per second (BPS). Most of the confusion about these two terms arises because at low speeds, BPS and baud have the same value. For instance, a 300 BPS modem transmits data at the exact same rate as a 300 baud modem. Baud measures the line-switching speed of a communications line. Thus, a 600 baud modem can transmit or receive 600 frequency or voltage changes on a line in a second. BPS, on the other hand, measures how many bits of data can be sent or received on a line per second.

So, how can a modem pack more information (BPS) into a line than a given baud? The secret is in the encoding. By modulating the baud—making changes in amplitude, frequency, or phase polarity of a line's carrier wave—more

BPS can be stuffed into a single baud. For instance, 1200 BPS modems actually use a 600 baud connection. The most common techniques for inserting more BPS data onto a baud are Differential Phase Shift Keying (DPSK), Frequency Shift Keying (FSK), Quadrature Amplitude Modulation (QAM), and Trellis Coding Modulation (TCM). If you can say all of these quickly and without fainting, congratulations: You're a techie!

If all those acronyms just gave you a case of alphabet soup indigestion, don't worry about it. The important lesson here is that baud does not equal BPS. When you next buy a modem, ask your salesperson to explain a modem's speed rating. This is a quick way of telling if they know their modems from a hole in the ground.

For webrunners, the important standards are the ones listed below in table 4.5.

**Table 4.5: Modem Standards**

| Designation | Defines |
| --- | --- |
| V.22 | 1200 BPS |
| V.22bis | 2400 BPS |
| V.32 | 9600 BPS |
| V.32bis | 14,400 BPS |
| V.32ter | 19,200 BPS [Not TSS; avoid!] |
| V.34/V.Fast | 28,800 BPS |
| V.34bis | 33,600 BPS |

| V.FC | 28,800 BPS [Not TSS; avoid!] |
|------|------------------------------|
| V.42 | Error Correction |
| V.42bis | Data Compression |

Today, almost all general purpose modems include V.22bis compatibility as a fallback for when lines are too noisy for higher speeds. If you're having so much trouble that your modem has dropped its speed to 2400 BPS, it's time to disconnect and call your telephone company, because something has gone badly wrong with your line.

With V.32, we start moving into the fast modem crowd. V.32 uses TCM, and optionally TCM encoding, to boost full duplex data transfers to 9600 BPS. Some folks still think that they're being financially sensible by sticking with their old V.32 modems. This is a case of being penny-wise and pound-foolish. You'll make up for the price of a newer modem over a V.32 within a few hours of jumping aboard the Internet.

V.34, known to friends as V.Fast, takes modems to a top speed of 28,800 BPS. V.34 took its time getting approved but was finally given official blessing in 1994. Some modem manufacturers, irked by the slow moving CCITT, decided to jump the gun. In mid-1993, Rockwell International, the most important modem chip manufacturer, released its V.FC (V. Fast Class) chipset. V.FC is not a TSS standard, but it is based on the proposed design of V.34. For example, V.FC uses V.34's multidimensional trellis coding and line probing to produce a top speed of 28,800 BPS. Modem manufacturers jumped on V.FC like shysters after an ambulance. More than a hundred companies, including major players like Hayes and Supra, rode the V.FC "standard."

Take a look at your "fast" modems carefully. If you find that you have a V.FC and not a V.34, check with the vendor to see if there's any way to upgrade them to V.34. If there isn't, junk 'em.

The last pair of standards that are important for modem commuters has confused more than its fair share of users: V.42 and V.42bis. V.42 defines the use of several error correction protocols. These protocols attempt—and for the most part succeed—in making sure that no noise creeps into data, no matter how noisy the line.

V.42's primary error-correction protocol is Link Access Procedure for Modems (LAPM). LAPM borrows from the X.25 High-level Data Link Control (HDLC) protocol. As the names indicate, both correct errors at the data-link level. When a V.42 modem connects with a modem that doesn't "speak" LAPM, V.42, it can also work with the earlier non-CCITT error correction protocols, MNP Classes 2 through 4. Regardless of the error correction method, V.42 can be used with modems using V.22, V.22bis, V.32, V.32bis, and V.34.

The V.42bis protocol uses data compression to speed up data communications. Usually, V.42bis compresses data at about a 3.5 to 1 ratio. In effect, V.42bis makes data communications go much faster. The proviso here is that this works well with simple text. If you're also working with large images, shipping spreadsheets across the net, or anything else that's in a binary file, you're not going to get anything like that much of a speed increase. Be wary of modem manufacturers that claim speeds higher than 33,600 BPS: They're using V.42bis to fatten up their speed claims to unrealistic levels.

Don't dismiss V.42bis; it can help speed things along. It's just not as good as it appears in some advertisements. Finally, V.42bis is also compatible with the older MNP Level 5 data compression protocol. V.42bis does have one shining advantage over the MNP-5: V.42bis constantly analyzes the data stream and stops trying to compress it when such efforts would be in vain. MNP-5, however, doesn't have this feature, and can actually slow down the transmission of compressed files by trying to shrink the unshrinkable.

With this information at your fingertips, you should be in a much better position to make an intelligent modem buying decision. Remember, always ask about the modem's standards support, and don't settle for wrong or evasive answers. Your modem is your gateway to the net—don't settle for anything less than the best.

# Network Cards

Even riding the slow boat to the Internet, you'll need to have Ethernet-capable network cards. For the most part, any network interface card (NIC) will do. There are exceptions to this rule. For PC users, this means any proprietary NIC, such as those of Moses LAN and Artisoft's LANtastic/Z product. Mac users must steer clear of PhoneTalk.

When you're shopping for a network card, there are a few things you, or more specifically your network administrator, should check on. First, on PCs, a 16-bit card will be faster then an 8-bit card. Even faster, if you have a PC with extended industry standard architecture (EISA), Video Electronics Standards Associa-tions (VL-Bus), or

Peripheral Component Intercon-nect (PCI) slots, is an NIC that can use one of these slots. A PCI board will leave the competition eating its dust. Before buying, remember that these three are incompatible standards. You can't use an EISA NIC in a PCI slot, and so on. Depending on the make of your motherboard, you may not be able to use certain PCI cards in your PCI slots. This is a problem that I, every other day an expert, ran straight into. Check with your NIC vendor before buying your cards.

If you're planning on buying new PCs for your intranet, make sure they have PCI slots. Systems with the other standards are still available, but they grow less supported by the day. It's hard enough as it is to keep up with the mainstream of computing. There's no point in burdening yourself with already out-of-date equipment.

Mac users should also consider upgrading to a Mac with a PCI bus. PCI cards are much faster then their NuBus cousins. Again, that same caveat about making sure the PCI card will work with your system's motherboard holds true.

Another feature to look for is memory on the NIC itself. You don't need a lot of memory on the board, but even 16K worth will help buffer network traffic. This insures that if your computer is busy with a job in the foreground, it won't lose any Web traffic that's arriving in the background.

# Audio Hardware

Audio requirements are perhaps the easiest for Web users to meet. Macintosh users already have all the sound equipment they need to deal with Web audio files. PC users must get Sound Blaster compatible sound cards. Since almost all PC audio cards are Sound Blaster compatible, that's a cinch. Bigger and better speakers are nice, but they're not immediately useful. There are only a handful of sites that demand higher-quality audio equipment than what can be found in a cheap boom box.

# Software

Your software is as important as your hardware. Unless everything works together, you'll be unable to connect with the Web. For example, it's not audio hardware that's usually a problem with net sound connections, it's finding the right software to play it.

Intranet software consists of four parts: the networking software, the operating system, socket software that lets network applications connect with the Internet, and the applications themselves. For now, let's leave the applications be, and look at the parts that glue together your applications and the Internet.

# Network Software at the PC Level

If you already have a TCP/IP-based network, you're home free. Connecting your network to the Internet will be child's play for any TCP/IP network administrator. If you're running Novell NetWare, Artisoft LANtastic, or Microsoft's Windows for Workgroups (WinWorks), expect some headaches.

The exceptions to this rule are Macintosh owners. Since System 7.5 includes MacTCP, hooking up a Mac to a

TCP/IP network, while not child's play, is a straightforward operation. That's anything but the case for PC users. Just be certain that you're running the newest version of MacTCP (2.04 or higher). Older versions, especially the 1.x editions, have a serious memory bug.

Your chief problem will be getting your current network stack to coexist with the TCP/IP protocols. Your first move should be to make sure that there's a TCP/IP that works with your network operating system (NOS). Most major LANs have TCP/IP supplements. For example, Novell NetWare, **http://www. novell.com**, has NetWare/IP and LAN WorkPlace. And as I've already mentioned, most of today's operating systems come TCP/IP-ready. For the down and dirty details of networks, see the next chapter.

# Beyond the Wire

Small businesses and home users can wed their systems to the Internet by using TCP/IP protocols that work over ordinary modems and telephone lines: SLIP and Point-to-Point Protocol (PPP). To use either one, you're going to need information from your ISP. After that, you'll need to know the phone number to call for user services. This will almost certainly not be your ISP's main number used for other data calls. With a full-time account, you'll get a number dedicated for your use alone.

Using this method, you're going to have an account name and password. These work just like a shell account's name and password, except they identify you as a SLIP/PPP user to your Internet Point of Presence (POP). Next, you'll need to know the IP address to your gateway server. This is the IP address of the machine that you've called into, and it's your first link to the Internet.

You'll also need the IP address of your Domain Name Service (DNS) Server on hand. The DNS is a distributed database system for resolving host names into IP addresses. For example, if you want to telnet to delphi.com, chances are you'd much rather type in "delphi.com" than "192.80.63.8." Without a DNS server to resolve domain and HTTP addresses, navigating the net is much harder. With a full-scale net connection, you might as well keep a DNS at your site. Since you're going to be going with a slow speed solution, it's almost a lead-pipe cinch that you're going to be using your ISP's DNS.

When putting this together, be sure to ask if the system supports Van Jacobson compressed SLIP (CSLIP). Many systems now use CSLIP in place of SLIP, but still call it SLIP. You don't have to have this parameter in sync to work, but you'll achieve higher throughputs if you can use CSLIP.

CSLIP is something of a misnomer. Unlike data compression standards like V.42bis, CSLIP doesn't try to squeeze down every byte that passes through it. Instead, CSLIP increases throughput with two tricks. The first is that it checks to see if long series of repetitious fields in TCP headers are being sent in datagrams, which is often the case. CSLIP doesn't send this duplicate data. Also, CSLIP analyzes the data stream and arranges it so that packets for interactive applications like telnet are sent before those for non-interactive programs like ftp. The result is a pronounced performance boost.

Next, we come to parameters that directly control how SLIP/PPP runs between your modem and your POP's modem. These are Maximum Transmission Unit (MTU), TCP Maximum Segment Size (TCP MSS), and TCP Receive Window (TCP RWIN). Some SLIP/PPP connections let you directly manipulate these values, while others keep them out of sight.

If you can change them, your Internet provider may have suggested values for these numbers. Otherwise, the rule to follow is to set TCP MSS to 512 for SLIP and less than 255 for CSLIP. MTU should be to set to about 40 above your TCP MSS. This would be 552 in the case of SLIP. TCP RWIN should be set to three or four times TCP MSS' value, or as in our example, 2048. These numbers are the sizes in bytes for these parameters.

**Table 4.6: Requirements For Low-Speed Intranet Connections**

| Item | Where to Find It |
|------|------------------|
| Modem/NIC | ISP, VAR, & for the brave, buy direct |
| Network Software | ISP |
| SLIP Phone Number | ISP |
| Domain Name | You and your ISP |
| Netmask | ISP |
| Account Name/Password | ISP |
| Server IP Address | ISP |
| DNS Server IP Address | ISP |
| Time Server IP Address | ISP |
| CSLIP or SLIP | ISP |
| MTU | ISP/Docs |
| TCP MSS | ISP/Docs |
| TCP RWIN | ISP/Docs |
| COM Port | Check Modem Connection |

There's an almost limitless number of things that can go wrong during a SLIP/PPP installation. Fortunately, most of the same problems, and solutions, show up again and again.

First, double-check all your information. It only takes one character out of place for the whole connection to crash like a semi on a slick road into a Jersey barrier. Intranet installations don't know the meaning of the word forgiveness. Once in place, thank goodness, things seldom go wrong.

Next, check that you and your SLIP provider are in tune on communication configurations. A modem that's set up for an eight data bits, no parity, and one stop bit connection will never reach a POP's modems that expect to find seven data bits and even parity. You may also ask if your POP has modems set for the other configuration. Unless you have a permanent connection, you can forget about having them change their configuration to match yours. There's no profit for them in doing anything like that.

Line noise, even with error-correcting modems, can still make life on an online slipper miserable. If you're always getting connections interrupted with static or disconnections, have your local phone company check your lines. If you have call waiting, get rid of it. You can deactivate call waiting with other commands, but why pay for it at all if you don't need it?

Once you have a modem/POTS connection going, the Internet is yours...provided, of course, that you have software that can link your Internet programs to the Internet. For that, you'll need a method of enabling sockets and socket-compliant software. To most of us, that means we need WinSock and programs that can work with it.

# Socket to Me

Sockets are TCP/IP's way of implementing Inter-Process Communications (IPC). An IPC enables programs to trade information with each other. The most familiar of these is Microsoft Windows' Dynamic Data Exchange (DDE), which is supported by most Windows programs.

In a TCP/IP network, sockets provide a way for TCP/IP-aware applications, like Mosaic, to communicate via TCP/IP with other TCP/IP servers, such as a Web server. A single socket provides a full duplex communication tunnel between a local application's virtual port address and its IP address to a remote application's socket. With this setup in place, your application and its remote server can work reliably with each other.

Specifically, for Windows, you'll also need a copy of the winsock.dll that's version 1.1 compliant. Here, WinSock not only implements socket services, it provides an application programming interface (API) that enables any WinSock-compliant TCP/IP application to work regardless of its maker. Real soon now, you're going to want to move on to the new standard of WinSock, 2.0; but in mid-1996, that's still optional.

Some older PC TCP/IP software is not WinSock-compliant and should be avoided. If you already have an existing base of this NOS, toss it. The time spent maintaining it, almost certainly fruitlessly, with modern socket-enabled applications just isn't worth it. With OS/2 Merlin, Windows95, and NT, this isn't a problem, since all three come with TCP/IP stacks.

When it comes to sockets, Macintosh users have it much easier. MacTCP includes the necessary sockets software, and all modern Macintosh TCP/IP applications transparently use these resources.

Before trying to connect, you must arrange with your Internet provider to set up a SLIP account. This may take several days. Internet service providers are notoriously understaffed, and setting up SLIP accounts is not much easier on the provider's staff than it is on you. Be kind: You're going to need these folks' help to get this done.

Why? Ah, for that information, net-hopper, we need to move on to the next chapter. To put it succinctly: Hooking together a LAN and the Internet ain't easy.

# From LANs to an Intranet

## Local Area Pains in the Neck

Chances are you're going to have to live with more than one protocol on a card. If you're one of those lucky sons of a net who already uses exclusively TCP/IP, feel free to skip the next section. As for the rest of you, flex your techie muscles, because there's no way to sweeten the bitter taste of Hard Technology. If it's any consolation, those of you who are using advanced operating systems will find many of these steps much easier—unless you run into a problem, and then you can join the rest of us in networking misery.

# How Many Protocols Can You Balance on a NIC?

The answer is: Not enough. There are three basic ways to get dueling network protocols to live with each other on a given card. The oldest is to use a packet driver. A packet driver is a program that translates between your NIC and your TCP programs. Packet drivers work well—once they're installed properly. That first step can be a doozy. To use them properly, you must understand vectors, Interrupt ReQuests (IRQs), and I/O addresses.

A vector is a number on an x86 architecture chip that ranges from 0 to 255. These vectors are used by software to communicate with the underlying hardware. Normally, these numbers are expressed in hexadecimal numbers. For example, 0x10 calls to the video basic input/output system (BIOS). These numbers may also appear as decimal numbers. In either case, the packet driver must have a vector number from 0x60 to 0x7F that is not used by another equipment or program. The default number is 0x60.

Your packet driver must also have a free IRQ and I/Obase address for its work. The IRQ is one of 16 numbers (0-15) on an 80286 or higher PC which the hardware uses to "interrupt," or get the attention of, the CPU. Once the CPU is paying attention, the IRQ is used to communicate data from a modem, scanner, or, here, a packet driver to the CPU. The I/Obase is the specific hardware address that's reserved for a particular piece of equipment or program. If any of the three are shared by another program or piece of hardware, chances are the TCP/IP session will abort. Finding just the right combination of vector, IRQ, and I/Obase can be a tedious task.

Most network cards come with their own packet drivers. In case you have one that doesn't, you're not out of luck. An enormous collection of public domain packer drivers is available from the Crynew Packet Driver Collection, **ftp://www.crynwr.com/drivers/**.

In essence, packet drivers work by sharing a network card as if it was a duplex house. That is, the TCP/IP packet driver lives on one side of the house, and has nothing to do with the protocol living in the building's other wing. That's one reason why packet driver solutions are being eclipsed by Microsoft's Network Driver Interface Specification (NDIS) and Novell's Open Data-Link Interface (ODI). These two NIC interface standards support up to four different network protocols on one NIC. Many network companies write drivers for these interfaces. This enables companies to write a driver for ODI or NDIS and not have to worry about writing or building packet-drivers directly to each card's hardware.

No matter what drivers you have at hand, avoid older (1993 or earlier) Ethernet cards like the plague. Your circa 1991 3Com 3c503 NIC may run just fine, but I wouldn't put any money on it. Usually, older cards get downright contrary when asked to run more than one protocol at a time.

The one bad thing about ODI and NDIS is that they're not compatible with one another. While you can use both ODI and NDIS NICs on one LAN, a driver written for one standard will not work with the other. Novell does have a program, ODINSUP, that will let you use some ODI drivers to work with NDIS interfaces; but I wouldn't count on being able to pull this trick off.

For intranet users, the standards make it much easier to run TCP/IP with other NOSs. That said, it's still no walk in the park getting different networks to live together on one NIC. Always check your documentation and keep the technical support number handy when trying to get TCP/IP to work in tandem with another network protocol.

Before sitting down and rolling up your sleeves, there are some things you can check to ensure that your setup will go as smoothly as possible. First, make sure you have the newest versions of your network software. Network companies are constantly updating their drivers. The newer the version, the more likely it is to work under the stressed conditions of running multiple protocols.

Next, read the documentation and any "readme" files. There's almost no one out there who doesn't have the bad habit of installing first and reading the manual afterwards. With network software, especially when you're trying to run more then one NOS at a time, that's a sure path to trouble.

Some NICs, even with ODI or NDIS, still require the use of a packet driver. In that case, you'll need not only a packet driver but another program, called a shim, which enables the packet driver to connect with the network interface software.

## Next Generation NICs

Of course, if you had unlimited funds, the best thing to do would be to upgrade to 100MB Ethernet cards. In late 1996, the price difference between a new Fast Ethernet or 100VG card and an ordinary card is only about 25 to 50%. That's not much of a premium for sustained performance ten times better than your current equipment.

As with everything else, there are some hidden costs. For example, Fast Ethernet and 100VG won't work with each other. The only way you can to mix and match them is with a bridge or the like, and that's a totally unnecessary expense. You may also have to change or upgrade your wiring plant. Both technologies require 10BaseT wiring, usually high quality 10BaseT at that. When your company is already using thinnet wiring, a.k.a. 10Base2, that can add up to a lot of wire. Wire itself may be cheap; but pulling the wire is dirty, unpleasant work that almost always has to be done on overtime, since no one can work with people crawling through the plenium passages dragging cable and dust behind them.

# Making the Net Connection

Okay, you've made it this far; your PCs and your LAN are ready to go. Now for the big step: moving to an intranet. You're going to need at least one dedicated server for your intranet and, if you plan on publishing on the Web, another server for sending out Web pages to the world. Your server hardware, no matter what the operating system, should have the fastest possible processor and massive amounts of memory and hard disk space.

How fast? How big? The answers depend on three factors: 1) how many users do you expect to use your intranet; 2) what do you expect them to use the intranet for; and 3) what kind of applications will you be running on the server?

My rule of thumb is: For each internal user, a server needs to have 1MB of RAM and 5MB of hard drive space. With external users, I usually figure on them using 500K of

RAM. With heavy-duty users, maybe running a DBMS for both internal and external use on the server, you need to multiply whatever the DBMS or what-have-you vendor tells you are the practical requirements for system resources by 1.5. In summation, I think the minimum memory requirements for an intranet server should be 32MB of RAM. Small companies can get by with less, but don't say that I didn't warn you. As always, if you have a choice between more RAM and a faster processor, go with the RAM—you won't regret it.

## Picking a Server

The easiest way to get the right server is to buy a preconfigured one. Several companies already have such ready-to-intranet machines on the market, and there are dozens more coming. The best of the lot, as I sit here writing in mid-1996, are Sun's Netra Internet Servers, **http://www.sun.com**, and Silicon Graphics' WebForce server family, **http://www. sgi.com**. With both, you get all the hardware and software you need without the aggravation of putting it all together.

Some people might balk at this because both systems run Unix. To be more precise, Netras run Solaris, and WebForce machines run IRIX. For my two pennies, Unix is still the operating system of choice for Internet or intranet servers. The Internet has spent most of its life running on Unix servers; and even now, the vast majority of sophisticated Internet tools exist in their highest forms in Unix versions. Unlike their equivalent tools on other operating systems, the Unix TCP/IP and Usenet programs give you enormous control and power over exactly how your Internet server behaves.

While knowing Unix well is a prerequisite for getting the most out of an Internet Unix box, today's ready-made boxes with their graphical controls mean that you don't need to be quite the wizard at sendmail arcania, PERL programming, and the like that an Internet guru had to be in the past. Still, it won't hurt if your network administrator does know his "at" command from a hole in the ground.

Of course, those of you who are already sold on NT as your server software of choice won't be hurting, either. There are many good freeware and inexpensive commercial programs out there that will make using NT for your net server immensely practical.

Other network operating systems are more troublesome. While many tools exist for NetWare, I've been rather underwhelmed by them—and occasionally overwhelmed by the difficulties of joining NetWare with the Internet. The best product for making that leap from IPX to IP that I've found to date is Firefox's Novix for Internet, **http://www.firefox.com**. On the whole, I've found Unix and NT to be far more manageable.

That said, when you've invested your company's resources into NetWare for an entire decade, I can't blame you for balking at the notion of giving up your NOS. I can only say that you should allow ample time for retrofitting your existing NetWare 3.1x or NetWare 4.x servers for the intranet. As for Netware 2.x, please, just upgrade now and put yourself out of your misery.

The only other viable intranet NOS, in my opinion, is Warp Server. The problem here isn't that you can't put up an intranet. When all is said and done, you'll be up and running before your NetWare competition on the next floor is. No, your headache, as always with OS/2, is that you simply won't have too many programs to choose from. Getting the existing internet tools to coexist can be done— I know, I've done it—but it's a slower process than working with Unix or NT.

As for other operating systems that can support intranet programs, just say no. There are Web servers available for everything from AmigaDOS to Windows95. The software itself can be quite workable. If programs were all there was to a functioning intranet, you'd be fine. Alas, it's not. You also need an networking operating system that's not going to break down under dozens of users and processes. None of these other NOSs are really up to these challenges.

# Across the Great Divide: LAN to the Internet

At this point, internally, everything is as good as it's going to get. Now you need the equipment and the connection to seal the gap between your LAN and the Internet. Exactly what you'll needs depends upon your connection type. Generally speaking, these can be broken down into three classes.

**Table 5.1: Speed Limits**

| Class | Speed | Enabling Technologies |
|-------|-------|----------------------|
| Low | 56Kbps-128Kbps | Switched-56; Basic Rate ISDN |
| Medium | 256Kbps-1.536Mbps | Fractional T1; T1; Primary Rate ISDN |

High        44Mbps-2,488Mbps        T3; SONET

> You'll notice that I'm not even looking at modems any-more. Modems are okay if you're willing to settle for just e-mail; but for anything more serious, like the Web, you need at least 56Kbps; and no modem today can handle that.
>
> Each technology level requires different equipment. So when you pick a technology, keep firmly in mind that, for the most part, you're not going to be able to upgrade to a higher speed down the road without replacing your exist-ing equipment.
>
> With that warning in mind, let's take a closer look at the different technologies at your beck and call.

**Table 5.2: Faster! Faster!**

Here are the most commonly available Internet physical network types and their speeds.

| Link Type | Speed Ranges |
| --- | --- |
| Modem | 28.8Kbps-33.6Kbps |
| Switched 56 | 56Kbps |
| Basic Rate ISDN | 56-64Kbps |
| Basic Rate BISDN | 128Kbps |
| Fractional T1 | 64Kbps-1.344Mbps |
| T1 | 1.536Mbps |

| | |
|---|---|
| Primary Rate ISDN | 1.536Mbps |
| T3 | 44.736Mbps |
| SONET | 51.84-2,488.32Mbps |
| FDDI | 100Mbps |

While people used to modems will think even the lowest of these speeds breathtakingly fast, for a LAN full of net users, they're merely adequate. Remember that 56Kbps is twice as fast as the speediest practical modem connection—for an individual user. If you have a dozen users all trying to use the net connection at once, that speed gets split up between the number of people using the connection at the same time. You can do the math. Still, for small or lightly used networks, low-speed connections are the way to go. You should also consider several other factors in deciding on your net connection's speed.

First, how many other companies will be using your ISP's POP? If your ISP won't give you this information, you can count on its being a crowded POP; and you may never get full advantage of your connection's speed because the POP itself is a chokepoint. How crowded is too crowded? That's a complicated question and highly dependent on your ISP's equipment. My feeling is that you should have no visible contention with other users. If there are somewhere between 15 and 50 other users, you'll feel the pinch at times, but for the most part you'll be okay. If, on the other hand, there are fifty-plus companies stuffed into the same POP, you're in trouble—unless there are some seriously powerful servers, Ethernet switches, and the like on the ISP's end.

Another critical question is, how fast is your ISP's connection is to the Internet? Ideally, your ISP should have at least T3 connections to the Internet. If they've got even faster roadways to the net, like SONET or FDDI, so much the better. You can also probably live with an ISP who has multiple T1 connections to the net. Does your ISP have only a single T1 connection, or—god forbid—less? Then cross that company off your list right now. One T1 may have been fine for modem connections; but it just won't cut it for serious intranet connectivity.

Another element which affects your connectivity speed that almost everyone misses is, when will you be using your Internet connection? If you're a medium-sized company, but you only have a small company's number of employees at work at any given time during the day, you can get by with less speed. Internet traffic also tends to get heavier during the midpoint of the work day. If you can distribute your load—say, by updating remote Web sites at night, or only picking up Usenet news at 3:00 a.m., 9:00 a.m., 9:00 p.m., and midnight—you can get the performance you want without paying for a higher speed connection.

# Connection Types

Regardless of the physical network, another issue you must deal with is what type of connection you are going to run. What this comes down to is a choice between dedicated connections and technologies that let you use bandwidth on demand.

For all practical purposes, the difference is between price and service. A dedicated line will guarantee you the bandwidth you want whenever you need it for a higher price. Other technologies, like frame relay and Asynchronous Transfer Mode (ATM), will usually give you the same speed; but because you're sharing lines with other enterprises, you may not get that full speed at all times. Your wallet, though, might appreciate the fact that frame relay and ATM are cheaper than their equivalent dedicated line brothers. My thought is that, everything else being equal, frame relay for up to medium speed networks and ATM for middling speed intranet connections and up is the way to go.

# Speed Spins

Whether yournet connection is switched-56 or T1, you'll need at least three additional pieces of equipment. These are:

· Network Termination Unit (NTU)

· Multiplexor, a.k.a Channel Service Unit/Data
   Service Unit (CSU/DSU)

· Router

An NTU is almost always the property of your local teleco. It strengthens your data signal, and adds your phone company into the crew of people figuring out if there's a problem.

The CSU/DSU serves as the physical breakpoint between your intranet and the telephone's networks. A CSU/DSU also handles low-end details (the first two layers of the ISO network model) to ensure that your connection is clear. Despite the fact that a CSU/DSU really does handle two jobs and has this weird name to emphasize it, these units are universally bundled in a single box. Unfortunately, a CSU/DSU that will work with one kind of connection, say a switched 56Kbps connection, won't help a bit with a fractional T1 connection.

The router works exactly the same way internal routers do (described in Chapter 2). A router's lot in life is to shift through the Internet's packets, move all outgoing packets towards their destinations, and make sure that incoming packets end up at the right service on your server. Unfortunately, this task is not as easy as it sounds. There are no fewer than seven kinds of data transfer protocols that an Internet router might have to deal with. These are:

· ATM

· Frame Relay

· High-level Data Link Control (HDLC)

· PPP

· SLIP

· Switched Multimegabit Data Services (SMDS)

· X.25

To the best of my knowledge, no single router can handle all of them. Frankly, even if one did, who cares? If such a solution existed, it would be much too pricey when you're only going to need support for two or three protocols at most. The trick is to make sure that your routers support the protocols that your ISP will be providing you with. You also must make sure that your router can handle its expected workload. A router that's meant for frame relay up to 128Kbps, for example, is just going to blink frantic error messages if you connect it to a frame relay full T1 connection. That way, you'll not only have a non-functioning intranet, you'll also be getting a splitting headache as well. Oh, joy; oh, rapture!

On the LAN side of your router, you must make sure that it can hook into your network. For example, some routers will work with 10Base 5 or 10BaseT but don't come ready for 10Base2. A little "oopsie!" like this will leave your intranet dead in the water...and you, quite possibly, without a job.

# Switched-56

The oldest popular business Internet connection is showing its age. A switched-56 line uses a unique blend of analog and digital signaling to give you a maximum speed of 56Kbps. Many businesses have been using this dedicated line technology for years now. It's time for a change.

Switched-56 simply isn't fast enough to keep up with its upkeep costs. Also, all you need is one person pulling data out of your Web site while someone else inside your company is extracting data from somewhere else on the net, and your system performance is going to drop down to the speed of bad synchronized swimming.

# Frame Relay

Frame relay is a low- to medium-speed packet switching protocol that was orginially used for WANs. Now it's an Internet darling for cost-conscious net users. Even a low-end 56Kbps frame relay line can be as much as one-sixth cheaper than a switched-56 or a dedicated 56 line.

Frame relay doesn't have much in the way of error checking; but then, it was built that way, because it relies upon having a solid physical network underneath it. Frame relay works well for speeds from 56Kbps to T1 rates of 1.544 Mbps. The lack of error checking is one shortcoming for an intranet that has its difficulties dealing with realtime voice and video due to its variable length packet architecture.

What it doesn't have any trouble doing is working with most of today's routers. Frame relay has become the packet-switching technology of choice for T1 speeds and below. Also, frame relay services tend to be cheap and reliable. If you need decent speed, but can't afford fractional T1 or a dedicated line service, frame relay is the technology for you.

Fractional T1's advantage over frame relay is that it does work much better with realtime information. If you're getting an intranet for cheap videoconferencing, you'd really be better off in the T1 and up range; but fractional T1 is the best technology for anyone who wants to do Internet TV on a budget.

# ISDN

The technology that everyone is talking about at the low end is ISDN (Integrated Services Digital Network) connection. This telecommunications standard lays the groundwork for local digital telephone connections that are capable of transmitting voice, video, and data at a minimum rate of 64Kbps.

ISDN comes in two varieties: Basic Rate Interface (BRI) and Primary Rate Interface (PRI). BRI is suitable for small businesses. With BRI, you get one or two 56 to 64Kbps data lines, called B channels, and one 16Kbps D channel for data control. Essentially, the D channel (no matter how much you may want to think of the "d" as standing for "data") keeps the B channels in sync and transmitting data at the highest possible speed. Most ISPs and telephone companies will sell you this service in a form called Bonded-ISDN (BISDN) that lifts your total throughput to 128Kbps.

PRI is on an entirely faster and more expensive level. Often used for voice services, PRI uses 23 B channels to push you up to throughput levels of 1.5Mbps. Its pricing, however, usually means that you'll want PRI for your Internet connectivity only if you're going to be using it mainly for its voice capabilities.

While many people talk about ISDN as a single-user technology, it's also ideal for intranets. There are numerous ISDN routers available, although in my opinion the ones from Ascend Communications' Pipeline series, **http://www.ascend.com/**, are the best.

Unlike other low-speed connections, BRI doesn't require a CSU/DSU. You will still need a NTU; but in ISDN idiom, an NTU is called a Network Terminator, or NT1. In the past, this was almost always a separate piece of equipment; but more and more manufacturers are putting it in with the ISDN router. Always ask: One without the other is completely worthless.

For high-end users, ISDN is cost-efficient. While ISDN is cheapest for power users, ISDN for an intranet will cost more. Nevertheless, its pricing tends to be lower than traditional lease-line costs. Also, unlike frame relay, within its speed boundaries, ISDN delivers the kind of steady service that's required for low-end videoconferencing.

Sounds great, doesn't it? There's just one problem: ISDN services can be very difficult to get even when you have the bucks. Many places, even in the middle of major cities like New York City and San Francisco, have no ISDN services. The phone companies are dragging their feet at making ISDN widely available; so if your area doesn't have it, don't hold your breath. On the other hand, it doesn't hurt to check. Remember, though, even if you can get ISDN, unless your POP also has ISDN lines, you'll gain no speed advantage at all.

# T1

Odds are you're not going to have any choice about what kind of connection you'll be getting with T1—dedicated lines are almost the only way it's sold. That said, it can't hurt to ask if frame relay or ATM services are available. Simply by omitting this question, you may end up costing your firm a pretty penny.

Those pennies will come in handy, too, because T1 equipment and service are always more expensive than the technologies we've already looked at. Like PRI, T1 uses twenty-four 64Kbps channels to deliver its data throughput wallop. Also, as with PRI, if you're foolhar—brave; yes, brave—and you're getting your Internet service directly from the phone company, you can use a channel bank to try to combine ordinary analog phones with your digital network. A channel bank is a multiplexor that converts analog voice to digital on the way out and then reverses the procedure when someone calls in.

The major advantage of T1 is that you get enough speed to host a serious Web server—that is to say, one that's going to get more than a thousand hits or so a month. Anything less is really only suitable for tiny user communities.

# T3

A T3 line takes more of those 64Kbps channels and combines them into the fastest common Internet connection. With six hundred and seventy-two 64Kbps channels, which add up to over 45Mbps of bandwidth, you've got the kind of connectivity that a large company—or one with an extremely active Web site, one that gets more than 20,000 hits per month—needs.

At this point, there's another piece of equipment that you're going to need to add to your LAN room—and by this point, you are going to have a dedicated room for just the servers and routers, or you're just begging for a major corporate disaster. This piece of hardware is usually called an M13 multiplexer, after the type of framing it uses to manage the roaring flood of incoming and outgoing data. Other framing types are becoming popular, but no matter what frame protocol it's using, you can count on having an additonal multiplexer to the one you already needed for anything up to about 56Kbps speeds.

With T3, you can also use ATM (we've left frame relay behind at these speeds) to maximize your throughput without maximizing your data bill. Check with your ISP to see if ATM is available. The one caveat here is that you're also going need to pay for an ATM box up front, usually a hefty price. The plus side is that it's very likely to work out cheaper for you within a year.

I don't suppose I need to tell you that T3s are expensive. What you may not realize, after you see what your ISP and telephone company want to hit you up for in installation and monthly maintenance speeds, is that for only about four to six times the price of a T1, you get 30 times more bang for the buck. Some people will try to convince you that multiple T1s are a better deal than a T3. They're just plain wrong.

# Zoooommmm!!

Want more speed? It's available. Here, in the land of Synchronous Optical Network (SONET) and FDDI, we're talking about major megabucks. T3 services aren't available everywhere; and SONET and FDDI are hardly available anywhere. Unless you're living in a major metropolitican area, don't even bother thinking about these technologies—not this year, anyway.

These technologies are fresh enough from the cutting edge of technology that their pricing will vary wildly. It will all be high, mind you; but even some major Internet providers won't be able to supply you with it unless they install their first SONET connection just for you. Being the guinea pig can be a painful experience, and it's always costly.

Let's say that you have hundreds, maybe thousands, of employees and expect your main Web site to get hammered with more than 500,000 hits per month. You'll want to take a serious look at these high-end technologies. In your situation, you just might need to spend the kind of money that this warp-speed technology demands.

Before we leave connecting Internet and intranet behind, there's one last subject I must cover. This one doesn't have much to do with technology, but it does have a lot to do with your business: putting your company's name on the Internet.

# The Naming of Domains

For an Internet-connected intranet, you must pick a domain name. You should also be ready to have your first few choices turned down by the InterNIC, **http://www.internic.net**, the organization that controls domain names and addresses.

The sad truth is that a lot of people have already signed up for a domain name before you, and the name you want may already be gone. There are some ways to address this issue, but don't count on them working. In particular, no matter what your ISP promises, there may be no way in hell that you can get anything even close to your first choice in names. I've run into ISP sales reps who will guarantee you that they can get your name for you—usually when you've made it clear that getting the name is essential for you to close the deal. The plain truth is, they can't.

Before setting yourself up for a fall, you can check for yourself to see if a name is available. You can pull this off by hooking up with a Unix system on the Internet with either the telnet or rlogin programs (more about those in Chapter 8) and entering the command:

```
whois fully_qualified_domain_name
```

That odd long phrase means that you have to enter a site's full domain name. For example, if you looked for just "vna1" with whois, you'd get nothing back, and you might think that vna1 was free to use. Wrong. You have to check for the full domain name. The same search with "vna1.com" will reveal that someone with a name suspiciously like your author has a domain by that name; and that the name stands for his company, Vaughan-Nichols & Associates. Why didn't yours truly use just "vna"? Because (sigh) like you, my first pick had already been taken.

What you don't want is a random string of letters or numbers for your domain name. You're in business. If someone has to fumble in "EBBB60A" to access your site, you know darn well that they're not going to bother. If that kind of junk is the best thing that your ISP can offer, find another ISP.

You'll need to know your domain name, of course, and its corresponding IP address. An IP address is a 32-bit number that's represented as four sets of decimal numbers separated by periods. For instance, the IP address to vna.digex.net, another of one my domains, is 164.109.213.7. As the Internet grows more crowded, even larger numbers are required; and other IP addressing systems are being built that will further pin down your IP address. These will likely look   like that odd set of four numbers again with another number delimited from the rest of the address by a comma.

The IP address, not your domain name, is your domain's actual address. The address is read from left to right, with the more specific information to the right. For example, the 164.109 above tells the informed reader (who had nothing better to do with his time than memorize IP addresses) that this is part of the access.digex.net domain. When your data moves through the Internet, this address is kept in your datagram's header. Armed with this information, the routers and DNS move your messages, connections, and data transfers through the net. This IP number is also your system's unique address on the net. If someone wanted to telnet to your system, they could do so by using your IP address.

You also need a subnet netmask. This IP number is used with your IP number to divide networks into smaller networks. For now, there are four IP classes.

**Table 4.6: IP Subnet Classes**

| Class | Purpose | Address Range | Notes |
|-------|---------|---------------|-------|
| A | Large Nets | 1.0.0.0 to 128.256.256.256 | Not available |
| B | Medium Nets | 128.0.0.0 to 191.255.255.255 | Not available |
| C | Small Nets | 192.0.0.0 to 223.255.255.255 | Few available |
| D | Multicasting | 224.0.0.2 to 239.255.255.255 | Site irrelevant |
| E | Reserved | 240.0.0.0 to 247.255.255.255 | For future sites |

The Class C ranges are used for almost all new domains appearing on the Internet.

There is one little problem with IP addresses: Just like the most popular domain names, we're beginning to run out of them. In fact, for almost all practical purposes, we are out of them for Classes A and B. That's also the reason that, even if you're a gigantic company, you're still going to get a Class C subnet, if that.

One proposal, known as IP Rev. 6 or IPng enclosed in RFC-1752,`http://ds.internic.net/ds/dspgli ntdoc.html`, is to move up from a 32-bit addressing system to a 128-bit system. This will almost certainly be the one that makes the jump from paper to reality. It will also make obsolete all addressing currently used on the net. Won't that be fun?

# Circuits Closing

That's enough technology and politics for now; but don't go away. In the next chapter, we deal with far more important issues. I get to tell you all about the fun of getting your ISP and your phone company to work with you and not against you. Trust me, if you thought a general introduction to routers was bad, just wait until you get to a general introduction to phone company technical managers: It's much scarier! But don't worry; I'll be there to hold your virtual hand all the way.

# The People Principle

## Working Together

People will cause you more headaches than hardware and software combined. It's tragic but true. If everyone worked together in harmony with their eyes on the goal, you could have anything short of a T3 up within 48 hours. Fancier, faster network links would take about a week.

Forget it. That fantasy scenario isn't going to happen. Even if you can throw money at your Internet connection like cash was Post-It Notes™, it's not going to help. That's because there are at least three groups that need to get in sync in order to get a net connection running: your own LAN personnel, the ISP's people, and your local teleco's employees. There's more red tape in that scenario than Post-It Notes™; and unfortunately, red tape never sticks together the way you want it to.

So the first thing to do is relax and realize that bringing up an Internet connection, for all but the smallest companies, is going to take at least two months. Yes, I know everyone will tell you that they can do it quicker than that. I also know they're lying through their teeth.

# LAN Personnel

If your company is like most, then your own internal LAN people are overwhelmed with work. Getting them to switch over from their existing LAN model to an intranet model is going to be a slow process. Keep in mind that even after the circuits are circuiting and the packets are packeting, no matter how much you may want to pull the switch on the old LAN, you're going to need to run both systems in parallel for at least a month, possibly even years, while you're getting your intranet to do all that your LAN did and more.

This, needless to say, is going to put even more of a burden on LAN workers. In other words, you're probably going to want to hire additional personnel for your LAN, unless you want people burning out trying to teach an old network new tricks. Some may stick around just long enough to learn the new technology and then jump ship to jobs where they can use their new skills without the additional burden of keeping the old LAN going.

Finding new people is never easy. It's even harder when you're looking for intranet pros. You can stick all the ads you want in the papers saying that you want someone with two or more years of experience in intranets, HTML, and HTTP; but you're not going to find anyone. Intranet and Web technologies are changing by the minute. I can count on the fingers of both hands the few people in the business who actually have that much experience in all those technologies. The best you can find will be workers who have substantive experience with TCP/IP and, if you're very lucky, other networking technologies. If you can't find even that, you're going to have to grit your teeth and call up their references. The good ones will have short but solid networking backgrounds.

More than anything else, though, you're going to want people who learn quickly. The Internet and the Web are changing far too fast for anyone but quick learners. This ability is far more important than whether they have the right buzzwords in their resume.

Management often treats support personnel badly. (If you don't believe me, pick up a copy of Scott Adams' *The Dilbert Principle* [ISBN 0-88730-787-6] and see how much of it looks familiar. It's scary!) If your company has such habits—expecting as a matter of course that network administrators will work 60-hour weeks for no extra pay, giving out recognition certificates instead of cash bonuses, and the like—now is the time to change that. Like it or not, you have to start treating your network personnel like they're the most important people in the company; because for these purposes, they are.

You know the standard company lie, "people are your company's most valuable resources?" Well, it's a good idea to live your words rather than just mouth them. In the case of networkers during a network transition, it's not just a good idea, it's a necessity. After all, do you want your senior LAN administrator—or, frankly, anyone who does more than pull cable—to up and leave in the middle of an intranet upgrade? I think not.

The reason for this (aside from the ideal one of treating people decently) is that for every important LAN person you lose, your company is going to spend at least another two weeks getting up to speed. Does your company have the time to waste? We both know that the answer is no.

If you're going to do the job right, you'll also need to get management, users, and LAN people together to figure out exactly what it is you want from an intranet. Now, I hate committees: I usually find them to be real time-wasters. But here, you're going to need input from everyone. If you and the LAN department are set on building a low-end intranet, but Marketing and your CEO want a Web site that will attract thousands of customers every day, it's better to find that out before you go charging ahead with your intranet plans—all the way to the unemployment office.

Your LAN crew is going to need to learn TCP/IP and Internet networking in a hurry. In the best of all possible worlds, they'd have months to pick up the information. In the real world, they'll be lucky if they have weeks. You should investigate training classes for TCP/IP and Internet administrators. Many companies and ISPs now offer these as a matter of course. They won't be cheap, but they'll be cheaper than having your people make their beginners' mistakes on the job at everyone else's expense.

I wish I could say that you could learn everything you need to learn from the Internet itself. Alas, while there are many excellent net resources, I've yet to find a good, coherent, and thorough introduction to TCP/IP networking on the Internet. Nevertheless, here are some of the more valuable documents about TCP/IP and the like that are available on the Web.

**Table 6.1: The Useful Web/Usenet Resources**

Title

**URL**

Introduction to TCP/IP

`http://pclt.cis.yale.edu/pclt/comm/tcpip.htm`

PC-Mac TCP/IP & NFS FAQ list

`http://www.rtd.com/pcnfsfaq/faq.html`

TCP/IP FAQs

`http://www.cis.ohiostate.edu/hypertext/faq/bngusenet/comp/protocols/tcp-ip/top.html`

TCP/IP Port Numbers

`http://www.con.wesleyan.edu/~triemer/network/docservs.html`

TCP/IP RFCs

```
http://www.yahoo.com/Computers_and_Internet/Softwar
e/Protocols/TCP_IP/RFCs/
```

<u>Usenet Newsgroups</u>

```
comp.os.os2.networking.tcp-ip
```

```
comp.protocols.tcp-ip
```

```
comp.protocols.tcp-ip.domains
```

```
comp.protocols.tcp-ip.ibmpc
```

Fair warning: Usenet groups often have more questions than answers. They're still useful; but you do have to go through a lot of chaff to get to the wheat.

Finally, ready or not, your LAN people are going to need to work closely with both your ISP and your telephone company. This will not be easy. An important thing for you and your LAN personnel to remember is that while you do have a common goal, both the ISP and the telephone people have different priorities than you. You can't expect personnel from these companies to respond with the same alacrity as your in-house staff.

This is, in my experience, especially true of telephone company employees. Many telephone staffers have a great deal of expertise with voice technology; but all too often, they may only be starting to earn their stripes in data communications. Smaller ISPs, who almost always take on more work than they can manage, also often fall prey to the problem of slow response time. Patience is a virtue, and you're going to get to exercise it a lot.

That doesn't mean you have to put up with crap. If your calls aren't answered within two or three days, climb up the management tree of the ISP or teleco until you get someone who will address your concerns. If you have to wait a week or more, think about switching to a different ISP. For that matter, now that the long-distance companies are getting into the Internet business, you don't need to put up with your Baby Bell throwing tantrums anymore.

# ISP Personnel

An Internet connection isn't a one-size-fits-all proposition. There's a host of other services beyond IP connectivity that you may or may not want from an ISP. These include:

- Datacomm Hardware

- DNS

- Domain Registration

- End User Technical Support

- IP Registration/Routing

- LAN Technical Support

- Network Maintenance

- Reverse DNS

- Router Maintenance

- Security Maintenance

- Usenet News Feed

• Web Server Hosting

We'll talk more about these issues and more in later chapters. For the moment, the important point is that there are a lot of issues you'll need to settle with your ISP before lifting a finger towards actually implementing anything.

When you talk with your ISP, you're going to start by working with the marketing people. Ninety percent of the time, the sales force can give you the answers you need. That other 10% can be a killer. If you get the feeling that your sales representative doesn't know what he's talking about, you're probably right. Ask to talk to someone from engineering, the network operations center (NOC), or technical support. For your part, make sure you have your LAN people on tap for asking the technical questions. What may sound like Greek to you might make perfect sense to someone who already knows networking like the back of her hand.

Some matters that fall into your ISP's domain may be beyond their control. For example, as I write this, there's a nationwide shortage of routers. Before you strike your deal, ask how much equipment for your project is already in stock. Don't be horrified if the answer is "not much"—everyone's in the same boat. On the other hand, do be sure to ask for realistic equipment shipping dates.

Once the deal is signed, you'll be talking almost exclusively to the technical staff. By this point, you want your own technical teams to be working hand-in-glove. In particular, when the week finally comes that your circuit is going to be turned on, you want your best people on the job. I say that not merely because you always want your top crew for the big jobs, but because this may be the only time that your technical people will be working with your ISP's top dogs.

Most of the time, before and after your installation, you're almost always going to be working with lower echelon people. Make the best possible use of this time, because trying to reach the ISP's technical bigwigs once your installation is done will be nigh unto impossible.

# Teleco Personnel

Telephony, the gentle science of making the telephone network do what you want it to do, is completely in the hands of your telephone company. Make no mistake about it: Even your POTS one-line phone at home is connected to a very complex network. It's also a network that's very hard to make changes in.

If you're lucky, you're not going to need to ask the phone company for anything more than they can already deliver. Do you feel lucky today? Me neither.

When you ask for a special kind of phone service, whether it's a Dataphone Digital Service (DDS), the technology underlying all connections up to T1 levels, or a pure optical SONET line, it's going to take the teleco a lot of time to get the service to you. And when I say a lot of time, I mean a lot of time. Getting DDS shouldn't take more than a day or two; but don't be surprised if a T1 takes up to two weeks. T3s can take up to a month; and for the really nifty stuff, just go ahead and put another quarter into your PERT plan, because it's simply not going to happen in less than several months.

If you hate that notion, all I can do is ask you to remember a certain Lily Tomlin comedy routine from the late '60s. The punchline was: "We're the phone company; we don't have to care." It's not quite that bad today.

Badgering the telephone company isn't likely to help you. The only time you should bug them is if you think the person you've been talking to really doesn't understand what it is you're asking for. This, alas, is more common than you might think. It's due to the fact that, until recently, telephone personnel spent almost all their time working on audio problems. Data is a whole new world for most of them. You don't want to step on anyone's toes; but you do want to guard your own interests. I've seen companies spend tens of thousands of additional fees simply because their phone contact didn't know about the alternatives.

In particular, if you're using ISDN, SONET, or FDDI—that is, any of the newer technologies—don't be shocked if the first few people you talk to don't have the slightest idea what you're talking about. Seriously. Your best move in this situation is to ask, repeatedly, for the person in charge of business ISDN or whatever it is that you need.

Still can't get anywhere? If you've settled on an ISP, try having them deal with the problem. Better still, let them deal with the phone company entirely. Well, actually, that's being a little too trusting, which can lead to other communication problems. The ISP may not get it wrong; but, for instance, you don't want the ISP telling the phone company to come in on Columbus Day to install the hardware if your company is open on Columbus Day.

Finally, just as with your ISP, when the people from the telephone company come in to do the actual installation and other teleco employees call to check on the installation's status, you're dealing directly with the most important and knowledgeable technical people that the phone company has to offer. Take advantage of this opportunity to get to know them better and gather any expertise you can from them. You're not likely to see or hear from them again after they ride out to take care of the next installation.

# Your People

Lest we forget, you also have your own employees to educate about the new way of doing things. Some of them are going to love working in an intranet. They're almost certainly the same people with 28.8Kbps modems at home and a SLIP account at Joe's Bar & ISP. Everyone else, like the people who still haven't figured out how to program their VCR, is going to hate changing to a new network.

Welcome to human nature. It's not like you can blame them. If someone's spent the last five years getting Da Vinci e-mail to work just so for them, they're not going to take kindly to the idea of switching to an Internet-enabled version of cc:Mail or Pegasus Mail.

The key to overcoming this problem is information and time. Let your people know what the company is up to as soon as you can. You'll probably get a lot of pressure to keep legacy applications around. This is a good idea—up to a point. Yes, you want to keep the old programs around until you're sure the new ones work. After that, though, for every piece of old software that you've left on the network, you're going to have to devote some technical support person's time to keeping that application running. Frankly, it's just not worth it. Many, if not most, of your users are going to go through a lot of pain converting from the old way to the new way. Making the pain linger with a slow shutdown of older applications isn't going to help any in the long run; and in the short run, it'll drive your support people batty.

Naturally, you also want to make absolutely sure that just because you're leaving your legacy applications behind, you're not leaving your legacy data behind. You must be triply sure that your new programs can use your old data!

Fortunately, intranet programs tend to be easy to use. No, stop laughing and rolling on the floor—they really are! Okay, you probably see my point: No matter how simple a program may be, you still have to teach people how to use it. Of course, you could let them learn on the job; but, hey, if you want to waste your company's productivity that way, that's your problem. Personally, I wouldn't advise it.

Beyond the specifics, what it all comes down to is working well with people. Yes, there are times you'll need to be forceful; but your best approach will be to treat everyone involved with respect, and listen to them carefully. If you do this, you're that much more likely to have a working intranet within the minimum period of two months instead of two years.

# Making Contact

## Getting Access to the Net

Finding a connection to the net used to be like a trip through Death Valley with no water: Some people made it; most didn't. That was because there was simply no way to get an Internet connection for love or money. These days, ISPs are popping up like violets after a spring shower. Today's question isn't, "how do I get Internet service;" it's, "how do I get good Internet service?"

One way not to do it is by word of mouth, or by reading the postings in the **alt.internet.**

**access.wanted** newsgroup. All ISPs get slammed on a regular basis for poor service, high prices, and so on. The terrible truth is, that comes with the territory. Every ISP is desperately trying to keep up with demand; and I don't know of a one of them which is succeeding. Some do better than others; but demand is far outstripping ISPs' supply.

If a service has always had a bad reputation, then stay away; otherwise, you'll want to give them the benefit of a doubt. You can, if you have the time for it, check on a service's long-term reputation by going to one of the Usenet news search engines like AltaVista, **http://www.altavista.digital.com/**, InReference, **http://www.reference.com/**, or DejaNews, **http://www.dejanews.com/**, and carefully doing a search for reports on the various news services. I emphasize "carefully" because if you don't do it right, you're going to end up with megabytes of useless information.

For an ISP, good service isn't just a matter of having enough routers on hand, though that is part of it. It's also a matter of having experienced, skillful personnel. There's a saying in the ISP biz that goes: The better the person, the more likely they are to be hired by someone else. The best people often go scampering from company to company or job to job chasing after ever-increasing salaries. You can't blame them; but in the meantime, this means that even the best ISP's level of service will vary from month to month. The best you can hope for is to find a reasonably stable ISP. How do you find such a marvel? Read on, my friend.

# What to Look For in an ISP

Any good ISP has a T3 or faster connection to the Internet's main lines, or backbones. The Internet's backbone starts at T3 speeds and howls on up from there. The very best ISP won't just have fast connections to the backbones, it will actually sit on the backbone itself, or be no more than one hop away from the backbone. The closer your ISP is to one of the main backbones, and the faster your ISP's connection is to it, the faster your overall service will be.

You also want an ISP that provides good service. As illustrated above, that's easier said than done. Despite this, there are some quick and dirty ways to find out if your prospective ISP is on the ball in the service lane.

First, does your ISP maintain e-mail addresses for reporting various types of trouble? What's that, you say—all they have is a mailbox labeled "help"? GONNNGG!! That ISP's a loser. You want an ISP that has dedicated mailboxes for different problem types. When I report a problem with the DNS server, I want it to go to someone who knows DNS, not someone who's trying to shuffle their way through bad modem connections, Web woes, and the nutcase who wants a T3 connection to their farmhouse in Outer Nowhere for a $100 a month.

Much as I hate voice mail, I also want my ISP to have separate connections for ordinary technical support ("How do I get my news server to get alt.sex-whoops, here comes the boss!"), serious technical support ("My news server just stopped serving!"), and five-star technical support ("We've just lost all Internet access!"). Need I say that while ideally, I always want to talk to a living, breathing person, that last call *must* go to a real person—at once!

Another, more subtle point is that your ISP must make a clear distinction between network operations support (NOS) and technical support. NOS should take care of physical and data link problems, and that's it. Trust me, that's more than enough. Technical support should be in charge of dealing with things like: what is the news server up to today, how do I get a message to someone on CompuServe, and other lighter issues. Without this distinction, you'll eventually wind up with a company that handles an "If we don't fix this, we're dead" problem after helping someone having trouble downloading cartoons from a newsgroup.

The bigger and better ISPs will also have a 24-hour a day, seven days a week network operating center (NOC) for its NOS. A simple yes or no to that question will tell you all you need to know about whether this ISP is good enough for you. If they don't, they're not. It's that simple.

You also want an ISP that has a clue about billing. Strange as it may sound, some ISPs have grown so fast that they long ago outstripped their ability to bill effectively. What you want from an ISP is either monthly or quarterly billing. Some companies will want their payments up front. I tend to put these companies at the back of my line.

In any case, you'll also want a 60-day cancellation clause. Less than that simply isn't practical for either party; and more is just asking for a bad relationship to grow really nasty.

One final way to find out how your prospective ISP is doing is to give their other corporate customers a call. In particular, find out what companies seem to have about the level of Internet activity that you expect to have, and ask them how they've been doing. Yes, it is a little underhanded; but ISPs simply haven't been around long enough to build up much of a track record. I'd rather have my instinct about an ISP supported by the opinion of someone who has already worked with the company than put all my faith in my ability to judge a business after only a few hours with their sales people and a four-color brochure.

# Finding Internet Providers

Before you can build an intranet, you have to find a connection. Specifically, what you're going to be looking for is an Internet provider that enables you to hook in with a network connection. Online services like America Online, **http://www.aol.com**, and Prodigy, **http://www.prodigy.com** that provide a vendor-specific Internet interface cannot be used for an intranet. Other online service companies, like CompuServe, do offer direct TCP/IP services.

The Baby Bells and the major long distance companies are also moving into the Internet business. The saying used to be that you couldn't be fired for recommending AT&T for your long-distance phone services. That stopped being true a long time ago; and it doesn't look like it will ever be true for Internet services. The phone companies know plenty about voice telephony, but they display an amazing degree of cluelessness when it comes to Internet services. That will change over the years, and maybe your local office does have its act together; but for the time being, I'd avoid AT&T WorldNet, **http://www.att.com/worldnet/**, MCI's networkMCI, **http://www.mci.com/**, and the like.

That said, some of the regional Baby Bells are doing well. In particular, Bell Atlantic, **http://www.bell-atl.com/html/business/**, and PacBell, **http://www.pacbell.com/**, know more about the Internet biz than their fellow belled babes in the woods. That won't help you in Cleveland, but it's good to know if you're in the mid-Atlantic states or the Pacific coast. Of course, it can't hurt to bug your own Baby Bell with a quick, "Why can't you make this as easy as Bell Atlantic does?" If enough of us hit them with a clue-by-four, eventually they'll get the idea.

## Nationwide ISPs

Before you pick an ISP, you need to know who provides Internet connections in your area. Here, people in suburban and urban areas have the advantage over their country cousins. Even the biggest ISPs don't have much in the way of connectivity in places like Alaska, West Virginia, or Arkansas (sorry, Clinton). If your business is in a rural area, you're probably going to be stuck with whatever ISP you can find.

The best guide to the national ISPs is, believe or not, 16-year-old Jay Barker's Web site, Online Connection, **http://www.accessone.com/~shwaap/onlinec/index.html**. It includes not only a comprehensive listing of national ISPs, but price comparison charts as well. As someone who's been following the industry for years, getting hard pricing for anything beyond minimal services out of an ISP is like pulling teeth from an angry tiger. The site's only weakness, from our point of view, is that it's more consumer- than business-oriented.

Many nationwide ISPs, like GNN, **http://www. gnn.com/**, Netcom, **http://www.netcom.com/**, and Pipeline, **http://www.pipeline.com/**, are meant for end-users and not companies. You can pass these by without a second look. The fast way to find out if an ISP is right for your business is to see if the ISP's Web site mentions business services within the first page or so. If it doesn't, you don't want to deal with them. If the company does have business services, but they're buried somewhere down in its virtual root cellar, do you really want to get your net connection from someone with those kind of priorities? I didn't think so.

**Table 7.1: National Business-Ready ISPs**

| <u>Name</u> | <u>URL</u> |
|---|---|
| <u>Speed</u> | |
| Digital Express | **http://www.digex.net** |
| Up to 34Mbps SMDS | |
| Earthlink | **http://www.earthlink.com/** |
| Up to T1 | |
| IDT | **http://www.idt.net/** |
| Up to T1 | |
| MSF Comm. | **http://www.mfsdatanet.com/** |
| Up to 2.488Gbps SONET | |
| PSI | **http://www.psi.net/** |

Up to T3

SprintLink                    **http://www.sprintlink.net/**

Up to 100 Mbps FDDI

UUNET                         **http://www.uu.net/**

Up to 34 Mbps SMDS

Notice how I keep saying "up to?" That's because no one has the same level of service across the country. SprintLink, for example, can only give you 100Mbps if you're in the New York area. To most of the country, SprintLink can only deliver T3 speeds.

# Regional ISPs

Why would you want a regional provider? The easy answers are more personalized service and greaterspeed. If your provider is just down the road, they'll be more familiar with any particular problems that you may face in bringing the Internet to your site. The companies' employees may very well be more willing to help a local business than a company that's just another name in a monster file.

Frankly, a local business may also be more hungry for your coin than a larger company. If you can make a better deal with a smaller company than with a multimillion dollar corporation, so much the better.

If you're in or near a city, you may be able to find an Internet provider by looking in the business section of your local newspaper. If that doesn't work for you, your next step should be to ask around your circle of friends. I'd bet serious money that at least one of your fellow business people already has an intranet.

Still on the hunt? Well you could look to some of the Internet magazines, such as *Internet World*, **http://www.internetworld.com/index.html**, and *Net Guide*, **http://techweb.cmp.com/techweb/ng/current/**, for occasional features on the state of ISP; but with the rate of ISP change, even the online versions of these magazines are hard-pressed to stay current. Still, such articles make excellent starting points for your own ISP search.

# Online ISP Hunting

Your next stop in the Internet access hunt should be either of the following Internet resources. The List, **http://thelist.iworld.com/**, is an excellent listing of worldwide ISPs. You can look through The List by state, country, or area code, or by pointing and clicking on a map. None of that thrills you? Well, you can also search for ISPs by their corporate name or their domain name. The List is maintained by Mecklermedia, a major Internet magazine publisher, and it's always current.

Another resource that's more specific to the needs of commercial buyers is Providers of Commercial Internet Access (POCIA), **http://www.celestin.com/pociaindex.html**. While this list is much smaller, and it's not kept as up to date as well as The List, it does have the virtue of being primarily for business users.

If I were looking for a new provider, I'd use both lists for my quest. They're both easy enough to use that double-checking my work isn't going to cost me any significant time; and I'm more likely to find just the ISP I need.

# How Much?

Now it's time to answer the question you've been wanting to know all along and no one, but no one, will give you a straight answer to: "How much is this intranet thing going to suck out of the corporate checking account?" You're going to hate this answer, but it's the only one I can give you: It depends.

Here are the items that are likely to appear on your bill with estimates based on average third quarter national 1996 price packages. The amount you'll end up paying flat-out is going to vary wildly. However, if you're paying more than 50% over the numbers listed here, I suspect you're either being overcharged or you're in a particular circumstance—such as living in a poorly-connected area—that's jacking up the price.

**Table 7.2: Services & Dollars**

| Item | Payment Frequency | Estimated Cost |
|------|-------------------|----------------|
| CSU/DSU | One Time Payment | $250-$3,000 |
| NTU | One Time Payment | $300-$1,000 |
| Line Install | One Time Payment | $300-$4,000* |
| Service Fee | Monthly Payment | $300-$3,000* |
| net Install Fee | One Time Payment | $300-$3,000 |

| | | |
|---|---|---|
| Router | One Time Payment | $1,000-$2,500 |
| Server | One Time Payment | $2,500-$10,000 |
| DNS | Free/Monthly Payment | Free-$100 |
| News Service | Free/Monthly Payment | Free-$500 |

*Combined ISP and Teleco prices

No doubt you've already figured out that the "cheap" prices are for 56Kbps frame relay services and that the highest ones are for T1 service.

This chart covers the range from 56Kbps leased line to T1 and PRI. Past T1 speeds, just about everything is open for negotiation—expensive negotiation, mind you, but wheeling and dealing nonetheless. If you've got someone on staff who got their start by selling the archtypical refrigerators to Eskimos, now's the time to beg, borrow, or steal him from sales and put him on the ISP negotiation team. You're going to need him. (On second thought, make that someone who sold surfboards to people in the Sahara. Alaskans, including Eskimos, do buy refrigerators regularly—to keep their food from freezing.)

At this point, you may be hitting your calculator keys and asking yourself, "Is this really worth it?" Well, yes, it is. In the next chapter, I'll look at some of the ways you can adjust who's getting paid for what to get the most out of your money. After that, I'll get into some of the nifty tools out there that you can use for turning an intranet from a capital expense into a company asset. So stick with me; the best is yet to be.

# Managing Your Intranet

## Intranet Management 101

In this chapter, I'm going to make a not-too-big presumption: You want to run your your newly running intranet site as a Web site. Oh, worry not, I'm going to go over some of the concerns of just running a plainjane intranet site as well; but the Web concerns are much more compelling.

Once you have the equipment up and have chosen an ISP, someone's going to have to have the job of intranet manager. If your company is of any real size, say over 25 people, that job going to be a full-time position.

Now, if you're switching over from a LAN to an intranet, you may already have just the woman for the job: the network administrator.

The first few months, when both systems will be running in parallel, are not going to be kind to your network administrator. Running a LAN or an intranet is a big job. Don't think for one moment that just because the jobs are a lot alike that it won't be putting that much of a demand on the netadmin: It will be.

You can make a netadmin's job much easier by supplying her with assistants for the grunt work of networking. Besides, do you really want to pay someone fifty Gs a year just to crawl underneath the floor hooking cables together all the time? A network administrator has more important things to do than the menial work of networking.

You'll also ease a network administrator's burden a great deal by giving them the tools they need to get the job done. The widgets and gizmos of network troubleshooting may not get used that often; but when you need them, you really need them. My particular favorite in this line-partly because it's software only—is Cinco Network's, **http://www.cinco.com**, NetXRay, a network analysis program. In general, though, don't just take my word for what you should get. Let your network administrator decide for herself. Network troubleshooting tools are idiosyncratic beasts; and one that works great for me might make another administrator's lot a living hell. The one key is, of course, that the program be able to deal with TCP/IP.

Other programs in the network administrator's toolkit are always in use. Your LAN administrator should have programs at hand for server monitoring, easy software distribution and licensing tracking, and tracking IP addresses.

Below is a listing of some of the programs I've found useful. Your bits per second may vary.

**Table 8.1: Good Network Administrator Tools**

| Name | Company | URL |
|------|---------|-----|
| Norton Admin. Suite | Symantec | `www.symantec.com/` |
| LANDesk | Intel | `www.intel.com` |
| IPTrack | On Tech | `www.on.com` |
| Systems Management | Microsoft | `www.microsoft.com /smsmgmt/` |

# Webmaster and Webweaver

Webmaster. It's a job title that gets bantered about a lot, but few people ever focus on what the job is and isn't about. Your Webmaster will be in charge of maintaining the hardware, software, and HTTP connectivity of your Web server. Maintaining the server's actual connections to both your intranet and your Internet is the network administrator's job. The jobs can be combined; but if you're doing a lot with your Web site, you'll find that's an impossible job to ask of anyone. If your Web business takes off in a big way, Webmaster will be a full-time position. In a small business it can be done on a part-time basis.

Another job, which many companies combine with Webmaster, is Webweaver. In one word: Don't. The Webweaver is the person who actually produces the Web documents. To do that job well, the person needs to be a good designer, editor, and writer. Did you see a word in that description about being able to dissect IP packets? Nope. You don't expect your desktop publishers to be network engineers, or vice-versa; and the same holds true for the net.

The jobs used to get confused because building and maintaining a Web site and its pages used to look like the same technical job. We've long left that point of Web page development behind; but many people still have the silly notion that just because someone can write HTML code in vi (a popular, but terse to the point of being cryptic, Unix text editor) means that anything they write in HTML is going to be worth reading or looking at. I don't mean to be nasty—many people did a great job of filling both positions. But technical expertise is no longer a requirement for Webweavers. Webmasters, yes; Webweavers, no. If that confuses you, think of it this way: Do you expect writers and editors to know how to run printing presses, or printing press technicians to know how to write solid prose? I think you see my point.

Being a Webweaver may take up anywhere from a few hours a month to 40+ hours a week. One thing it never is, however, is a temporary, one-shot job. Your Web pages will change and grow with your business. If they don't, then your online business will die. Just like advertising, Web pages must be ever-changing or they lose their appeal.

You should plan on changing at least the front page, or "home page," of your Web site at least once a month. At the same time, you don't want to alienate your customers. For example, you don't want to change how your customers reach technical support or place an order, except to make substantive improvements. You want to look new and innovative, but not so new that old customers get lost or run into the dreaded 404 error, which means that the Web server can't make heads or tails of an old URL.

Do all these jobs sound like a bit much for your company to carry? You're not the only one. Many other businesses have come to this same decision. Luckily, there's an alternative to adding more people to your staff. The name of this game is outsourcing.

While you could have someone from outside of your intranet take care of all your Internet needs, I don't think this is an optimal solution. If you're moving on to an intranet, you really need at least your network administration to be done in-house. Maybe you're willing to trust all your company's data and programs to a contractor's hands. Call me paranoid; but the essential control over the intranet itself I would want firmly in my employees' hands. Again, this is a personal call. You may have always had contractors in charge of your networking and never had a problem. More power to you. When it comes to maintaining your Web presence, well, that's another matter.

# Outsourcing

If you decide you'd rather have someone else take care of your Web pages for you, you have three choices: a company that will build your Web pages for you, something like a graphics shop; a business that will both provide you with Web pages and put them up on their server for you; or a company that will do all the above, plus put your pages on the equivalent of an online mall.

Each approach has its advantages and disadvantages. First and foremost is cost. The lower the level of service, generally speaking, the lower the price. Web service pricing at all levels is still sorting itself out, so there are no hard and fast rules on what's a good price and what isn't.

In addition to price as a guideline, you should make your decision based on the quality and reliability of your possible contractors. With the Web being as new as it is, none of the companies are going to have a very long track record. Generally, you should go with the business that produces the best material and has happy customers. If they've done well by others, they should do well by you.

Let's take a look at the three basic levels of service in turn. Briefly, they are:

* Pages Only

* Internet Presence and Pages

* The Whole Enchilada: Presence, Pages, and Malls

# Pages Only

If you've outsourced much advertising, you probably already know about graphics and layout shops that produce nothing but finished ads and then leave it up to you to place them properly. Most Web shops work pretty much the same way.

Quality of workmanship and timeliness are the critical factors to look for here. If the page about your sale looks great, but your sale ended yesterday, that Webweaver is a waste of your time and money. At the same time, you certainly don't need an unattractive page, or worse, one in which all the links don't work even if it is a week early.

As you go into this, realize that you're looking for a long-term partner, not a quick fix. Good Web pages are dynamic. You want your customers checking in every now and then—not just because of a new product or service, but because they want to be entertained by a new look. If you keep your customers' interest, you'll keep their business.

Since you're going to be looking for a Webweaver to have an ongoing relationship with, ask to see a sample of his work built around some of your company's information. Any competent webweaver ought to realize that they're only going to stay afloat with long-term customers, so they should be willing to do this. Don't, however, expect him to do complete Web site layouts for you based on a hand-shake and a promise of work tomorrow. A fool is born every minute, but good Webweavers only show up about once a week. Don't blow his goodwill by trying to take advantage of his talents.

Given a choice, you're going to want to work with a small webweaving company. (There are no large ones—yet.) Many people are just getting started in this business; but unless they have a proven track record, you don't want to put all your company's links into one weaver's basket. Even with the best of intentions, it's all too likely that a solo operation won't come through for you someday when you really need them to.

Keep in mind that if you're going this route, you're the one who's ultimately in charge of your Web server. If you change your system setup, you can't blame the webweaver when links suddenly stop working. When you outsource only Web pages, you're committing yourself to a partnership in which the weaver must have some access to your systems. If you're particularly security-conscious, this can be a problem.

# Internet Presence and Pages

When you go this road, you're letting another company handle the technical details of both connecting with the Web and making the pages for you. Chances are you're probably using this same company for your business' own Internet access-e-mail, Usenet news, and so on. You don't have to, though: Some companies run their own intranets and have an entirely separate entity run another machine just as an external Web server. The advantage, of course, is that you have complete control over what your company does and doesn't make public to the outside.

Besides the usual issues of quality workmanship delivered in a timely fashion, technical and financial reliability are the critical factors here. An Internet site that spends 5% or more of its time down for repairs is only going to frustrate your customers.

Two things you should look for when talking to these providers are the size of their help desk staff in comparison to their customer base, and whether they have a 24-hour network operations center (NOC). You want a company with a large help desk staff compared to the number of their customers. That's harder to figure out than you might think. Most Internet providers are being overwhelmed by the volume of business; and a company that's staffed up properly in August may be swamped by late September.

As for the NOC, this simply tells you if the company has an engineer on site 24 hours a day, seven days a week. Internet servers are sensitive beasts that can and will go offline at the oddest times. Internet providers that know their stuff realize that they have to have someone always available to coax ill-tempered Internet hosts back into going online.

When you're talking about a Web site that's a vital part of your company's public image, this is even more important. After all, look at what happened to IBM's reputation after their engineers dropped the ball with their Olympic coverage. IBM's proud boasts of having a perfect Web site went down the toilet, along with its credibility of being a top-of-the-line Web site host.

Sometimes, such failures can sink an entire company; and if that corporation also happens to host your Web site, you're really in trouble. That, by the way, is not an idle threat. For all that the Internet business is booming, some Internet providers have gone out of business leaving customers high and dry. WebTech Advertising of Clearwater, Florida, for example, filed for bankruptcy and went out of business, simultaneously leaving nearly 100 Web advertisers high and dry.

The moral of the story is to know your Internet provider. All the hard work and goodwill in the world won't prevent a business from failing if it's undercapitalized.

## The Whole Enchilada: Presence, Pages, and Malls

What if you don't want to fool with any of this Web stuff yourself, but you still want a presence on the Web? You can do that, too. Several companies will build your pages, hook you up into the Internet, and place you in an online mall so your pages will get noticed.

These services are brand-new, so there's almost no track record to go by. The majority of them are national in scope. The most important of these are:

**Table 8.2 Virtual Malls**

| Names | URL |
|-------|-----|
| Access Market Square | `http://www.icw.com/ams.html` |
| Branch Mall | `http://branch.com:1080/` |
| EINet's Galaxy | `http://galaxy.einet.net/galaxy/` |
| eMall's Home Page | `http://eMall.Com/Home.html` |
| Internet Shopping | `http://www.internet.net/` |
| The Internet Mall | `http://www.mecklerweb.com:80 /imall/` |
| WWW Advertising | `http://www.xmission.com/~ wwwads/index.html` |

If you don't want to reach a national audience, there are electronic malls with a regional emphasis. For example, Blacksburg, VA, is the home of:

| BizNet Center | `http://www.biznet.com.blacks burg.va.us/shopping.html` |
|---------------|----------------------------------------------------------|

Check around online with Yahoo `http://www.yahoo.com`), an Internet catalog that is especially well-suited for finding local malls, and see if there's a mall for your hometown.

You can expect the national services to charge you more, but their pricing is flexible. If you can supply your own pages and Web space, you could get a much better deal, as you'd only be paying for your virtual store's placement in an online mall. Of course, now you're back to running some of this work in-house; but hey, no one ever said creating and running an intranet and Web sites would be easy—least of all me.

Still, if you want none of the headaches of Web and Internet and all the benefits, writing one check to an online mall is a very attractive proposition. Just be aware that your whole Internet presence is now resting on the success or failure of another company. For you, that one headache may be worth the multiple headaches of other answers. Just be damned sure that you know exactly who you're dealing with and what you can expect from them.

# Getting Noticed

Okay, one way or the other, you've got your site. It looks great. The last pixels have been polished and the datalines have been dusted. Now what?

Well, letting people know you've got a site, that's what. The easiest way to do this is to get your site as quick as humanly possible onto the main Web catalogs and search engines. These are:

**Table 8.3: Prominent Web Sites**

Where to find places for others to find you.

| Name | URL |
|------|-----|
| AltaVista | `http://www.altavista.digital.com/` |
| InfoSeek | `http://www.infoseek.com/Home` |
| OpenText | `http://www.opentext.com/` |
| Lycos | `http://www.lycos.com/` |
| Webcrawler | `http://webcrawler.com/` |
| Yahoo | `http://www.yahoo.com/` |

There are other sites that do similar jobs; these, however are the best.

All of these sites let you enter your own Web site into their indices. It may take a week or two before your site appears, but it will happen. Of course, that involves a lot of typing. If you'd rather announce your site to as many different Web sites as possible, the best answer is PostMaster `http://www.netcreations.com/postmaster/index.html`. PostMaster uses its own online form to send your Web site's birth announcement to several hundred sites at once. Other services try to do the same thing. Some of them are free, but they're worth exactly what you pay for them. PostMaster is the only program that actually does get the word out. It costs, but its worth the dough.

# Advertising

Lest we forget, if you're looking to generate business from your Web site—and, who isn't?—then you need to look into advertising.

Were we working with a traditional information/advertising model, there wouldn't be many questions. Welcome to the Web, where all things are new and different. Web pricing is so irregular that it's downright scary. On paper, general interest publications will run you from $30 to $60 per 1,000 readers, and a trade magazine or newspaper would cost you $100 to $150 for an advertisement. On the Web, though, even advertising agencies will admit they're not sure how to properly price their products. Ad agencies, Internet providers, and the businesses that monitor media circulation, like Nielsen Media Research and Audit Bureau of Circulation, are even now pounding away at coming up with good numbers for measuring how many people see a Web page and how much attention they might pay to a link from that page to your page.

To give you an idea of the going rates in the summer of 1996, HotWired **http://www.wired.com**, a popular magazine and Web site for the technically hip, was asking for $15,000 for a month of ad links on their pages. Netscape, arguably the most recognizable name on the Web, was guaranteeing 1.5 million "impressions" (that is, customer viewings) for $30,000. Time Inc.'s popular Web site, Pathfinder, was also asking—and getting—$30,000 per months of ad placement on its service. By the time you read this, expect all those rates to have gone up.

Just as in magazines, prominent Web sites are beginning to charge more for select placements on their services. If you want to be the first thing anyone sees on Netscape's site, for example, you'll pay the top rate of $30,000. If you're on a budget, you can still appear on Netscape's site...somewhere...for $10,000 a month.

The advertising model isn't the only one that Web vendors are trying on for size to make money, but it's the most popular one. To keep up to date on what's what in the world of Internet advertising, you'll want to put The Internet Advertising Resource Guide, `http://www.missouri.edu/internet-advertising-guide.html`, on your hot list. For the latest on who's charging what, check out the IPA Advertising Index, `http://www.netcreations.com/ipa/adindex/`.

Those are just prices for placing a Web ad, and they're far beyond the reach of most small companies. On a lower level, there really aren't any good answers to the bottom-line question of how much your Web presence will cost you. Your best approach is to study the Web carefully. Look at your competitor's Web sites, talk to your customers, and get a feel for just how being on the Web can help your business. Once you know what you're looking for, it will be much easier to decide how much you want to pay for it, even if market prices are as jumpy as a Mexican jumping bean.

But enough of Webbing it for now. In the next two chapters, we'll take a look at what we can do inside and outside of your intranet, sans Web.

# Introducing Usenet Tools

## Welcome to Usenet

E-mail is the application that makes the Internet world go around. Oddly enough, e-mail isn't really an Internet application at all. It's part of a larger network, often confused with the Internet, called the Usenet.

The Usenet is what I call a metanetwork. Technically speaking, it's not really a network at all, because there's no networking protocol binding the system together. Instead, network independent protocols for sending e-mail and Usenet news are used to send messages and news over the Internet as well as any other network that's connected with the Internet and recognizes the mail and news protocols.

# Moving Mail

When packets must leave the Internet proper to access a non-TCP/IP network, a gateway computer routes the packets across the network to either its destination or to another gateway. Gateway computers also translate information from one native format to another. The most common of these are the mail gateways that bind the Usenet together by translating e-mail address headers.

The mail servers do this job by normally using two of three protocols. These are: Simple Mail Transfer Protocol (SMTP), Post Office Protocol 3 (POP), and Internet Mail Access Protocol (IMAP). Of these, the first two are by far the most popular. IMAP, for all that it has more than two years of solid work expereince behind it, is still regarded by most people as semi-experimental, and few mail servers and clients support it.

Protocols aside, which server will work right for you? Well, it depends on your operating system and your existing e-mail system. Many familiar LAN e-mail systems are turning over a new Usenet leaf. Banyan's BeyondMail, `http://196.11.117.2/docs/banyan/213e.htm`, DaVinci's SMTP eMail, `http://www.on.com/on/products.html/tigb88a`, Lotus' cc:Mail, `http://www.lotus.com/comms/ccmail.htm`, Novell's Group-Wise SMTP Gateway, `http://www.novell.com/groupwise/prods/gwise/gateways/smtp.html`, and Microsoft's Exchange, `http://www.microsoft.`

`com/exchange/`, have all incorporated SMTP and POP in the last few months.

If you want to move directly to Usenet-style mail, that's perfectly possible too. For example, FireFox's Novix Mail for NetWare brings SMTP to NetWare LANs. For NT, my personal favorite out of more than a dozen programs is Digital Equipment Corporation's AltaVista Mail Server, `http://altavista.software.digital.com/products/nfintro.htm`. Some people—although I'm not one of them—are very fond of Netscape's Mail Server, `http://home.mcom.com/comprod/server_central/product/mail/index.html`.

For those of us who are already committed to Unix, the mail server of choice, even if it is one of the annoying programs in the world, is the SendMail program already on the disk. SendMail is a pain, make no mistake; but its nigh unto infinite flexibility makes it the all-time champion when it comes to moving the Unix mail along.

Once these servers are in place, you just need a client side e-mail program for your users, and you're in business. Traditonally, e-mail programs have almost always been standalone products. Some of the best ones, such as David Harris' Pegasus Mail, `http://www.pegasus.usa.com/`, still carry the flag for single-purpose e-mail applications.

For the most part, though, these programs are being brushed aside by Web browsers with built in e-mail tools. For example, Netscape has a fine built-in e-mail facility. Other programs, like the groupware favorite Lotus Notes, have always had a strong e-mail component and are now incorporating Usenet e-mail standards. Eventually, all Web browsers and serious groupware products—which will be almost impossible to tell apart—will become all-in-one Internet/Usenet interfaces.

For today and tomorrow, there are many things you need to know about Internet mail that have nothing to do with the interface. Whatever the look and feel of a program, there are many things about Internet mail that hold true regardless of the application.

# Working With Mail

E-mail has always been a better solution than any of the traditional means of business communications. It's faster, and its hardware is easier to integrate into a PC. In the past, e-mail's Achilles' heel has been that it's difficult to use. If you can dial a telephone, you can learn to use a fax machine. E-mail, on the other hand, required expert-level computer users.

Times are changing. Currently available e-mail programs make it possible for even computer novices to send messages across the continent as easily as across the hall. The fall of fax, with its gigantic installed base, won't happen overnight; but it's long been my opinion that by 2001, fax machines will be as quaint and old-fashioned as rotary-dial phones are today.

Unfortunately, you simply can't stop using paper mail, telephones, and fax machines in favor of e-mail. This has little to do with technical concerns: E-mail interfaces are as friendly as a golden retriever pup. No, the real concerns are with legal and privacy issues.

# Mail Problems

E-mail is not the US Postal Service. There are large gray areas in the law when it comes to privacy rights regarding e-mail. If you're using your company or school's Internet system, the system owners may claim that they have a perfect right to peek into your electronic mailbox. Whether they do or not is still a matter that's being hashed out in the courts.

As the person in charge of all this, you need to sit down now and spell out your company's policy. Having done that, you're going to need to run it by the company's attorneys. In your copious free time, you should keep in mind that making too many restrictions is just asking for employees' morale to sink faster than the Titantic.

You probably don't want employees running their own businesses over their corporate e-mail. (Don't laugh; it happens every day.) Still, you have a choice: You can either let your people talk over e-mail like they do in the lunchroom or by the coffee machine, or you can annoy the heck out of them. I think you know which choice I favor. Go ahead and let your people gossip, romance, and tell tales of last night's game onscreen. They're going to do it anyway, so you might as well as relax about it.

At the same time, you don't want things getting out of hand. One effective way to limit e-mail extravagance is to set a policy that any mail sent on the company's system can be looked into by the proper authorities (and spell out who that is). Even if you'll never peek into someone's mail under ordinary circumstances, openly stating your ability and authority to do so should be sufficient to keep most people from spending their days sending messages to sweetie-pie and snugglewuggums.

# Mail Security

Users may also have a problem with someone unofficially snooping into their mail. This can be a serious threat. Your confidential mail, whether it's romance or business, may be vulnerable to the online versions of cat burglars.

Another problem is that someone may use your e-mail address to send bogus messages out to the world. In a recent case, someone sent out thousands of racist messages from a (thoroughly non-racist) college professor's mail account. How would you like your CEO to find out that nastygrams have been sent to half the world from your account? Sound unlikely? It can happen; and as sure as I'm sitting here, it will happen to some business someday.

Now, this might sound so unlikely as to not be worth worrying over. Let's move the problem down a couple of magnitudes. Consider: One rude note to your boss with your name on it, by someone else's hand, could put an end to your career.

To combat online peeping toms and forgers, you must employ some security basics. I'll talk about security in more detail in later chapters; but here I'm talking about the real basics that don't have a darn thing to do with security protocols. Frankly, you're much more likely to have something bad happen to your company by ignoring these than you ever are from having S-HTTP not set up just so.

Security starts with people. An old cracker joke that's painfully true is that the easiest way to break into a system is to make friends with someone in the office.

If you want to make sure that your secrets don't walk, you can start by making sure that your password isn't easy to guess, changing it on a regular basis, and not telling anyone what it is. Oh yes, and above all, don't write it down on a piece of paper on your desk! Everyone does this, and every snoop knows it.

After you've done that, you can look into encryption programs. By far the most popular of these on the Internet is Philip Zimmerman's Pretty Good Privacy (PGP). PGP encrypts your mail so that nobody but the intended recipient can read it.

You can also use PGP to sign your public messages with a unique digital signature. You use this option when you want to make certain that there can be no mistaking that you're the author of a message. If you want to know more about PGP, look for the FAQ in the **alt.security.pgp**, **alt.answers**, or **news.answers** newsgroups.

# Mail Addressing

Most people will find e-mail addressing to be their biggest headache. For all of e-mail's virtues, getting mail from one system to another can be monstrously difficult.

It's not that e-mail addressing is really that difficult. It's just that with dozens of different e-mail systems out there, it can be a wee bit tricky figuring out which method is right for getting mail from one system to another. For instance, sending messages from one user to another on the Internet is pretty straightforward. Sending a message from the friendly confines of the Internet to someone on MCI Mail or CompuServe is a pony of a different color.

The crux of the problem is that the who, what, and how of e-mail addressing is hard to come by. Most systems hide this vital information away in obscure help files. The trick is finding out how to address properly in the first place, which we'll learn later in this chapter.

No man may be an island, but e-mail systems once were. One of the forces behind the intranet revolution is that more and more workers are finding incompatible e-mail systems inaccessible. Even in the bad old days of mailing systems that wouldn't talk to each other, you could send messages to users on other systems if you knew either the RFC822 or X.400 mail addressing protocols.

Then, as now, most e-mail users, whether they know it or not, used the RFC822 protocol. RFC822's real name, "Standard for the Format of ARPA-Internet Text Messages," bears witness to its age. Today, RFC822 is still the standard of choice for the Internet, BITnet (Because It's Time Network), and almost all academic, business, and scientific networks.

RFC822 defines not only how messages are addressed, but their format as well. For instance, all RFC822 messages must consist of either ASCII, or on BITnet, Extended Binary Coded Decimal Interchange Code (EBCIDC), an IBM mainframe binary code for representing data.

An RFC822 address consists of two parts: a mailbox name and a domain name. This address can be represented in many formats. For example, were I to send you a message from the Internet, my address might read:

**`sjvn@access.digex.net`**    (Steven J. Vaughan-Nichols)

or:

Steven J.Vaughan-Nichols    **`<sjvn@access.digex. net>`**

or, for that matter, the plain but cryptic:

**`sjvn@access.digex.net`**

Whichever way you type it, the important part of the line—called a header, because it heads an e-mail message—is the section containing the 'at' (@) sign. My full name is there purely for your convenience. The information to the left of the 'at' sign is the mailbox address. On many mail systems, this is usually a version of your name, or in my case, my initials.

Some mailbox names contain percentage signs(%) or periods. This usually means that the mailbox name is a forwarding address. When you send a note to a forwarding address, the address will be expanded to its full size by the receiving machine. Frequently, this is the solution used within an internal network. For example,

**`sjvn.Notes@mail.zd.ziff.com`**

sends a message to my Lotus Notes mail account, which is connected to the Internet by the mail.zd.ziff.com gateway system.

There are fundamental problem with using full names. Some e-mail systems are unable to deal with very long names. Others, like BITnet systems, can't hack mixed cases in addresses. A message sent to the hypothetical mailbox,

**Esther_Schindler@testcase.bitnet**, would generate an error message from the BITnet mailer because it couldn't figure out—or, as we say in the business, "resolve"—the address.

Another concern with mixed-case addresses is that these addresses are usually treated very precisely. If you sent a message to **sjvn@access.digex.net**, I'd get it; but if you sent one to **Sjvn@access.digex.net**, I wouldn't. That's because to most mailers, "Sjvn" is not the same thing as "sjvn." To prevent confusion, most users go with e-mail handles in all lowercase letters. You'd be wise to adopt the same convention.

On the right side of the address, we come to the domain address. At the extreme right, you'll find the top-level domain. Other elements in this section of the address are referred to as sub-domains.

Domain addresses normally resemble the US mail system of addressing. The more specific address elements come first, and the most general ones come last. There are thousands of ".com" sites, for instance, just as there can be thousands of homes in any given state or zip code area. The next sub-domain, as you move closer to the 'at' sign, tells you more specifically where the user's e-mail account can be found. Hard to see? In table 9.1, we have syntactically similar addresses for your author.

**Table 9.1: RFC822 Addressing Examples**

| Postal Address | E-mail Addresses | |
| --- | --- | --- |
| Steven J. Vaughan-Nichols | **sjvn@** | **sjvn@** |

| 123 Some Street | **well.** | **access.** |
| New York, NY 21202 | **sf.ca.** | **digex.** |
| USA | **usa** | **net** |

As with every rule, there are exceptions. In the United Kingdom and New Zealand, some mailers read the address in reverse. These systems expect to see something like: **example@uk.oxford.history**. Fortunately, modern mailers can cope with either address form.

You'll notice that there can be more than one sub-domain. These can represent geographical entities, as you can see from The Well address in San Francisco, California. A sub-domain can also represent any particular computer in a network, or a department inside any one business or organization. For example, another of my addresses reads:

**sjvn@vna.digex.net**

In this case, vna is a single computer within the larger 'digex' organization. This is an especially popular addressing scheme in university communities, where addresses like **test@history.mit.edu** abound.

In our example above, the mail server would point your system's addressing inquiry to digex.net. Finally, digex would supply the details on how to send message a first to it and then to the vna computer. The mailer would the delivers your message as directly as possible to the target system.

Not every system that uses RFC822 style addressing actually uses RFC822 within its own confines. The two most important systems that hide their own addressing systems behind RFC822 are the UUCP (Unix to Unix Copy Program) networks, used by some of Usenet in the US, Europe's Eunet, and BITnet. Many LAN mailing programs still use gateway programs for the same job. These programs, almost aways called gateways, are usually extra price options that aren't included in a LAN program's basic package. Never assume that just because your existing mail system could connect to a net mail system means that the copy you have is in any way capable of pulling this feat off.

The UUCP networks use, surprise, UUCP to maintain system connections instead of the TCP/IP. In practical terms, this means that UUCP networks' internal addresses look like:

```
say!this!is!an!example!sjvn.
```

What that translates into is not an address as such, but an actual listing out of the path that a message should take to reach sjvn at the 'example' machine. Sounds messy, doesn't it? It gets messier. Most of any UUCP system's intersystem mail is actually devoted to updating UUCP topology maps. Fortunately, even between UUCP sites, you can normally just use RFC822 addressing and not worry about the precarious underpinning that makes it possible.

BITnet's addressing looks much like RFC822. The only easy difference to spot is the use of '.bitnet' as the top-level domain. BITnet addresses, however, do have their quirks. Besides the aforementioned mixed case problem, BITnet puts an eight-character limit on mailbox names.

# X.400 Addressing

The X.400 standard was supposed to be the universal answer to e-mail interconnectivity. Born of a desire to solve such recurring problems as binary file transfers with the intent to produce a single, consistent addressing scheme, X.400 promised much and, to date, delivers little. X.400 belongs to the OSI standard family. The OSI standards are meant to make maintaining connections between heterogeneous networks easier. Well, that was the idea anyway.

In this country, X.400 was given a boost when the federal government mandated its use in government internetworking projects rather than RFC822. Government Open Systems Interconnection Profile (GOSIP) was the driving force behind X.400 in the United States for years. When the government woke up to the fact that almost every federal agency was ignoring the directive in favor of RFC, the Feds finally dumped its X.400 requirements.

In theory, X.400 and its universal directory system, X.500, can handle any kind of communications: fax, paper mail, binaries, you name it. In practice, it's proven to be another matter. You can't, for instance, send binary files or faxes reliably between X.400 systems. You're taking your file into your own hands if you use X.400 to send a binary file, say your annual report, from MCI Mail to SprintMail.

So while you may run into X.400 mail ocassionally, for most intranet administrators, it's a non-issue. My only recommendation for you is: Whatever you do, *don't* get an X.400 gateway or server. X.400 is taking a long time to croak, but there's no question that it's on its way out.

# Mailing Lists

Do you want to get valuable information by mail for free? And, no I don't mean electronic junk mail; I'm talking about the real thing. If your answer is yes, then you need to look into mailing lists.

A mailing list is, quite simply, two mail addresses. The first address, the broadcast address, sends your message to multiple e-mail addresses. Thus, when you send a message to a mailing list, it's automatically forwarded to everyone on the list and vice-versa. Mailing lists are used for everything from keeping weddings organized to socializing DOOM players to keeping workgroup members in sync with each other.

If a list's subject matter sounds interesting to you, you'd usually ask to be added to the list by sending a message to the subscription address. Do not make the exceedingly common mistake of sending a subscription note to the broadcast address: Everyone on the list will get a copy of your note; and if you're lucky, maybe as many as 1% of them will not be annoyed at you and send you a nasty note in return. Subscription addresses come in two flavors, personal and automatic. A personal subscription list address almost always looks something like:

**subtle-request@vna1.com**

Notice the hyphen followed by the word request? That's the usual telltale of a manually maintained subscription address. This one ends up sending me a personal note which I would take as a request to join the list I keep for people who play in my role-playing game. (Before you try it out, I can already tell you: Sorry, but the answer is no. We've nearly got too many players as it is.)

Once you have permission to set up a mailing list from the network administrator, you can use similar formats to organize your own lists for everything from the totally informal, like I just did in the example above, to more serious purposes, like organizing your company's Web page.

Other lists use programs to automate list management. These lists have mailbox names like listserv, majordomo, listproc, and mail-serv. Each of these uses a slightly different command syntax. To discover the incantation that will make them work for you, simply send the mailing list a note with the single word "help" in the subject header. For the basics, the following table will steer you right.

**Table 9.2: Popular Mailing List Program How-tos**

<u>Mailing List Software</u>

ListProc

| | |
|---|---|
| *Subscribe:* | subscribe list_name first_name last_name |
| *Unsubscribe:* | unsubscribe list_name |

ListServ

| | |
|---|---|
| *Subscribe:* | subscribe list_name first_name last_name |
| *Unsubscribe:* | signoff list_name |

Majordomo

| | |
|---|---|
| *Subscribe:* | subscribe list_name |
| *Unsubscribe:* | unsubscribe list_name |

With all these programs, you leave the subject header empty. Many mailers will ask if you really want to send a message without a subject. In these cases, the answer is yes.

If you're running a small list, doing it by hand is fine. I've run lists with up to one hundred members manually, and it wasn't a big deal. Once you go over a hundred people, however, you really need to get a list management program. Fortunately, there are several good ones available. Unfortunately, none of them are cheap. Majordomo is free; but you'd better be a darn good hand at the PERL scripting language and mail administration before you try installing it. For the latest information on the big three programs, check out their Web sites.

**Table 9.3: Major List Processing Programs**

| Program Name | URL |
| --- | --- |
| ListProc | `http://www.cren.net/www/listproc/` `info.html` |
| ListServ | `http://www.lsoft.com/listserv.stm` |
| MajorDomo | `http://www.greatcircle.com/majordomo/` |

Which one is best for you? I favor MajorDomo myself; but you can read a full, blow-by-blow account of list server versus list server on a very technical level by reading Norm Aleks' study of popular list servers at `ftp://ftp.uu.net/usenet/news.answers/mail/list-admin/software-faq`.

Once you're on a mailing list, you'll automatically receive a copy of all mail sent to the list, including any mail that you send. Some systems will also let you set up your own lists. Check with your Internet provider to see if this is possible. Small lists are easy to maintain, and can be invaluable for keeping people with common interests in contact.

Mailing lists can be so useful that, for many people, they're reason enough in and of themselves for some people to use e-mail. For example, in my own writing and journalism business, I find my membership in the Internet Press Guild list, **ipg-l@netpress.org**, a list for professional online/Internet journalists, and **online-news@plane-tarynews.com**, for keeping up on what's what in the world of online publishing, to be invaluable. No matter what your profession, there's almost certainly an e-mail list out there that can, at the least, keep you in touch with other people in your particular business, and at best, give you invaluable advice in record time.

Considering how many online journalists are out there, you may not find either of my examples very useful. But if you turn your Web browser to Stephanie da Silva's Publicly Accessible Mail Listings, **http://www.neosoft .com/internet/paml/**, or tile.net/Lists, **http://tile .net/listserv/**, I'll betcha a dime to a dollar that you'll find a mailing list that's right for you.

# User Mail Basics

There are too many Internet e-mail interfaces to go into much detail on how to use them. Here are the basics for two of the most basic Internet mail programs. Check your manual or your Internet provider's help desk for more information.

Almost all Unix systems will give you access to the spartan mail program, elm. Elm, which is short for elementary mail, gives you an easy-to-use menu-driven interface, which can be seen in figure 9.1. If you've never run elm at your command prompt, give it a try: You may just be pleasantly surprised to find it there.

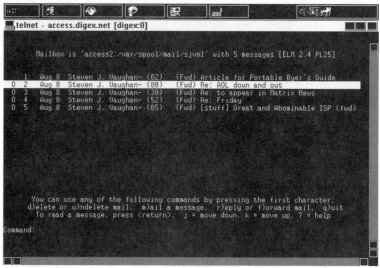

**Figure 9.1**: There are fancier mail interfaces than elm, but it's a good beginner's e-mail program.

For specific instructions on how to use either mail, elm, or other Internet programs, simply type:

`man program_name`

at your Internet provider system's command line prompt. This will present you with an online manual for the command. This information is meant for Unix power users, so be prepared to spend some time studying the manual online. Better still, print out the manual pages with your communication program's print option so you can refer to it as you start working with the program.

There are also a wide variety of text editors that work with the mail interfaces. If you're working with a system that gives you a native Unix interface to the Internet, your menu of text editors will almost certainly include EMACS and vi.

If that's the case, before starting with either one, read the documentation on your pick of the editors. EMACS is very powerful, but is also very complicated. Vi, on the other hand, has a bare minimum of commands to learn; but its learning curve is very steep, because there's essentially no online help available while vi is running.

Most folks will want a fancier mail program. I've tried many of them. You'll see my pick of the best in table 9.4.

**Table 9.4: The Best E-Mail Programs**

| Program | OS | URL |
|---------|-----|-----|
| Embla | Windows | `http://www.pro.icl.se/*` |
| Eudora | Windows & Macintosh | `http://www.eudora.com/` |
| Pegasus Mail | MS-DOS & Windows | `http://www.pegasus.usa.com/` |

*Supports IMAP

When sending mail, there are several problems that always trip users up. If you avoid these common mistakes, you'll be a long way toward successful use of intersystem e-mail. Here are some helpful ways to avoid getting tangled in the crosswires.

The first rule is, send only ASCII text. Word processing files may look like ASCII to you, but they're actually loaded with formatting codes which will turn them into gibberish if you send them as is. If you need to send a file from your word processing system, first save it into ASCII format. Then you can cut and paste the ASCII text into a mail message that won't look like a cat walked over your keyboard.

You can send binary files, like graphics and spreadsheets, over Internet mail; but you can't send them as ordinary mail. That's why trying to send a WordPerfect document as the text of your message will lead only to garbage on the other end. To send binary files, you need to use Multipurpose Internet Mail Extensions (MIME) and send it as an attachment to your message. MIME is a set of additions to the SMTP format that enables it to carry digital data. To use MIME, you need a mail interface that supports it. Almost all modern mail clients support MIME. Whatever else you do, don't get a mail program that supports only older mail standards for sending binary files. UUENCODE, for example, was great in its day; but its day came to an end about three years ago.

Of course, before you can send someone a message, you need to know their address. How do you find out what someone else's address is? Really and truly, the best way is to simply to ask them or have them send you a message at your address. None of the attempts at Internet white pages are anything like complete.

Once you've gotten the hang of net addresses, they're easy to use. You can also use Internet mail to send mail to users on other networks or online services. For the address format for several of the most popular online services around today, see table 9.4.

## Table 9.4: Online Service Address Formats

| Service Name | Address Format |
| --- | --- |
| America Online | `user_name@aol.com` |
| AT&T Mail | `user_name@attmail.com` |
| BIX | `user_name@bix.com` |
| CompuServe* | `user_number@cis.com` |
| Delphi | `user_name@delphi.com` |
| MCI Mail | `user_number@mcimail.com` |
| Netcom | `user_name@ix.netcom.com` |
| Pipeline | `user_name@pipeline.com` |
| Prodigy | `user_number@prodigy.com` |

*Note: To send mail to CIS users, use a period instead of a comma in the user number. CIS and Prodigy are both trying to move to a kinder and gentler user name system, but they're not there yet.

One final note: Even when leaving the Internet, address case is still important. For example, "fred.com" is not the same thing as "Fred.com." While some mailers—programs that actually do the grunt work of forwarding mail from one system to another—can cope with mixed case addresses, older ones still throw up at the very thought. You can make the mailers' job easier, and insure that your message will arrive where you want it to go, by making sure that your addresses are in the right case.

## Getting a Mail Interface

There are several things you should look for in a mail program. First, it should be capable of using aliases. No one wants to type "ladedadedadedadeda@somewhere.or.the. other.com" every time they want to send a message. A good mail program will also have an address book, so that you can keep all your aliases and addresses in one place. The best mail programs will also let you store more than one name to an alias, so that you can easily send out mail to a group of business associates or friends at once.

Another important feature is the ability to place your mail in various folders. If you're on a mailing list or two, it won't take long for your mail to get too unwieldy for a single virtual mailbox. For example, in figure 9.2, you can see that Pegasus Mail lets you set up a complete system of mail folders.

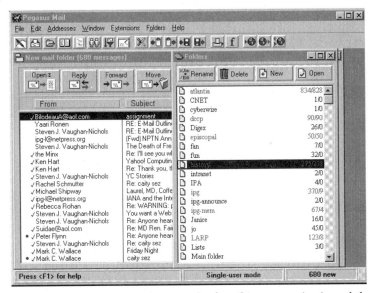

**Figure 9.2:** The only way to keep track of mail is to organize it, and the easiest way to do that is with folders.

If you're like me, you'll also want a mail program that can run in the background and gather your mail automatically on a regular schedule. This way, you always get your mail within minutes of its arrival, and you don't have to strike a single key.

A good mail program is also capable of letting you sort your mail in a variety of different ways. Some people like their mail sorted in date order by "last in, first out" order, while others prefer an alphabetical order by mail address listing.

The best mail programs can filter your mail for you. Say, for instance, that you don't want to read any more junk mail from the jerk down the hall who wants to keep the entire office up to date on his football pool. An excellent mail reader can be used to set up a "twit-filter" that automatically dumps his messages into the bit-bucket. An absolutely top-of-the-line mail program could also be set to sort your mail. For example, my copy of Pegasus Mail is set to send mail from my editors and friends to my new folder, while everything else, such as messages from a computer history mailing list that I belong to, gets automatically moved into the history folder.

While not essential, one bit of chrome you'll almost certainly want from a mail program is the option of having your mail program automatically attach your signature to your messages. A signature is a short (no more than four lines) declaration of who you are and how you can be contacted. A standard signature—or ".sig"—file might include your name, title, e-mail address, and perhaps a pithy (read: bright but brief) quote of the day, or QOTD. Many people take this chance to personalize their mail. That's great. What's not so great is using .sig files to send people large ASCII graphics or long, rambling lines of wisdom. Far too many people do this; and even more people get emphatically tired of seeing their dreary, attentuated signatures.

## Working With Usenet News

Usenet newsgroups are collections of messages on a single topic—or as closely related to a single topic as anything can be in the semi-formalized anarchy we call the Usenet. Whether you're working on Web page design or chasing C++ coding tips, there's a newsgroup for you.

Many people get tangled up by the syllable "news" in newsgroups. Except for the claris family of newsgroups (i.e. "claris.whatever"), few of these groups actually carry formal news at all. The closest equivalent to a newsgroup in the real world is a conference call with keyboards. Everyone can, and will, talk. In theory, there's an agenda; but like many a badly managed teleconference, things usually go quickly off-topic. Unlike the most horrible teleconferences, though, multiple conversations can and will go on at once.

With thousands of topics, hundreds of thousands of networked computers, and millions of readers, it doesn't take much to turn Usenet reading into drudgery rather than a joy. There's valuable information hidden away in net news. The only problem is finding it.

If you think that sounds bad for the user, consider, if you will, the poor network administrator. It's bad enough just keeping up with a few newsgroups. Now consider trying to manage 15,000 or so of them on a Network News Transfer Protocol (NNTP) server.

Oh, it's easier than it sounds. If it wasn't, Usenet news would have imploded long ago. Still, it's a load on the administrator and, far more importantly, it's a tremendous burden on your Internet connection and your server. Do you have a gigabyte a day to spend on Usenet news? Even if you do, do you have the throughput to cope with that kind of load? Or, for that matter, with the hundred megabytes or so of news a day that even a very limited news feed will give you, do you really have enough room on your net connection for it?

Also, keep in mind that people are going to want news to stick around on your local server for at least a week or two. You can't expect everyone to read their news daily (*sigh*); and they need context for the news articles they read to make any sense of them. At that 100MB a day rate that I mentioned earlier, that means that your "small" feed will require—ouch!—about 1.4 gigabytes of storage.

Did I mention that you'll have probably have to pay to get the feed? There are public sites where you can get free news feeds, but—surprise!—they tend to be as slow as running a marathon through Georgia mud. Still, if you want to give them a try, you'll find the most current listings for them in the Yahoo Public Access Usenet News listing, `http://www.yahoo.com/News/Usenet/Public_Acc ess_Usenet_Sites/`.

I think you get the idea. Usenet news is popular, it's amusing, and, occasionally, it can be informative. That said, it probably isn't worth your time to bring an NNTP server and a news feed to your intranet.

You can expect a howl of outrage from your firm's long-time net users when you announce that your new Internet connection won't be including news. To be frank, though, Usenet newsgroups long ago grew too popular to be worthwhile for most people. As we say in the biz, the noise to signal ratio has grown so large that spending time in most newsgroups is a waste of time.

Of course, that's not true of all of them. Many of the tightly focused newsgroups, such as comp.unix.admin, for Unix administrators, and comp.compression, for people who need to know the input and output of data compression programs, are very useful. If your people need access to such groups, then go ahead and get a small feed.

To use a feed, you'll need your own NNTP server. I've listed some of the best of them in the table below. Be warned, however, that even the best NNTP server software—which is what I've listed below—can be cranky, especially when its first installed; so be ready to spend some time getting an NNTP server up to speed.

**Table 9.5: NNTP Servers**

| Name | OS | URL |
|---|---|---|
| DNEWS | NT, Unix | `http://world.std.com/~netwin/dnews.htm` |
| INN | Unix | `http://www.math.psu.edu/barr/INN.html` |
| Netscape News Server | NT | `http://home.mcom.com/comprod/server_central/product/news/index.htm` |
| NNTP | Unix | `http://www.academ.com/academ/nntp/index.html` |

Generally speaking, the broader the topic, the more worthless the group. This is true in particular of any group that involves anything in the least bit controversial. Here, you'll find most of the postings are actually "flames"—loud, hot-air-filled diatribes in which more heat than light is shed on any given subject. Even narrow-cast groups can go rotten. If you find you have groups like that on your intranet, save yourself some bandwidth and unsubscribe from them.

The simple truth is that real, person-to-person information exchange and intelligent discusssions long ago passed from Usenet newsgroups to mailing lists. You may be able to justify a small news feed for the people involved in one of the topics which still has a viable newsgroup. For many companies, however, it's not worth the trouble of putting up an NNTP news server and news clients.

A good news reader makes it possible to wade through the net news swamp and get only the information you want, instead of spending hours online becoming a Usenet news zombie. Don't think it won't happen. An old funny-serious joke in college circles is that when someone first finds Usenet news, you can add another year to their expected graduation date.

## Getting a News Interface

When you shop for a news interface, there are a number of features you should look for. First and foremost, the interface must be capable of threading messages. In threading, messages are presented to you in both time and conversational order. For example, when you read a conversation, or thread, on Sun's latest version of Java, you'll read the thread first by its subject, then in the order that the messages arrived. Without threading, reading news is almost pointless, because you can never tell where a subject begins or ends and who's saying what in response to whom.

If you want a more sophisticated newsreader, the newsreader of choice for Windows users is Forte's Agent, `http://www.forteinc.com/`. This full-featured program is also avaialble in a free version, named—appropriately enough—Free Agent.

Agent stands so far above the common mold of newsreaders that there's no comparison. If you're going to use Usenet news in a Windows environment, this is the news reader for your company to standardize on. Agent lets you work online or off, download headers on one pass, disconnect, and tag topics for retrieval on a second pass. While that's good enough, far more interesting are its abilities to extract binary files from multiple news articles with a click of a mouse, and its search capacities. If Usenet news ever had a killer application, this would be the one.

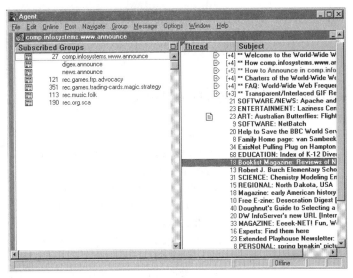

**Figure 9.3**: Agent gives you all the news all the time, the way *you* want to read it.

The reason for this is very simple: Agent makes it easy to *not* read news. The trap of Usenet news is that you'll find yourself reading everything and anything—and learning nothing. Programs like Agent can be set to automatically weed out irrelevant topics, primarily using "kill" files, so that you can read only the information gold in the Usenet ore. Kill files are exactly what they sound like—they toss out anything you don't want to read so it never comes back. Alas, as far as I can tell, there's nothing on this level for Macintosh users. Mac news fans will be best off sticking with Netscape Navigator's built-in news browser.

Now, if only there were more in Usenet news that was worth getting! Oh well, enough of that. Let's take a look at some of the Internet applications that will be at your beck and call on your intranet.

# 10

# Introducing Internet Tools

## Internet Toolkit

The Web is what gets people excited about the net; but there are many other useful Internet tools for intranet users. Some of these, like ftp, are almost as old as the Internet, while others, like Internet telephony, are as new as yesterday. These programs include:

- archie

- audio

- chat/talk

- ftp

- gopher

- IRC

- telephony

- telnet

- time

- veronica

- WAIS

You can use most of these services without having a server program for them; but a time server and telnet services are essentials for your intranet. The former lets you synchronize all your computers' clocks, while the latter gives everyone a limited way of logging onto your network from a remote location.

Some of these programs, like ftp and gopher, can do useful work on your intranet servers. Others should never be run on your network's servers because they hog system resources and provide scant returns. Of the latter, veronica is the preeminent example. If you want to use archie and veronica, you're much better off pointing everyone's clients towards servers on the outside rather than placing these services on your own LAN.

With most of these utilities, there are two ways to use them. One is to use them in character mode via telnet. The other is to run them as client applications on your PCs to your intranet server or a remote server. We'll be looking at both.

# Archie Action

File transfer protocol (ftp), which I'll talk about in a minute, enables you to search through a public directory for files. Of course, if the files you're looking for aren't there, hunting for them won't do you much good. If you think looking for a needle in a haystack is tough, just try finding a file with ftp when you're not sure of the file's name: Now, that's hard. Luckily for you, archie gives you a magnet for pulling publicly accessible files out of the virtual haystack. It's still not easy; but it's no longer quite as impossible.

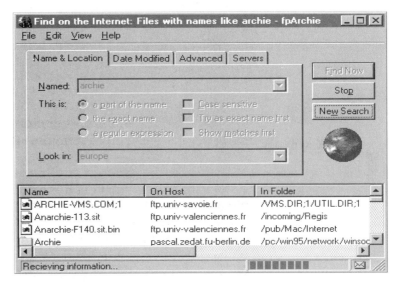

**Figure 10.1**: Today's GUI applications make archie much more usable than it's been in the past.

Archie is a client-server database program that does the hard work of finding and indexing files throughout the Internet. Instead of tracking down elusive files by blindly blundering from ftp site to ftp site, you can contact an archie site and use archie to find your elusive quarry.

There's only a handful of archie sites for the entire world. [See Table 10.1] While you can use any archie server, it's fair play to use the one allotted to your geographical area. Not only should this take up less online time, but by spreading out the load across a number of servers, the service is less likely to be overburdened by user demands.

**Table 10.1: Prominent Archie Server Sites**

| URL | Area Served |
| --- | --- |
| `archie.ans.net` | Eastern US |
| `archie.internic.net` | North America |
| `archie.rutgers.edu` | Eastern US |
| `archie.sura.net` | Eastern US |
| `archie.unl.edu` | Western US |
| `archie.bunyip.com` | Canada |
| `archie.cs.mcgill.ca` | Canada |
| `archie.doc.ic.ac.uk` | Great Britain/Ireland |

Why so few servers? The answer is very simple: Keeping an archie server's database up to date requires a lot of time, more bandwidth, and even more storage space. That's why archie is not a program you want to run as a server application on your intranet. Archie's handy, but not so much so that you'll want to sacrifice an entire server—not to mention a T1's worth of bandwidth—to its requirements.

Besides, while archie is still useful today, with every day that goes by, more of its thunder is stolen by Web-based search engines like AltaVista, Open Text, and Lycos, **http://www.lycos.com**. With that in mind, it's clear that new archie servers simply aren't worth the time and investment.

To make the most of archie, you have three choices. The old-fashioned way is to telnet to the closest Internet site with an archie client. This process works just fine; but only people who feel at home with a command line will really like it. Unadorned archie is a very persnickety program.

Instead, you're going to want to provide most of your users with a local, graphical archie client. While archie servers eat up resources like there's no tomorrow (which, come to think of it, there isn't for archie servers), archie clients are cheap and don't stress either your people's PCs or your in-house servers. The best of these programs are listed in table 10.2 below.

**Table 10.2: Archie Achievers**

| Title | OS | URL |
|-------|-----|-----|
| Anarchie | MacOS | **http://www.share.com/peter lewis/anarchie/anarchie. html** |
| fpArchie | Win95 | **http://www.euronet.nl/ users/petert/public_html/ fpware/** |

| | | |
|---|---|---|
| WS Archie | Windows | `http://dspace.dial.pipex.com/town/square/cc83/wsarchie.htm` |

and if you really, really must have an archie server, check out:

| | |
|---|---|
| Archie Home Page (various) | `http://services.bunyip.com:8000/products/archie/archie.html` |

The final way is to use a forms-enabled Web browser to visit an archie gateway. This method has the dual advantages of not requiring any additional software on your end or any additional training, which would be a must if you went the character-based route. You'll find a comprehensive list of Form-Based Archie Services at `http://pub-web.nexor.co.uk/public/archie/servers.html`. Just pick the archie site that's closest to home, click on it, and make yourself at home.

# Audio

Few people realize it; but Mosaic, the first graphical Web browser, actually paid more attention to the audio possibilities of the net than the graphic. It didn't come to much then because audio files were so huge, and inline images were much more immediately appealing. Several years later, though, audio is coming into its own on the Internet; and it can play a role on your intranet as well.

Many people would rather listen to something than read it. That's where realtime audio finds its niche on the intranet. With the right applications, you can broadcast company announcements and the like over your intranet rather than a dusty old intercom system.

There are several competing technologies for your audio dollars. In my opinion, only two of these have a real future. These products are Progressive Networks' RealAudio, `http://www.realaudio.com/`, and Xing Technologies' StreamWorks, `http://www.xingtech.com/`.

Behind these and the other clients and servers exploring this new range in the Internet is a single technology: streaming audio. Streaming technologies start playing audio files after a short buffering period and continue to play until the message is done. This technology is much more responsive than the older download-and-play techniques, both for listeners and broadcasters. With some implementations, it's even possible to make realtime broadcasts over your intranet.

You have to admit, realtime audio is one heck of a way of letting everyone know that the snowstorm is coming and everyone can go home now. As time goes on, all but the most low-end programs will include realtime options.

If nothing else, your webweavers will want to see about adding audio to your external Web site. Audio gives Web sites an immediacy that captures the attention of even the most jaded Web users. Any company that plans on staking out a claim on the Internet must seriously consider adding some audio to its Web site. On the other hand, audio's no miracle cure for dull Web sites. Plenty of sites try to overwhelm users with sound and wind up chasing them away instead.

Your weavers and marketers should also realize that making effective use of audio requires enormous bandwidth. A site that could get along with just a T1 for an ordinary graphics and text-based Web site should consider upgrading to a T3 if it needs to support audio as well. That's not a cheap jump. The reason is that even though streaming audio pushes data compression to its maximum, you still need oodles of bandwidth to handle multiple requests for audio data. External users will already have trouble getting high-quality audio with 28.8Kbps modems. If they get only 14.4Kbps worth of signal from your site, they're not going to be happy. All audio companies will tell you that they can work with speeds as low as that. True, they can; but what they don't tell you is that the signal sounds like something from a south of the border 500,000 watt AM station…from a thousand miles away. You want to do better. Trust me.

# Chat/Talk

Internet Talk is not an audio application. Internet telephony is a topic I'll take up later. Talk, also known as chat, is a program that enables you to write back and forth with a correspondent in real time over the net.

Doesn't sound so hot, does it? Many folks, and I'm one of them, find it very useful. Ever been in a situation when someone wants to tell you that you're making an ass of yourself on a teleconference, but it's a call that you don't dare leave? I have; and short of using American Sign Language, you're not going to get your message to me--at least not without letting everyone else know that I've just overestimated the company's revenue by a factor of ten. Unless, that is, you're using talk, in which case my coworker can send me a note that will flash on my screen. Then I can try to dance my way out of my earlier mistake. Talk also works well for short conversations which would be too disruptive if they were over the phone and are too time-critical for e-mail.

Talk programs are so small that, in many situations, you don't even need a server for them. The mini-clients can work as both client and server sitting on your people's PCs if they're running the TALK protocol. The ones I recommend are Talk for the Macintosh OS, **http://www.share .com/peterlewis/talk/talk.html**, and WinTalk, **http://www.elf.com/elf/wintalk/wintalk.html** for Windows.

# Flexing FTP

Ftp, as I've mentioned, stands for file transfer protocol. The name says it all. Ftp enables you to download files from remote systems to local systems over your intranet.

Many systems around the world keep file archives, usually in directories named 'pub', for ftp access. Ftp is the tool you need to get copies of these files. Any file that can legally be freely distributed is available for anonymous ftp, a process where you login to the foreign server as "anonymous" and use your e-mail address in lieu of a password. Unlike telnet, which is most useful when you have full-fledged accounts on remote systems, ftp comes in handy even if you have only a single account.

As with archie, you can either user a character-based interface to ftp (via a telnet session) or use a client program. There are several ftp clients available; but almost all Web browsers can deal with ftp servers as well as any dedicated ftp program can.

Unlike archie, however, ftp servers require very little from your intranet server. For that matter, you may already have ftp capabilities without even knowing it. Many Web servers include ftp server abilities as a matter of course. If so, consider using them. With ftp, you can distribute files and documents across your organization even to people using running-on-their-last-byte Amiga 500s and XTs. Ftp is fast, it's cheap, and almost any system with a CPU can handle it.

If you do want a dedicated ftp server, here are the best I've found to date.

**Table 10.2: Dedicated ftp Servers**

| Title | OS | URL |
|-------|----|----|
| NetPresenz | Mac OS | `ftp://mirrors.aol.com/pub/info-mac/_Communication/tcp/web/net-presenz-401.hqx` |
| Penguin FTP Daemon | OS/2 | `ftp://hobbes.nmsu.edu/os2/network/tcpip/pfpd108.zip` |
| WU-FTPD | Unix | `http://wuarchive.wustl.edu/packages/wuarchive-ftpd/` |

# Flashless Character-Based FTP

Character-based ftp is what makes it possible to make ftp the lowest common denominator file exchange mechanism for your company. God knows it's not the easiest way, although the opening command is deceptively simple:

```
ftp remote_host_name
```

After you enter that, you'll be prompted for a login and password. Most systems will let you use the anonymous or e-mail approach to enter the ftp server's directories. If you as the network administrator don't want people having such free access, you can set up your operating system's normal blocks against unauthorized entry. Beyond that, you'll find a barren approach without even a character-based menu to be seen.

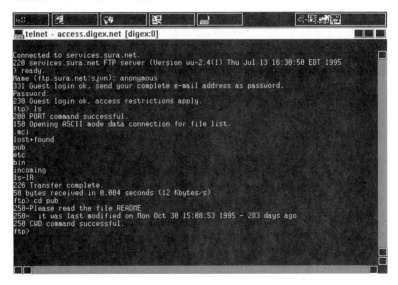

**Figure 10.2**: Ugly, isn't it?

Once you reach ftp, you'll find that you're in the "pub" directory or its local equivalent. From here, you can use the "ls" command to list available files. Some systems will use the "dir" command for the same purpose. As an administrator, you can change this if you want to, but I wouldn't recommend it. These defaults have worked well for decades and there's no good reason to change them.

Unix ftp servers often have a file named "ls -lR" for file directory information. If it does, the best way to handle it is to ftp the file home to examine it at your leisure using Notepad or another simple word processor.

The ftp command you'll get to know best is "get." From the user's perspective, get works a lot like Unix's cp or MS-DOS' copy command. Instead of copying a file locally, "get" copies a file from the remote system to your local system.

In many ways, ftp's "get" is a lot like the asynchronous file-transfer protocols of dial-up connections like X-modem, Z-modem, and Kermit. The critical difference is that ftp only works across network connections. While it's possible to use ftp over an ordinary modem connection using SLIP or PPP, these are examples of networking across phone lines rather than the asynchronous connections offered by proprietary services like CompuServe or your local Bulletin Board System (BBS).

To copy a file using ftp, you'd enter a command like:

```
ftp> get cool.game.file
```

Whoops—we are on the company intranet, aren't we! Let's make that:

```
ftp> get serious.marketing.file
```

For binary files, like programs or compressed files, you must enter the binary command at the ftp prompt. For example,

```
ftp> binary

ftp> get cool.marketing.game.zip
```

will successfully bring home this compressed file. No binary command, though, no file. Or, to be more precise, no file worth reading. Ftp's default is to send ASCII files, not binary. More time has been wasted and tears shed over that simple mistake than any other in the ftp command collection. Some older ftp servers also refer to binary mode as image mode. In these cases, you can use image instead of binary.

# Local FTP Clients

As you might have guessed from this short visit to the LAN of ftping, your users, unless they're stuck on bottom-feeder machines, are going to want an ftp-capable browser or ftp client software. Raw ftp just isn't very tasty for even character-line fans. These days, a Web browser is really all you need. There are good standalone ftp clients; but what's the point? If you support a separate ftp client, it will just be one more program for in-house technical support to keep running; and we all know how exactly eager they are to learn and support yet another new program, don't we? Still, if you must have an ftp client, here are the features to look for and some of the best titles on the market today.

**Table 10.3: Important FTP Client Features**

Features

Automatic Name Translation With User Control

Drag-and-Drop File Copying

File Sorting By Name, Extension, and Type

Ftp Site Address Book

Multiple File Retrieval

**Table 10.4: The Best of a Dying Breed: FTP Clients**

| Title | OS | URL |
|-------|-----|-----|
| Anarchie | Macintosh | `ftp://mirrors.aol.com/pub/,`<br>`info-mac/comm/tcp/anarchie-`<br>`16.hqx` |
| CuteFTP | Windows | `http://www.cuteftp.com/` |
| Fetch | Macintosh | `ftp://ftp.dartmouth.edu/pub/`<br>`mac/Fetch_3.0.1.hqx` |
| FTP-IT | OS/2 | `ftp://hobbes.nmsu.edu/os2/`<br>`network/tcpip/ftpit211.zip`WS- |
| FTP | Windows | `http://www.ipswitch.com/`<br>`pd_wsftp.html` |

Finally, no matter how you're pulling files from an ftp server, if you're saddled with an older operating system, beware of long file names. You're most likely to run into this brick wall on operating systems that still use MS-DOS' old file allocation table (FAT) directory system. If your disk is FAT, then you can use file names with eight-character names and three-character extensions. When try to you get a hold of a file with a name like "amazinghowlongsome-filenamesareisntit," the operating system can't deal with its long title and truncates it into something it can manage. If you're dealing with multiple files whose names are both long and similar, you may inadvertently overwrite the last file in as the next one roars down the pike because it's been assigned the same short-name.

# File Types

One headache that no file hunter can avoid is dealing with a bewildering array of data compression and archive types. Here are the basics of what file types you can expect to find and what to do in order to open them up.

Way, way back when 300 BPS modems were the fastest things on telephone lines, people had trouble moving files because it took so darn long. Another woe was that then, as now, many programs required multiple files, and there was no way to neatly package them into one file. The answer to the first question was data compression. To settle the matter of bundling files together, people came up with the idea of file archives or libraries. We have much faster Internet connections now, but the problems remain.

The fact that these are two separate problems with two answers is an important point which is often missed in the

PC/Macintosh world. This is because most of the data compression programs on these platforms do both jobs. On the Internet, that's not always true. Some file collections are compressed by one program and then tied into one file by another program.

Finally, there is another file type that's used primarily to make it possible to ship binary files through e-mail. The most important of these for ftp users is ".hqx." This is a Macintosh file type known as binhex.

If it's humanly possible, you'll want to standardize on one compression format for your intranet. My suggestion is to make it "zip." PKWare's zip format, `http://www.pkware.com/`, has been ported to every operating system known; and it's also highly effective in wringing the last bit of space out of even the most tightly packed files. If you don't, you can count on at least one technical support employee spending part of her day explaining how to decompress arc, zoo, or the like to a coworker without a clue. I can think of better uses for both employees' time, can't you?

There are two types of data compression. Lossless, so called because no data is lost, is used for text and binary files. Graphics files are often compressed with "lossy" programs that help shrink the file down by actually dumping some of the data. Both methods work; just make sure that if you ever compress a file, you use the appropriate type of program. A lossy program would make hash of a binary file, since even one bit lost is enough to ruin the program. A lossless compression program will only shrink graphics down by 5% or so, which is close enough to nothing in data compression to make no substantial difference.

To deal with binary and ASCII compressed files, you need the appropriate software. In table 10.8, you can see the most popular compression file extensions and their corresponding programs. Compressed graphics are covered later.

## Table 10.5: Data Compression/File Archive Types

| Extension | Program | OS |
|---|---|---|
| .arc | arc, pkarc | DOS/Windows |
| | arc | Unix |
| | arcmac | Mac |
| .arj | arj | DOS/Windows |
| | unarj | Unix |
| | unarj | Mac |
| .gz or gzip | gzip-msdos | DOS/Windows |
| | macgzip | Mac |
| | gzip | Unix |
| .hqx | xbin23 | DOS/Windows |
| | binhex | Mac |
| | mcvert | Unix |
| .shar* | (None) | DOS/Windows |

| | | |
|---|---|---|
| | (None) | Mac |
| | (Not needed) | Unix |
| .sit | unsit | MS-DOS |
| | Stuffit | Mac |
| | unsit | Unix |
| .tar | tarread | MS-DOS |
| | tar-30.hqx | Mac |
| | (Not needed) | Unix# |
| .tar.Z, .tar-z, or taz | | |
| | (Not needed) | MS-DOS% |
| | (Not needed) | Mac% |
| | (Not needed) | Unix% |
| .zip | PKzip | DOS/Windows |
| | Unzip | Mac |
| | zip | Unix |
| .Z | comp | DOS/Windows |
| | macompress | Mac |
| | compress | Unix |

*.shar files are opened in Unix with the command line: "sh foo.shar."

#tar files are opened in Unix with the command line: "tar xvf foo.tar."

%.tar.Z files are files that have been compressed with the Unix compress program and bundled together with the tar archiving program. Tar.Z files are opened in Unix with either the command line "zcat file.tar.Z | tar xvf" or, if you have GNU tar, with the command line: "tar xvzf file.tar.Z." Mac and MS-DOS/Windows users must first uncompress the program (see the .Z entity0 and then unarchive it using the tar programs.

&tar.gz files, like tar.Z ones, require the use of two programs to be extracted. For straight Unix, run the command "gzip -cd file.tar.gz | tar xvf". If you're using GNU tar, use "tar xvzf file.tar.gz" instead. For other operating systems, first pop the file open with the utility you use for ".gz" files and then untar it.

MS-DOS exe compressed files, Macintosh sea files, and Unix shar archived files are both popular and dangerous. Their advantage is that you can extract these files just by running the program. The danger is that you're running an unknown program with no idea of what you're letting onto your system. Take extra care when dealing with these files. Unfortunately, self-extracting files, for data extraction programs themselves, are a necessary evil.

Mind-boggling, isn't it? If you're an MS-Windows user, however, there's a delightful little program you must know about: WinZip. This program from Niko Mak Computing, **http://www.winzip.com**, can cope with almost all the various compression formats. It actually makes working with compressed files easy. If there's a must-buy compression program, this is it. Now, if only there were versions of it for other operating systems!

Compression programs are in a constant state of flux. To get the latest, most accurate information, get a copy of the **comp.compression** newsgroup's FAQ file.

When you have a file and its appropriate utility, make sure you have the newest available version of the archiving program. PKzip versions older than 2.04G, for instance, can't deal with compressed files made by 2.04G.

The important compressed graphic file formats are listed in table 10.6.

**Table 10.6: Graphics Compression File Types**

| File Extension | Full Name |
| --- | --- |
| GIF | Graphics Image Format |
| JPEG | Joint Photographic Experts Group |
| MPEG | Moving Pictures Experts Group |
| PCX | (None) |
| TIFF | Tagged Image File Format |

Graphic users don't have to run through several steps the way compressed file users do. Graphic file viewers always include the appropriate decompression tools and make them transparent to the user.

# Gopher It

Getting the most out of the Internet isn't easy. Archie only helps with one specific area of net use—finding and ftping files. With more of the right programs, like gopher, finding information on the net doesn't have to be like stumbling around in the dark blindfolded.

Unlike ftp and archie, gopher is a general purpose information tool. Gopher builds on the foundation of ftp, archie, and other data sources to provide an easy-to-use, menu-driven interface to the net's file and informational resources. Unfortunately, gopher predates the Web and has only a text-based interface. Compared to the Web search engines, gopher is downright dowdy.

In truth, gopher is on its way out. Web catalogs like Yahoo, covered in detail in the next chapter, have made gopher obsolete. Mind you, gopher still does useful work; it's just that Web catalog programs do it easier and in a more attractive fashion.

Gopher was born at the University of Minnesota, home of the Golden Gophers. (No, really, it's true!) A gopher's job is to "go-fer" information. Like the Web search engines, gopher doesn't depend on any particular data collection. Gopher doesn't know where a particular item is, but it does know how to search down information. In computing terms, gopher is a distributed client-server database system. Gopher's failing, compared to AltaVista, Lycos, and the like, is that its links must be explicitly and manually set up rather than being created on the fly. This puts gopher servers in the position of always being out of date, as opposed to an up-to-the-minute Web search engine.

Formerly, to get the most out of gopher, you had to have a gopher client on your system. These days, Web browser programs do a top-notch job of using gopher databases, so you don't need a dedicated gopher client. If nothing else is on hand, you can also telnet your way to a site with a publicly accessible gopher client and use its character-based menu system.

No matter how you get there, the end result always looks the same. When you reach a gopher server, you're presented with a set of menus. From there, you select the best path to your informational destination.

Gopher clients often come with a hardwired gopher server they first look to for information. This can, and often should, be changed to access your closest available gopher server. Some of the most important general purpose gopher sites are listed in table 10.7; but there are more than five thousand public gopher servers out there.

**Table 10.7: Worldwide Gopher Server Sites**

| Name | Area Served |
| --- | --- |
| consultant.micro.umn.edu | North America |
| ux1.cso.uiuc.edu | North America |
| panda.uiowa.edu | North America |
| gopher.msu.edu | North America |
| gopher.ebone.net | Europe |
| gopher.sunet.se | Scandinavia |
| info.anu.edu.au | Australia |
| tolten.puc.cl | South America |
| ecnet.ec | South America |

gan.ncc.go.jp                    Japan

When you and your client go to the server with your request, the server works on figuring out where to find the information. All you know, sitting at your desk, is that a few seconds after you start your inquiry, gopher has given you menu choices that take you closer to your destination.

These choices come in two forms: resources and directories. A directory, marked with a '/' at the end of its menu item, indicates that choosing this item will lead you to a sub-menu. Resources are actual sources of information. Browsers tend to mark these files in different ways, usually with different colors or icons. It should be quite clear which is which.

From the menus, you proceed to narrow down your choices until you can reach an appropriate resource. Eventually, you arrive at what you and gopher agree is probably the resource you were looking for. At that point, you can fetch the information or file.

When you access a resource, gopher takes over the job of logging on to the computer and service. Gopher also shields you from the local system. No matter what you're logged into, you use your gopher client's search interface, not the remote systems. Again, though, Web browsers and servers handle this job, the gopher file identification system, while roughly-hewn, is still used in gopher sites, MIMEd e-mail, and some Web sites.

## Table 10.8: Gopher Object Types

| Object ID | Object Definition |
| --- | --- |
| 0 | Text file |
| 1 | Directory |
| 2 | Phone-book server |
| 3 | Error |
| 4 | Binhexed Macintosh file |
| 5 | DOS binary archive (ARC, ARJ, ZIP, etc.) |
| 6 | Uuencoded file |
| 7 | Index (often a gopher or WAIS menu) |
| 8 | Telnet session |
| 9 | Binary file |
| g | GIF |
| h | HTML |
| I | Image type |
| i | Inline text |
| M | MIME |

| | |
|---|---|
| S | Sound |
| T | TN3270 session |
| + | Redundant or previous gopher server |

Gopher+, the next generation of gopher server software, was supposed to clarify these matters by having expanded object-type definitions. Gopher+ has added some advantages to gopher, such as a login system; but the program's file defining standards are being overwhelmed by Web's standards.

With all its flaws, you'll never mistake gopher for such powerful, single-purpose online information retrieval engines like the Web's AltaVista or Yahoo. Even so, gopher does have its good points. Gopher may have outlived much of its usefulness; but as a lowest common denominator tool for doing Internet searches, you can't beat it. While you may never need a dedicated gopher client for your office, you may still want a gopher server for your intranet. The reason is that gopher, faults and all, can make information available to even computers that are little more than dumb-terminals. Since many Web servers already include gopher support, it's not like you're going to be shelling out any more up-front cash.

If you need a couple of "go-for-it" gopher clients, two of my favorites are WS Gopher, `http://sageftp.inel.gov/dap/gopher.htm`, for Windows, and Hgopher, `ftp://ftp.ccs.queensu.ca/pub/msdos/tcpip/winsock/hgoph24.zip`, for Windows 3.x.

# Interactive IRC

Internet Relay Chat (IRC) is the cocktail-party program of the Internet. With IRC, anyone and everyone can write to each other in simultaneous conversations over multiple channels. Some people love this. Me, I find it annoying as all get-out.

Raw IRC isn't a useful intranet tool. There are simply too many online bores, and not enough focus to make even the best IRC channels worth your company's time. Where IRC does get interesting, however, is as an internal mechanism for brainstorming sessions. Other programs, like Netscape's Collabra, make this process much easier; but if you're on a tight budget, a set of freeware or shareware IRC servers and clients might be just what you need.

Give IRC a try. It's cheap, and it requires little in the way of network resources. If it works for your company, you're ahead. If it doesn't, it's not like you've lost much except some time. For full details on what IRC can and can't do, plus a comprehensive list of IRC clients and servers, visit Benso.Com/IrcHelp.Org's IRC site, `http://benso.com/`.

# Telephony

Here's the good news: Right now, a group of companies, which I'll refer to as Voice on the Net (VON) after these businesses' consortium, enable you to make free telephone calls over the Internet. VON includes not only the net telephony companies, but also software giants like Microsoft and Netscape as well as the unholy trio of AT&T, MCI, and Sprint.

Against VON stands a group of smaller telephone companies, the America's Carriers Telecommunication Association (ACTA). Right now, the two groups are wrangling in the courts over the VON's companies' right to offer free long distance over the Internet.

By this point, you're probably wondering: "Why this excursion into industry politics?" Remember much earlier in the book when I said it's not the technology, it's the other elements that determine who wins and loses in the computer and communication business? Welcome to another of those elements.

Net telephony is currently a hodgepodge of differing technologies, and there's not a glimpse of a telephony standard on the horizon. Oh, don't get me wrong; the programs work, but only if you use them with another copy of the same company's product. You can't, for example, call someone who uses Netspeak's Webphone if you're using Netscape's CoolTalk. In your own intranet, you can take care of this problem by establishing one standard and sticking it with it. Unfortunately, you probably don't have any control over what your business partners are using.

Another problem that most people refuse to hear is that net telephony does not produce a very high-quality sound. Unlike the streaming audio techniques of RealAudio and the like, with net telephony, you can't have communications that are constantly being slightly time-delayed. The result is a lot more like CB communications than it is telephone—and that's when things are going well. When the Internet is bogged down, a condition that will occur with only more and more frequency as time goes by, managing a decent connection only gets harder.

Technology aside, the pressing reason not to dream of a day when your telephone bills drop from five figures to three is that the Federal Communications Commission (FCC), or possibly another agency, will start restricting Internet telephony. As sure as a dropped hammer will hit the floor, the government will regulate Internet telephony; and about two seconds before that happens, everyone is going to start charging extra for net telephone service. It may have happened by the time you read this. It will almost certainly have happened by 1998.

Assuming I'm correct in all this, there are still reasons to have Internet telephony within your intranet. For one thing, while you won't be able to use net telephony to talk to the outside world without paying fees, you probably will be able to use it freely over your own internal network. That's no big deal if your business takes up one building; but if you're already using a wide area network (WAN) to hold transcontinental business together, we're talking big bucks worth of savings here.

Another noteworthy factor in your intranet telephony decision is that Netscape and Microsoft have already embraced net telephony. As I write this, Netscape has telephony capabilities, and Internet Explorer is charging up from behind with its own net phone. Since your browsers are almost certainly already going to enable you to make phone calls, why not make use of that ability?

In the meantime, here are some of the most important net telephony companies and their products. Go ahead and play with these programs today. By the time the federal regulators catch up with Internet telephony, you'll know whether they're worth keeping on your company's intranet.

**Table 10.10: Major Net Telephony Players**

| Product | Company | URL |
|---|---|---|
| FreeTel | FreeTel | `http://www.freetel.inter.net/` |
| WebPhone | NetSpeak | `http://www.itelco.com/` |
| Iphone | VocalTec | `http://www.vocaltec.com/` |
| Digiphone | Third Planet Publishing, | `http://www.planeteers.com/` |
| CoolTalk | Netscape | `http://home.netscape.com/` |
| WebTalk | Quarterdeck | `http://www.qdeck.com` |

# Telecommuting Telnet

Telnet provides direct communications with other computer systems via a TCP/IP network. In essence, telnet enables you to login on other computers on the network. It doesn't take a rocket scientist to see telnet's possibilities. If you're running a complex query on a slow Sybase database, but must work on something else as well, you can simply telnet to an idle system and start anew.

This is spiffy enough when you're working with your own in-house systems, but telnet knows no distance barriers. If you're logged into a system in San Francisco, you can telnet into one in Boston as easily as you can to an Internet system in the next cubicle.

Another way to use telnet is to run a remote program. For example, if you're working with a character-based interface and you want to visit the Web, but you don't have a local Web browser, you can telnet to a system with a character-based browser and use it. Normally, this is done by logging in as www and, if requested, using your mail ID as your password.

Working with telnet is almost mindlessly easy. To connect to another system, you just type in:

```
telnet remote_host_name port
```

and you're on your way. On most systems, the port is optional because the telnet daemon (a daemon is a program that runs automatically on the server) uses a default port, usually port 23. In figure 4.1, however, we see that telnet works like a charm without specifying a port.

For the name of the system you're trying to contact, you can usually use the system's host name—for example, access.digex.net; princeton.edu; or well.sf.ca.us. If that doesn't work, you may be successful by specifing the host's IP address. For instance, 192.132.20.3 is well.sf.ca.us' IP address, a site known in people-talk as The Well online system.

Some systems also restrict their users' ability to use telnet. If you're having trouble, check with your system administrator before you assume something is wrong. You simply may not have permission to use telnet or ftp.

Once you've logged into another system, you proceed just as if you were logged into the computer next door.

Everything you type in feeds directly into the remote system. If you need to issue a command to the telnet program, you precede the command with the escape character. This is usually set to '^]' (that is, control key and right-bracket key). For instance, to quit telnet and return to your local system, you would type:

```
^] quit
```

There are other possibilities, like using telnet interactively but these vary with the Unix shell you're using and the telnet implementation. With local telnet clients, though these methods have waned in importance

# Using Local Telnet Clients

Many companies make Windows and Macintosh telnet clients. In addition, one Web browser, Cello, already has a telnet program. If you don't already have a telnet program and you have an IP connection with the Internet, the table below gives you the features you should look for.

**Table 10.11: Important Telnet Features**

3270 Terminal Support

Adjustable Scroll Buffer

Capture Data to File

Capture Data to Printer

Enable Cut/Paste Operations

Telnet Address Book

Multiple Telnet Sessions

Multiple Terminal Type Support

I'm still looking for the perfect telnet programs. Among the better ones are those I've listed in the next table.

**Table 10.12 Terrific Telnetting**                    **Clients**

| Title | OS | URL |
|-------|-----|-----|
| NCSA Telnet | MacOS | `ftp://ftp.ncsa.uiuc.edu/Mac/Telnet/Telnet2.7/2.7b4/Telnet-2.7b4-fat.sit.hqx` |
| CKermit | OS/2 | `http://www.columbia.edu/kermit/os2.html` |
| NetTerm | Windows | `http://starbase.neosoft.com/~zkrr01/netterm.html` |
| CRT | Windows | `http://www.vandyke.com/vandyke/crt/` |

**Servers**

| | | |
|-------|-----|-----|
| SLnet | Win NT | `http://www.seattlelab.com/prodslnet.html` |

# Telling Time

Making sure that your intranet computers agree what time it is may not sound like much; but when it comes to tracking down which really was the last record entered into a database before the DBMS went screwy, or keeping track of whose document is the most recent version, you can't beat time servers and clients.

Both halves of these programs are tiny. The sole job of a timer daemon is to look up the time, using Network Time Protocol (NTP), at one of the public time servers that's tied to one of the atomic clocks that keeps accurate time for your country. A timer client simply checks in on your server's time server to update its own internal clock. While you could arrange for users to do this manually, you'd be better off putting the procedure straight into their power-up programs so that their PCs are always on company time.

For that matter, you don't need a time server on your intranet. You can enable the client programs to go directly to one of the public time servers. The problems with this approach is that it increases, albeit minutely, Internet traffic; and by not using your own server, you're increasing the chance that small but significant differences can creep into each computer's clock. You see, desktop computers aren't very good at keeping time. My philosophy is, why give them another chance to screw up? To pick your own NTP client and server, click on over to Time Servers **http://www.eecis.udel.edu/~ntp/** for everything you always wanted to know about time but were afraid to ask.

# Vamping Veronica

Veronica is one of the most useful Internet information hunting tools around. Unfortunately, it's also the one that has the fewest servers; so making a date with veronica can be a real hassle. Veronica is also much too much of a resource hog for anyone to consider using it on an intranet server.

Veronica stands for—get ready—"Very Easy Rodent-Oriented Net-wide Index to Computerized Archives." (Why, yes, Internet programmers do have a twisted sense of humor; how did you ever guess?)

You access veronica by using anything that can serve as a gopher client, such as a Web browser. From the client's point of view, veronica just looks like one heck of an over-grown gopher. Unlike gopher, however, instead of wading through menus, veronica lets you search for information with keywords. The advantage of this approach is that you cut out the gopher middleman and go straight to the gopher resource you want—if veronica can find it.

Most veronica servers offer two basic types of searches. The first is a keyword by title search. In this variant, you're searching all gopher resources for your target. The problem with this is that it takes a long time, and you can be swamped with misleading results.

If you're searching for common terms, like "Usenet" and "Web," you'd be better off using the second type of search: directory titles. Here, you'll only be searching the titles of directories. Your search will go faster and your results will be more manageable. Of course, narrowing down your hunt will take some effort on your part, as you'll need to open up the newfound directories to see exactly what you've laid your virtual hands on.

Since most gopher sites are indexed by veronica, the problem isn't that the information is not out there. No, the problem is that there are so few veronica servers and so many veronica users that the servers are almost always overloaded. If you can get into a veronica server on your first go, pat yourself on the back; you've just accomplished a minor miracle. As always, you should try to use your closest site, but don't be surprised if you have to go farther afield.

**Table 10.13: Veronica Server Sites Worldwide**

| Name | Area Served |
| --- | --- |
| gopher.umanitoba.ca:2347/7 | North America |
| gopher.unipi.it:2347/7 | Europe |
| info.psi.net:2347/7 | North America |
| serra.unipi.it:2347/7 | Europe |
| veronica.nysernet.org:2347/7 | North America |
| veronica.uni-koeln.de:2347/7 | Europe |
| veronica.scs.unr.edu:2347/7 | North America* |
| veronica.sunet.se:2347/7 | Scandinavia |
| wisteria.cnidr.org:2347/7 | North America |

*The easiest way to get to veronica servers is via <gopher://veronica.scs.unr.edu:70/11/veronica>. This takes you to a gopher menu of veronica sites.

After your search is done, you'll see a gopher menu style display of the gopher objects, files, directories, and so on that veronica has found for you. You can then simply select any of them to be transported there.

Veronica is capable of far more than simple, one-term searches. The latest version of the program supports Boolean searches. For example, you can search using a phrase like "Web AND Mosaic," which would only dig up references that contained both words. Actually, veronica is smart enough that you don't even need to use "AND." Merely placing two terms in the search box will cause veronica to search for a document with both words in it.

Veronica also tends to supports the NOT and OR operators. Note that these Boolean terms are only capitalized for emphasis. Veronica doesn't care about the case of your search or Boolean terms. Unfortunately, not all veronica servers will run these operators. The only way to find out if the server you're using supports them is to give it a try and see what happens.

You can also use some veronicas to make complex queries with the use of parentheses. For instance, the search:

**web server not (Netscape or Internet Explorer)**

would find only documents that were about non-Netscape and Microsoft Web servers.

If you want to know more about how to use veronica, look for its FAQ and the "How to Compose Veronica Queries" document at **gopher://veronica.scs.unr.edu**.

# The Way of WAIS

WAIS (pronounced wayz) works something like gopher in that it's a tool for finding information and resources on the Internet. With gopher, though, you need to point it in a certain direction using its menu-driven structure. In short, gopher's fine if you already have an idea where something is before you go looking for it; and veronica's often too busy to help. Furthermore, both gopher and veronica operate at a high level of information granularity. That's a fancy way of saying that both work at the title level. Neither can help you find a particular word or idea within a document or object.

WAIS, on the other hand, is a freetext DBMS. It works with the words inside documents, the same way that AltaVista can find words in Web documents. Of course, WAIS can't do everything. It's not capable of searching willy-nilly through public directories throughout the Internet universe. (A good thing it can't, or it would eat up network bandwidth like peanuts.)

For an intranet administrator, the problem with WAIS is that it represents a dead-end database technology. When WAIS first came out, it was hailed in some circles as the database engine for the '90s. In fact, WAIS was soon run over by the increasingly more powerful relational database managers I'll cover in later chapters. Today, WAIS remains an interesting and useful technology; but putting up a new WAIS site? Get real. Most of the programs I'll be talking about later do a better job, and they're a lot easier to install and manage than WAIS is.

WAIS relies on indexed data collections—or, as they're called, libraries. Most libraries are free. That's very sweet and idealistic, but it also means that WAIS database coverage can be pretty spotty. For example, you won't be greatly surprised to know that computer science subjects are well covered. If you want to know something about antique cars, however, you're likely to be out of luck.

Data hunters often find WAIS frustrating. That's because it doesn't use any of the Boolean search terms. While I can search for references to "Netscape and Xing," I won't get just documents that contain both terms. Instead, WAIS uses an internal weighing system that measures the value of each term for the search—including the "and!" The result is a table at the top of which are the most relevant articles measured by WAIS' 1 to 1000 score, where a higher number is better. An article that contains many "ands" and "Xings" may be tagged by WAIS as being more important than a short document containing "Netscape" in the title but with all further references to Netscape in the document being to "Navigator."

Why use WAIS, then? Because WAIS does just fine at simple, one-term searches; and more importantly, it has the unique ability to perform relevance feedback searches. Say you find an article on Xing's StreamWorks that exactly hits the spot. You can then pull terms from that document and use them to start a new search. WAIS gives you the ability, once you're on the right trail, to refine your search and track down even the most wary information to its lair.

The problem with WAIS, from many Web browser users' viewpoint, is that few browsers can use WAIS URLs directly. While they can access WAIS databases from some gopher sites, these programs are utterly unable to work directly with WAIS. The reason for this is that no one has built a good WAIS helper application or plug-in for browsers. This lack of development, more than anything else, tells me that while existing WAIS data is valuable, the DBMS itself has reached the end of the road.

# End Session ^D

In their day, all of these applications were valuable. Today, many of these programs are only useful for technically oriented users. Still, most of them can now be used directly from a Web browser, which makes them much more accessible. The Web alone is powerful. Combine the Web with the right mix of older Internet tools, and your company will be in a position to take full advantage of the information resources of the net. For many of these programs, though, night is falling while the sun continues to rise on the Web. What's up in the Web for your intranet? That, I'll be looking into in the next chapter.

# 11

## Making the Right Web Connection

## It's All in the Connections

Once upon a time, you had one good choice for a Web browser: NCSA Mosaic. Boy, was that a long time ago! Actually, it's been less than four years, but that's practically an eternity on the Web. Today, everyone and his uncle has a Web browser they want to sell you. What's a wanna-be Web explorer to do?

Well, forget any pre-packaged answer. I'm not going to tell you to use this or that. While I am going to look at specific browsers, browsers change so quickly that there's little point in making precise recommendations.

What's hot today is forgotten about tomorrow. What I am going to do is tell you what features a corporate intranet Web browser needs.

# What Browser Types Are Out There

There are four basic browser types. For an intranet's purpose, only one of them counts—the one that requires the use of a direct TCP/IP connection to the intranet, and from there to the Internet.

I'll fill you in on the three others, just so you'll know to avoid them. The most common ones are the online-service specific browsers. These include the early browsers of America Online, CompuServe, and Prodigy. A few ISPs—notably Netcom, with its NetCruiser—continue to use such service-specific browsers. None of these browsers were ever meant for general intranet use; and, frankly, none of them have ever been any good anyway.

A far less common type of browser is one that relies on a proprietary technique to imitate TCP/IP access using a Unix shell account, such as SlipKnot. While such browsers give you an inexpensive standard graphical interface, these browsers and the technologies underlying them are on their way out. They have no place in a business network. For individual users on a tight budget, SlipKnot makes sense. For a business, this type of browser is nonsense.

Finally, there are the tried-and-true character-based interfaces, like DOSLynx, Lynx, at `ftp2.cc.ukans.edu`, and www. While by far the most primitive of the lot, these programs still have their uses on a corporate intranet.

Why? Well, for starters, they're faster than any graphical browser around. While some sites with too much glitter and not enough substance make using character-based browsers impossible, most sites still reveal their information to these older interfaces just as well as to the fanciest new version of Netscape. Another reason is that these antique browsers can work on any system. If you're using a Unix server, even dumb-terminals can let your people have access to the intranet. Old doesn't necessarily mean obsolete.

# Browser Shopping List

Before shopping for a Web browser, stop and take a look at what's already on your computer. IBM's OS/2 Warp has a browser, Web Explorer, bundled with it. Microsoft's Windows95 comes with its own browser, Internet Explorer. Computer vendors are also getting into the act by bundling Netscape Navigator and the like with their systems. Why spend money when you don't have to?

There may be several reasons. Number one with a bullet is that the free browser might not do the job that you and your people need done. Like it or not, Netscape Navigator is setting all the browser trends. If you want a browser that can handle the newest HTML format and enabling technologies, Navigator must be your first choice.

Navigator also has the advantage of being available for more operating systems than any other browser. While it doesn't support OS/2, it does support Windows, Mac OS, and more Unix versions than you can shake a mouse at. If your net includes more than one operating system, for the sake of making life bearable for your technical support people, Navigator or other browsers with broad operating system support demand your attention.

How do you find the browser that's right for you? The ideal Web browser should:

* be easy to install

* be easy to customize

* enable you to easily navigate the Web

* enable you to view all common Web document types

* support secure transactions

* support other Internet/Usenet tools

* work quickly

# Easy Installation

Once, installing Web browsers was like wrestling bears for money: You'd probably get paid, but was it really worth the pain? Today, while making the initial intranet connection for a PC can be difficult, most Web browsers are a cinch to install. A quick and dirty way of deciding which one is easiest is seeing how many manual steps are involved in its installation. Usually, the more steps, the less friendly the installation.

For an intranet, you'll also want browsers that can be installed on the entire network from one workstation or from the server. Any browser that enables you to sit down at one place and automatically arrange for installation across the entire network is a big win in my book.

# Customizing Your Browser

Don't think for a New York minute that customizing a Web browser is an unimportant job. That's because customizing a browser isn't just making it look pretty, it's setting the browser so it will work successfully with the Web.

While much of the Web is written in HTML and about half of its graphics are in GIF, many documents and images are in other formats. To handle these foreign formats, your browser must either be able to work directly with these formats, or it must be customized so that you can use helper applications or plug-ins to view these formats.

Ideally, your browsers won't need such special treatment; but with everything from Notes databases to Word for Windows documents appearing on the Web, that's merely a pipe dream. The next best thing is to have a browser that makes it easy to add helper applications and plug-ins to deal with the ever-increasing number of new file formats.

Your best bet is to be able to adjust these settings from a centralized location, and then ship a single custom version of the browser and the appropriate helper applications to each machine. If you can't do that, you're looking at spending more than a hour at each person's PC: Yuck!

In some cases, you'll be completely out of luck. Character-based interfaces not only can't work with graphics by their very nature, they're also utterly unable to cope with such non-HTML text files like those in the PostScript or Portable Document Format (PDF) page description formats.

The best browsers let you pick and click your way to the appropriate helper application. Your ideal browser would suggest what applications would be appropriate for the foreign format document. Unfortunately, there are no browsers that are bright enough to figure that out on their own yet. Both browser and helper application designers are working on just that, so don't be surprised to see such capacities real soon now.

Another plus for the network administrator is to be able to lock down the selection of helper applications. Again, while many users will want the neatest new version of ShockWave, if your company doesn't need it, you don't want to be stuck with the job of supporting non-standard software. Making the files that control the helper application selection accessible only to the network admin is an excellent idea. If some new format comes along and sweeps the net world, your users will let you know about it; then you can find the best plug-in, install it on everyone's systems, and get on with running your intranet.

# Navigation Advice

Getting through the Web can be as tough as trying to hack your way through one of those nasty, sticky webs spun by monster spiders in B-movies. Your browser might be as sharp as a vorpal sword, cutting down all that stands between you and your information goal, or else it can be as useless as a dull putty knife.

A decent Web navigator will let you go back to previously visited sites with the click of a button. A better one will let you pick and choose exactly how far you want to backtrack along your route instead of forcing you to laboriously walk back step by step.

An excellent Web browser will also let you move about quickly and easily through frames. Frames are an innovative way of dividing up Web screens into several parts so that you can, say, keep a table of contents on the left side of the display while diving deep into the site in the main part, or frame, of the browser window.

The best ones of all enable you to keep a permanent record of your favorite Web destinations. This feature, often referred to as a "hot spot" or bookmark file, is invaluable if you spend any serious amount of time on the Web.

While such Web mapping is a common enough feature, Web browsers still have a ways to go to perfect it. For example, Netscape Navigator, an otherwise outstanding Web browser, doesn't let you put your favorite Web sites in any order except from first entered to last entered. Your users can edit this; but with native Netscape, it's a pain. A function that would enable you to automatically sort the sites into alphabetical order by name would be a vast improvement.

Be ready to pay cash money for a browser that will let your users to organize their Web sites into categories and sub-categories, too. To date, only one company has gotten close to getting this right, and that's First Floor Software's Smart BookMarks, **http://www.firstfloor.com/**. This handy program enables your users to organize their favorite URLs without having fits.

**Figure 11.1:** Smart BookMarks really are a smart way to organize your favorite URLs.

You can use this same software to build catalogs specifically for your business. That done, you can distribute these catalogs to the masses, and presto: Everyone can a find human resources page on the internal LAN, along with news about the competition from the Internet. This use of bookmark organization should not be underestimated! Instead of having to guide each user by hand, you can immediately set them up with the Web resources they need to get their job done effectively.

Better still, the program can use agents to track sites automatically. Instead of trying an old site only to find that it's moved, with BookMarks, the client program resets your bookmarks so that when you use them, they'll be pointing at the right site. I don't know about you, but anything that saves me time and aggravation is a major bonus.

Smart BookMarks (sigh) does have a problem: It only supports the Windows family of operating systems. While IBM has inked a deal with First Floor Software, when this book went to print, IBM still hadn't integrated the program with Warp's Web Explorer. In theory, the next edition of Warp, code-named Merlin, will have this invaluable feature.

# What Was That File!?

One of the biggest headaches of today's Web is keeping up with the flood of new Web formats. If this was limited to special-purpose files, like RealAudio's sound files, that wouldn't be a big deal. We're not that lucky. Now, even home pages are coming out in HTML versions that appear as gibberish to some browsers. Worse, several pages are being created using special format languages and graphic formats that are completely illegible without the right helper application.

The bare basics that a graphical browser must be able to read are HTML 1.0 and GIF89a. Once, that was all you needed. No longer. Today, a browser should also be able to handle HTML 3.0 and all earlier iterations of the language, plus PDF for text. Graphically speaking, your browser should be literate in GIF89a, GIF24, JPEG, and Portable Network Graphics (PNG). The well-equipped Web explorer will also want to have helper applications on hand to handle QuickTime and MPEG movies as well as Word for Windows and PostScript documents. These used to be optional, but they are swiftly becoming necessities.

Why does your browser need to be able to handle so many different formats? That's a good question. For a good answer, the next two sections briefly examine the world of text and graphic standards on the Web. I'll be looking at the question from the webweaver's point of view later in the book. After all, you too are going to become part of the problem—and, hopefully, the solution—for a Web that's quickly becoming less and less worldwide.

# Text Wars

There was a day when all of the text on Web pages was in HTML. Time moved on, and with it went the unity of a single hypermedia language. There are several HTML variants and other document formats being used in Web pages today. For Web readers, this means the Web is changing from a friendly place where any Web browser can be used with virtually any document to a hostile world where not all browsers will be able to cope with all Web documents.

This has always been something of a problem for Web browsers. That's why there are viewers, helper applications, and plug-ins. Like many problems, however, this one is only getting worse. "Pure" HTML is no longer the sole language of the land. Other file formats are being used to carry the basic textual information of the Web.

Before HTML was a twinkle in Berners-Lee's eye, there was Standard Generalized Markup Language (SGML). SGML is an ISO page description standard (ISO 8879). SGML itself does not describe how to format a document. Instead, it provides a set of rules, or a grammar, to create Document Type Definitions (DTDs). A DTD specifies how to identify structural items—such as keywords, endnotes, and words in italics—by specifying tags and their meanings for a class of documents. HTML is a variation on the SGML theme which can be thought of as a DTD for hypermedia documents. Purebreed SGML supporters think of HTML as something of a bastard child; but since they're in academia and we're trying to pull off an intranet, we'll leave them to their almost theological arguments.

What is true is that a purer SGML implementation would make universal documents that would not only act as hypermedia documents, they would look more like their authors had intended. The cost for this trick is complexity and size. Most webweavers find pure SGML too difficult to write and too bulky for Web documents where every kilobyte counts. Now, some webweavers are exploring the use of SGML on the Web. The SGML community is also lobbying for HTML to move closer to SGML orthodoxy. Their position is that SGML gives readers far more sophisticated textual resources, such as being able to bounce more easily from text to footnote to bibliography and back again, than does HTML. One company, SoftQuad, **http://www. sq.com/index.html**, has even released an SGML browser, Panorama Pro.

While SGML does have some advantages, it hasn't caught on on the Web. That doesn't mean, however, that you should rule it out for your intranet. Many companies have used SGML in-house for years for their internal documentation. If your company is one of them, then Panorama Pro may be just what your in-house editors need to make their lives a lot easier. SoftQuad only supports several SGML development tools for the Web; but if it turns out that SGML is right for your firm's internal documentation, it's worth it.

SGML's most likely fate on the Web is to fade into a document format hidden behind an HTML mask. For more information on SGML, the best place to stop is The SGML Web Page, **http://www.sil.org/sgml/sgml.html**.

Almost everyone else in the Web page production business is coping with the move from HTML 1.0 and HTML 2.0 documents to HTML 3.0, and trying to decide whether or not they should support Netscape's enhancements to HTML 3.0. The first version of HTML, HTML 0.9, while used with some documents, is now considered antique. HTML 1.0 is still the most popular Web document format. Fortunately, for those with hours invested in legacy documents, there's no need to update these items. Any Web browser will be able to read them.

HTML 2.0 gives the existing state of mainstream HTML usage the official blessing of the Internet Engineering Task Force (IETF). The IETF, in turn, derives its authority from the World Wide Web Consortium (W3C). This group, led by Tim Berners-Lee, the Web's founder, guides the development of HTML and the other Web standards: universal resource locators (URLs) and HTTP. In the case of HTML 2.0, rules for forms and currently legal character sets are now formally part of the standard.

That's not to say that all present-day HTML uses were grandfathered into HTML 2.0, or HTML 3.0 for that matter. Nothing could be further from the truth. The status of both Netscape's and Microsoft's proposed additions to HTML remains very much up in the air.

Because of this, no one knows if HTML will remain an open, viable standard. The main browser and server companies are well aware of the old axiom that he who makes the standards wins. Both Microsoft and Netscape have the potential clout to make their changes a de facto part of HTML 3.0 and any future standards. Both of them want to make such changes so that their system will be the one that wins the hearts and minds, not to mention the wallets, of the server- and browser-buying public. All of these changes, whether they're from companies or the W3C, have one goal: to give authors further means of controlling the look of their documents.

Microsoft has taken this competitive effort to a new extreme. Documents written with some of these Microsoft extensions crash Netscape browsers. These extensions are relatively minor and seem to only be there to make life difficult for Netscape users. This blatant attempt to get people to use Internet Explorer instead of Netscape is doomed to fail. While Netscape has certainly pushed other companies into adopting their standards, their changes never knocked other browsers for a loop. By making Netscape unusable for some pages, I believe that instead of gaining support from users, Microsoft is just going to harvest the bitter fruits of their anger.

Some webweavers wanting absolute control of document presentation are moving on to using Adobe's PDF, `http://www.adobe.com`. PDF gives authors the ability to send documents with PostScript-like fidelity to the original, but without the size and compatibility penalties that PostScript imposes. Since Netscape has embraced PDF as a supported format via an Adobe plug-in, some now believe that PDF will replace HTML for all but the most general purposes.

They may be right. PDF is gaining vast popularity. For example, the Internal Revenue Service uses HTML for their Web pages, but their forms are kept in PDF. Even the dreaded IRS 1040 form is rendered with enough PDF fidelity that the IRS will accept a printout of the form as the real form. HTML, no matter what you do with it, simply can't create such precise duplicates of documents.

For you, as the person in charge of your company's intranet, this means that you can count on needing to support PDF for your browser. You can get away with ignoring SGML, unless something drastic happens; but PDF support is a must. You may also want to support PDF as a company standard for your servers, but that's a story for another chapter.

As for HTML, what can you do but keep your software up-to-date? That doesn't mean installing every new beta that comes along, though. All the browser companies are fond of letting the entire world be their beta-test lab; but there's no reason you have to join in this foolishness. For example, as I write this in mid-1996, Netscape 3.0 and Internet Explorer 3.0 are both available in beta formats. Do you want to deal with these products' teeth-cutting problems in addition to all your other intranet tasks? I know I don't.

For now, while the potential for conflict exists, you can be relatively certain of reading any HTML document you find. As time goes by, this will prove to be the case less and less frequently. Eventually, the Web is going to be divided into incompatible sections. If there is popular support for standard HTML and open systems, your users will still be able to roam over most of the Web freely. If not, then you can expect an end to the days when you could explore the Web from hither to yon without restriction. Your only response will be to get a Web browser with the fullest possible support for foreign file formats.

# Graphics Battles

You may not believe it if you're new to the Web; but once, there was no question about Web graphics. The Web's inline graphics were written in GIF. Period. End of statement. Alas, all good things must come to an end.

Today, it's no longer a given that GIF will be the inline graphics format of choice. That's because Unisys, the patent owner on the Lempel-Ziv-Welch (LZW) data compression algorithm, began demanding licensing fees for programs using LZW. Three guesses as to what popular graphics format uses LZW. Yes, that's right: GIF. CompuServe, GIF's owner, then started charging fees for all programs using GIF.

Now, this doesn't affect webweavers or users directly. You can keep using and viewing GIFs in your pages to your heart's content, and no one's going to come pounding on your door demanding payment. However, this does affect the vendors that make programs which create, edit, or (and this is the important one) view GIFs, such as browsers.

When the licensing fee news first came out, the graphics and online services programming communities were outraged by the very notion. For years, the GIF format, while copyrighted by CompuServe, had been the free, de facto graphics standard of not only CompuServe and the Web, but of most of the online world. Graphic designers and programmers felt as if someone had changed the rules on them in midstream. Angry and betrayed, they started looking for alternatives to GIF.

Browser programmers' response to GIF licensing fees has been to add JPEG support to their browsers. JPEG is slowly become as important an inline image format as GIF. For webweavers, though, JPEG has its problems. JPEG isn't as flexible as GIF for design purposes. The short explanation is that JPEG is a fine end-product format, but it's lousy for editing.

The result? CompuServe, faced with furious developers, decided to dump LZW from GIF and come up with a new GIF. This new format, GIF24, will allegedly be a "free, clear and open format" for all developers. Despite this, GIF24 is only creeping onto the Web.

Other graphic developers have been working on a completely new alternative to GIF. The most popular of these is the Portable Network Graphics (PNG, pronounced ping) format. Its designers hope that PNG will replace GIF for inline images. PNG produces smaller graphic files than GIF. It also includes 24-bit truecolor support, and is free of any LZW licensing problems. For the down and dirty details, check out PNG's source code in **`ftp://ftp.uu.net:/graphics/png`**.

For you and your users, all this means that you might consider getting a browser that includes native support for GIF24 and PNG, but I wouldn't put it at the top of my list. While PNG and the new GIF have garnered the support of many graphics development companies, webweavers haven't done much with either format.

The Web browser designers, after some initial annoyance with Unisys, don't seem to be doing much to support these new formats. The consensus among both Web developers and users seems to be that JPEG's an acceptable substitute; and that the old GIF is worth the minimal licensing fees.

## Support Secure Transactions

If you're going buy or sell anything over the Web, your browser must support a secure transaction protocol. These protocols encrypt your private data so that no rogue spider on the Web can intercept your private data.

Currently, there are two important secure transaction formats battling for Web domination. These are Terisa Systems' Secure HTTP (S-HTTP) and Netscape's Secure Sockets Layer (SSL). While they go about their work in different ways, the goal is the same: encrypting the data that moves between your browser and a Web site. In both cases, both the server and the browser must be using the same security protocol.

While other businesses are warring over other standards, it doesn't look likely that any of us them is going to be able to push their alternatives forward enough to be in the running with S-HTTP and SSL. Companies have already lined up behind the security protocols. SSL, used in Netscape's Netsite Commerce Server, has been licensed by Digital, Novell, Bank of America, and Delphi Internet Service. W3C members, including AT&T, IBM, MCI Communications, Microsoft, Netscape, Novell, and NCSA, have all come out in support of S-HTTP.

No, that was no error: Digital, Novell, and Netscape are supporting both protocols. They can get away with this because the two technologies aren't mutually exclusive. For that matter, you can implement both methods on a single browser or server. Politically, of course, it could be a bloodbath between the two standards. Since Web software vendors realize that having a secure transaction war could kill the golden goose of Web commerce, peace talks rather than saber-rattling is the order of the day. After all, it's hard enough getting people to make purchases over the Web without making it harder for them.

The best thing you can do for your company is look for products that support both standards. If you can't find one—as I write this, none do—make sure your corporate browsers support one of these two main standards.

# Other Internet/Usenet Tools

All Web browsers can support some other Internet/Usenet tools. For example, ftp and gopher have always been supported by browsers. Web browsers are rapidly increasing the number of other programs they support as they move from being strictly Web browsers to being all-in-one Internet front-ends.

The other programs that you'll likely want your company's browsers to support are mail and, if you think it's worth it for you, Usenet news. You may also want to consider support for telnet and its mainframe cousin, telnet-3270.

# Quick Work

More than anything else, your browser's speed depends upon the speed of your Internet connection. That said, your browser can make it feel like you're moving faster on the Web than you're actually going.

While other browsers now employ similar techniques, this bit of magic began at Netscape. Netscape displays the text of a Web site first, and then takes its time bringing up the pretty graphics. It may not sound like much; but the overall effect is to make speedy browsers seem even quicker. Instead of waiting for a 20K GIF to appear, you can decide whether or not you want to stick around for it based on the words already displayed on the page.

Another performance wonder is to display information as it arrives. Some browsers do this poorly, showing you chunks of information in screen-blurring displays. The speed secret here is for the browser to smoothly show you information as it appears, not in jarring fits and starts.

Yet another speed magic feat to look for in a browser is keeping its own PC-based caches of frequently accessed pages. If you have the memory for it, these programs store out-of-sight pages in RAM; otherwise, they store them to disk. In either case, the effect is the same: Pages you've already visited come up much faster because you're accessing a local copy rather than a cached copy on the intranet server or, slower still, the actual Internet site.

The final touch to complete the illusion of greater speed is to allow you to stop an incoming page from fully downloading so that you can move on to other work. There's nothing quite as frustrating as waiting for a page to appear once you've realized it isn't the page you wanted. Most browsers now enable you to hit the escape key or a special button to escape from a partially loaded page.

Finally, there are some true speed differences between browsers. This normally shows up in how they handle graphics. Some programs, such as Mosaic, take their own sweet time to display a graphic, while others, like Netscape, quickly paint GIFs to your screen.

Since is everyone is working on making the fastest possible browsers, don't accept these comparisons as gospel. The best way to judge is to get copies of the browsers—almost all of them are available in freeware or demo versions— and run your own tests using a single PC with local or server-based files. That way, you won't need to worry about the differences caused by the Internet's highly variable speeds, and you'll get a fair idea of just how fast your intranet is with any given browser.

## Specifically Speaking

Next up, I'm going to briefly discuss specific Web browsers. I'm not going to spend too much time on this, because Web browsers change faster than Paris fashions. If you want to know what's hot and what's not, look for a recent copy of *Byte*, *Internet World*, *NetGuide*, or *PC Magazine* for an overview of the latest crop of Web browsers.

# 12

## Picking the Right Browser

## The Never-Ending Quest

Let me get this off my chest right now: I can't tell you what's the right browser for your company. What I can and will do is tell you some specifics about the best of today's Web browsers. By the time you read this, an entire new generation—that's about three months—of Web browsers will have appeared. As I said in the last chapter, the only way to pick the best browser for you is to try them out and look for the most recent review you can find in one of the respectable general computing or Internet-specific magazines. There is one specific publication that's dedicated to Web browser testing, and it's well worth your time to visit. This online magazine is BrowserWatch, `http://browserwatch.iworld .com/`.

I'll also repeat a warning from the last chapter: You don't want to switch browsers at the drop of a new release. In particular, avoid using beta versions. If you want to play with the cutting edge of technology at home, go for it. There's only so much damage it can do there. But you don't want your business to end up bleeding red ink because you switched the entire intranet to Company X's newest beta, which turned out to have a jagged cutting edge.

How do you tell if your browser is a good one or not? Other than testing the heck out of it for a considerable period of time, the best shortcut is to aim it at the following test pages.

**Table 12.1: The Web Testers**

| Name | URL |
| --- | --- |
| Browser Caps | `http://www.pragmaticainc.com/ bc/` |
| C-Net Torture Test | `http://www.cnet.com/Content/ Reviews/Compare/Browsers/ Test/index.html` |
| WWW Browser Test Page | `http://www-dsed.llnl.gov/doc uments/WWWtest.html` |

At these sites, you can give the browser of the day a quick checkup to see how it handles common text, graphics, audio, and video file types. If there's a quicker, better way to give a browser an unbiased functionality test than sending it through its paces on these pages, I haven't seen it.

Another question you might ask is: What are your peers using? Simple: Netscape. A basic analysis of data from Yahoo's home page, one of the most popular sites on the Web, shows that as of mid-August 1996, 65% of all the site's Web visitors were using Netscape. In second place was Spry Mosaic, a program based on Spyglass's Enhanced Mosaic, used almost exclusively by CompuServe users. Lagging far behind in 3rd place, despite all the hype, was Microsoft's Internet Explorer, with a miserable 6.4%.

Other sites that track what browsers are being used suggest that Microsoft is getting beaten even more soundly. The BenLo Park Research site, **http://emporium.turn-pike.net/J/jc/public_html/stats.html**, shows Netscape walking away with 80% plus of the mark, and Internet Explorer not even within spitting distance of a single percent of the market. If this was a softball game, they would have already declared Netscape the winner based on the mercy rule.

The Microsoft programmers and public relations machine are trying their damnedest with Internet Explorer. The plain truth is that they're going nowhere fast. Of course, if your staff includes a lot of people who live and die by Microsoft products and a programming group that knows what ActiveX is without looking it up in a book, you may want to give Internet Explorer a try. (Incidentally, ActiveX is Microsoft's revamping of the Object-Linking Embedding (OLE) 2.0 interprocess communications protocol in an attempt to make OLE Internet "sexy"—that is, exciting and appealing to the masses.)

That said, despite anything you read in the computing newspapers and magazines, there can be no question that Netscape, not Microsoft, rules the Internet. For browsers, that's not that important. Market share or no, Internet Explorer can do most of the things that Netscape can do. For your webmasters and webweavers, though, the numbers say it all. If you're going to write any browser-specific code, Netscape Navigator should be your target.

With those caveats in mind, let's take a look at what's out there.

# Macintosh

Macintosh users have two real choices for a Web browser: Microsoft's Internet Explorer 3.0 and Netscape Navigator 3.0. There used to be a host of other programs that were in the running; but even the best of them, like Intercon's WebShark, have fallen well behind the two browser giants. This is a story that you'll hear over and over again as we look at the browser markets. There are more than the big two out there; but the smaller companies' browsers are either being forced out of the market or trying to find niche markets by developing special purpose browsers.

With most operating systems, I give Netscape the nod for being the better pick; but for Macs, I actually prefer Internet Explorer. Why? Well, it's really quite elementary. Netscape puts most of its efforts into improving their Windows95, Unix, and Windows editions, in that order. Somewhere down at the bottom of the list is Macintosh.

Don't get me wrong; the Mac version of Navigator is great—it's just never quite as current as the other versions. For example, today's Internet Explorer can support audio formats like AIFF, MIDI, and WAV, and video formats like AVI and QuickTime on the Mac without helper applications or plug-ins. Netscape can't. Microsoft, of course, also has its own list of priorities, and Windows95 tops the Redmond crew's list; but the Macintosh isn't that far down the line.

Navigator continues to holds the advantage in some areas. Explorer, for instance, can send e-mail but not receive it. Navigator can do both. In either case, on the Mac, you'll want separate e-mail and, if required, newsreader programs. The browsers' attempts to do the job in these areas just don't cut it.

There are still other Mac Web browsers out there. Of those worth mentioning, my favorites are Tradewave's MacWeb, **http://galaxy.einet.net/EINet/MacWeb/MacWeb Home.html**. Today, this browser is only available as part of Tradewave's TradeVPI package. I'd rather be able to just get the browser; but as I mentioned earlier, the smaller browsers are being forced into finding new ways to make a profit. Tradewave's method has been to bundle it into a complete secure Internet package. The browser itself is old and slow, but it's also the only program that you can run on an SE/30. If you have older Macs, MacWeb's really your only decent choice.

With more of a machine, and more in your budget, you might want to consider Intercon's tcpConnect4, **http://www.intercon.com/**. This Swiss-army-knife of a program suite comes with everything from the TCP/IP stack to the Web browser to, on the enterprise edition, a Network File System (NFS) client. Of course, all of this comes with a price tag that soars above the others. Still, you can try it out first. For an office that's already committed to Macs, this package may be exactly what you're looking for in the way of a universal solution.

# OS/2

OS/2 Warp has the best in-the-box combination of Internet utilities of any operating system, including a solid Web browser. If you have an earlier copy of OS/2 than the Warp edition (version 3.0), you can also get a copy of its freeware browser, WebExplorer 1.1, directly from IBM, **http://www.raleigh.ibm.com/WebExplorer/**, or at many other sites on the Web.

The new version—which will be shipping with the next generation of OS/2, code-named Warp—is a step forward for OS/2 browsers. Older versions couldn't support such popular HTML 3.0 features as backgrounds, background colors, tables, or transparent GIFs. Warp can do all this and more. Admittedly, it does so at a turtle's pace compared to the twin hares of Netscape and Microsoft. WebExplorer is slow; and while slow and steady may win the race in the fairy tales, it doesn't win any kudos in the browser biz.

Until recently, though, the alternatives were few and far less effective. There's a GNUscape Browser that will work—at a frighteningly slow rate—if you have EMACS 19 or higher. WebExplorer will work on any operating system that will support EMACS, which is essentially all of them. EMACS, for those of you who haven't met it, started out as a programmer's editor and has evolved into being almost a high-level computer language in its own right. It's far too complex to be a contender for an intranet.

Other browsers, like Cello, **http://www.law.cornell.edu/cello/cellotop.html**, and early versions of Netscape Navigator, will work in Warp's DOS and Windows emulation modes respectively; but Cello is ancient, and getting less modern versions of Navigator to work correctly is an exercise in installation agony.

Since then, however, Netscape and IBM have joined hands to make Netscape Navigator for OS/2. While this version will lag behind Netscape versions on other operating systems, it won't surprise me a bit if Netscape becomes the browser of choice on OS/2 the same way it has on almost all other operating systems.

If you're using Warp or Merlin, you're most likely to be using WebExplorer. Considering that today's Merlin package includes a host of better-than-average Internet and Usenet tools in Internet Connection for OS/2 and TCP/IP for OS/2, things could be much worse. The bottom line: You can run a successful intranet with Warp clients. You may have hoped for more pizzazz; but Merlin and Web Explorer or Netscape will get the job done just fine.

# Unix

The operating system that gave birth to the Web also has the most browsers. For better or for worse, Netscape Navigator is again the program to beat for all the reasons it stands out so well on other operating systems: It simply works better.

Netscape also supports, without the need to compile source code, more Unix platforms than other browsers. A limited list includes DEC's OSF, HP's HP-UX, IBM's AIX, Silicon Graphics' Irix, Sun's SunOS and Solaris, SCO Unix, and even freeware Unixes like BSDI and Linux.

With Unix, however, there are other viable alternatives to consider. Sun, for example, has the HotJava browser, **http://java.sun.com/products/index.html** , for the SunOS/Solaris operating systems. This browser, as you can probably guess from the title, works better with the Java Web-enabled programming language than any other browser. HotJava is also likely to be the first browser with native support for WebNFS. WebNFS is a rival protocol to HTTP and offers the possibilities of vast speed increases over HTTP when it comes to large files. I'll talk more about that in later chapters.

To support low-end users, Unix also supports the best of the character-based Web browsers, Lynx, **http://kuhttp .cc.ukans.edu/about_lynx/about_lynx.html**. If you have users who can only access your intranet via terminals or low-end PCs, having Lynx available on your Unix server is a must.

If you like to live dangerously, you can give CNRI's Grail a try, at **http://monty.cnri.reston.va.us/grail/ #introduction**. This HTML 2.0 compliant browser works quite well in my experience. To use it, you'll need to have the object-oriented language, Python, and John Ousterhout's TK user interface. Since all of these are freeware, you're not going to spend a lot on this browser. Like most Unix browsers, this is actually an X11 Windows interface. It should work on any Unix that supports X, which in effect means almost all of them.

If you're lucky enough to have some people working with the NeXTStep operating system, then you should be good enough to get them one of the best browsers around: Omni Development's OmniWeb, **http://www.omnigroup. com/Software/OmniWeb/**. While OmniWeb only runs on NeXTStep, it's a real class act. OmniWeb supports essentially all HTML 2.0 and most Netscape and HTML 3.0 extensions. In addition, with OmniPDF, it reads Adobe's PDF files. It's enough to make you wish that NeXTStep had caught on with the masses. As it is, NeXTStep is likely to only be found on the desktops of top-flight developers, financial analysts, and graphic artists.

At one time, Arena, **http://www.w3.org/pub/WWW/Arena/**, the W3C's own Web browser for testing out HTML 3.0, was worth considering. These days, the W3C doesn't plan on putting any more effort into Arena; so I can't see any reason for business users to put any effort into the product either.

NCSA Mosaic, **http://www.ncsa.uiuc.edu/SDG/Software/Mosaic/NCSAMosaicHome.html**, and Spyglass' Enhanced Mosaic, **http://www.spyglass.com/index.html**, are also still available. But let's get real: Netscape beats the pants off both of them.

# Windows

By now you know what I'm going to say: Netscape rules. Internet Explorer tries; but for all its virtues, it's no Netscape. There are dozens of other Web browsers for Windows, but I won't bore you with the list. If you want a full list of Windows' and other operating systems' browsers, then click your way over to BrowserWatch's Browser List, **http://browserwatch.iworld.com/browsers.html** .

The features list alone for Netscape speaks for itself. The newest Navigator includes frames, plug-ins, Java support, JavaScript support, Progressive JPEG, client-side image mapping, and built-in telephony services. Internet

Explorer has its own list of tricks, such as built-in support for ActiveX and integration with other Microsoft products. Taken as a whole, though, I feel the advantage clearly lies with Netscape.

This also holds true in terms of performance. While with the 2.0 version, Explorer could occasionally edge out Netscape. That no longer holds true.

Other programs are eating the power pair's dust. Even as some, like Attachmate's Emissary Desktop Edition, **http://www.attachmate.com**, which includes most Internet tools in one seamless interface, inch ahead in terms of sheer integration, Netscape and Microsoft are still way out in the lead in all other respects. Further, their newer editions are well on their way to equaling Attachmate's level of integration.

When it comes to a heads-on comparison on issues of specific importance to businesses, Netscape again leads the way. All shipping versions of Netscape browsers for United States users, for example, come with 128-bit encryption to keep sales transactions over the Web secure. Like every other security measure, it will eventually be broken; but for now, it's orders of magnitude better than anything Explorer or any other browser can offer.

Both Netscape and Explorer are available in versions for Windows95 and NT. Oddly enough, Netscape keeps its Windows 3.1 edition more current than does Microsoft, where it's clear that 3.1 support is an afterthought.

# Netscape or Nothing

As I end this chapter, I can only tell you that short of a major market transformation, Microsoft, for all of its size and marketing dollars, is running a distant second to Netscape on almost all platforms. That isn't going to change any time soon. In particular, if you're running an intranet with multiple operating systems, there's not even the appearance of choice: It's Netscape or bust. The single exception is OS/2, where your choice is Web Explorer or nothing.

For my own intranet, which includes Macs, PCs running everything from Win 3.1 to Windows NT to OS/2, my browser mix of choice is Navigator on everything except the Warp machines, which run WebExplorer. It works for me; it should work for you as well.

Web servers, though—that's another kettle of fish entirely. There, as I'll show you in the next pages, there are some real selections to be made from a variety of good products.

# 13

## Introducing Web Servers

## The Heart of Your Intranet: The Web Server

The key component of your intranet will be your Web server. E-mail may actually be more important for internal matters; but it's your server that will be the cover to your company's book. For, despite the saying, people are going to judge you by your cover.

The crafting of that book is a matter for your web-weavers. What you need to do is make sure that they have the solid foundation they need to create the best possible Web pages.

A server's primary job is very simple. It takes in HTTP requests and returns data by HTTP. That's it. Even so, there's a great deal of differences between servers. The factors that you need to look at are:

* Speed

* Security

* Setup

* Management

# Server Basics

Your choice of servers is going to be limited by your major operating system. While you can choose a server that uses a different operating system than your LAN does, you'll be adding to your company's overall networking overhead if you do. You'll also be creating needless headaches for your network administrators-who, as I mentioned earlier, you're going to want to keep on your good side. The less headaches you can give them, the better.

If you plan on making your site the public heart of your business, then you may well want to pay the high costs of some of the more upscale options. For example, today's most trustworthy servers are built around Unix. NetWare and NT have their strong points; but if you want a server operating system that will keep going no matter what, Unix is your best choice.

That said, unless a server offers a particular service that others can't provide, the differences between operating systems aren't enough in and of themselves to demand that you switch. The one exception to this is that you must use a serious, heavy-duty network operating system (NOS) for your Web server. For all practical purposes, that means your choices are limited to Mac OS, Unix, Warp Server, and Windows NT Server.

Yes, there are servers for AmigaDOS, Windows 3.1, Windows95, and more besides. Don't be tempted by them. These operating systems simply aren't tough enough to handle the workload of a large corporate intranet.

Most people are tempted by servers for these operating systems because the operating systems are dirt cheap, if not free. The reason you don't want to bother with them is stability. On the other hand, if you lust after a low-priced Web server, you're in luck: Some of the free servers really are as good as any server you'll spend several grand on. The Apache server, **http://www.apache.org**, for instance, is one of the best you can get for Unix. For that matter, it's one of the best servers, period.

Be aware, though, that not all "free" things are truly free. More often than not, there's a catch. One prominent example is Microsoft's pricing for its Internet Information Server (IIS). IIS is, in fact, free. However, it requires NT Server for its OS, rather than NT Workstation. I won't go into a detailed financial analysis because by the time you read this, the numbers will have changed. The bottom line is, unless you're already running NT Server 3.51 or higher, it's going to cost you more to use free IIS than it would to buy Netscape's Enterprise Server. Caveat emptor, indeed!

# One More Standards War

What would any part of the Web be without a standards battle? For servers, the relevant one is the struggle between Web Network File System (WebNFS) and HTTP.

Some people will tell you that Web Network File System (WebNFS) is just what the Web needs. For them, the Internet is like a dirt road with a lot of potholes. WebNFS will fill in those potholes, providing commercial grade connection speeds that are 10 times faster than HTTP or ftp. This increase won't be as dramatic over modems; but even with 28.8Kbps connections, there will be a notable jump in your webrunning speed.

Sun's NFS has been the popular TCP/IP open network file distribution standard of choice for more than a decade. This architecture and operation independent file system is the glue that holds together heterogeneous file systems. The newsy bit here is that there's never been an open implementation that would work consistently over Internet connections—until now. Sun has already submitted WebNFS to the Internet Engineering Task Force (IETF) as a proposed open standard.

WebNFS springs ahead of the hypertext (HTTP) and data transfer (ftp) protocols because WebNFS sends a Web page, or any other document, as one whole package. WebNFS is all about moving entire documents quickly. HTTP, on the other hand, downloads a site a little at a time. This is because HTTP is designed for hypermedia, so it's always leaving windows of opportunity during which the user can click on an icon, focus only on the top of the screen, or fill in a blank. You'll notice, too, that most good browsers constantly switch back and forth between downloading the text and graphics of a given page. The result? HTTP: Slow, WebNFS: Fast.

WebNFS has found some marketplace support. Oracle and Spyglass are incorporating it into their browsers. Auspex, IBM, and Sequent plan to include WebNFS in their Web servers. Sun, of course, is putting all its resources behind WebNFS. The most visible sign of this support is the popular Netra NFS file server series. These Web servers depend as much on WebNFS as they do on HTTP for data transfer.

You'll notice that there are two prominent names missing from the WebNFS bandwagon: Microsoft and Netscape. Microsoft agrees that HTTP and ftp are lousy for seeking, reading, and writing. But Microsoft has its own idea: service message blocks (SMBs). SMBs are basically Microsoft's equivalent of WebNFS. The SMB protocol has already been incorporated into Unix, as SAMBA; and it's also an X/Open standard.

HTTP's not out of the race yet. HTTP 1.1 improvements, like Byte Read-Range and HTTP connection keep-alive, are evolving HTTP into a rival for WebNFS.

Like so many of these battles, the real heat is because of corporate politics and money, not technology. If Sun is successful, then Sun will succeed in setting a new and vital standard. In particular, Sun's winning here will hurt Microsoft's grand network plan, Normandy, which depends on HTTP.

WebNFS plus Java can also be seen as a direct competitor to HTTP and HTML. If Sun is successful in replacing the existing infrastructure, all the other major Web companies are in serious trouble. Remember, whoever controls the standards controls the marketplace; so this isn't just a technological religious war: WebNFS' success or failure will determine billions in Internet revenues.

Will WebNFS win out? Maybe. I wish I could give you a better answer; but that's the only answer there is at this time. A lot depends on whether Sun can gain the support of third party HTTP servers. For example, if WebNFS is ported out to popular freeware servers like Apache, WebNFS will appear everywhere. Even holdouts like Netscape and Microsoft's browser and server product lines will have to cope with third party add-ons that will retrofit their software with WebNFS. If that happens, then its Katie, bar the door, because the Web will be completely reinvented with WebNFS as its standard. (No one ever said that working in a time of technological transformation was going to be easy!)

# Speed

Let me make one thing perfectly clear: How fast users will see your site has more to do with the speed of your Internet connection than your server hardware or software. You want a site that sets world records for speed? Get the fastest possible connection you can afford.

Most server software does an equally good job at dishing out the bytes via HTTP. The real difference in servers is in how well they do at interactive jobs. If you want to really compare servers, take Common Gateway Interface (CGI) tasks—like handling form data, image maps, and interprocess communications (IPC)—and run them on each of the server programs under consideration using identical hardware. That will give you meaningful numbers for comparison. Better yet, since CGI is inherently inefficient, are servers that come with built-in IPCs to DBMSs, image maps, and forms. A server that's gone beyond CGI will be inherently faster than a model that has to resort to CGI to translate between input and output.

Anything specific I could say about a given product's speed would be out of date by the time you read this, so I'm not going to waste your time by giving you answers that we both know will be wrong. The only real answer is for your people to come up with the kind of interactive work you think you'll be doing the most of on your server and then run head-to-head comparisons.

# Security

Right after speed, security should be your greatest concern. I'll go into far greater detail on security in a few chapters, but there are a few basics I can already tell you.

Before anything else, your server must support S-HTTP or SSL. Both would be even better. Right now, just like everything else in the Web business, there's a lot of jockeying around as vendors try to push their own security software as the answer for your Web serving needs. Horse pucky. When all is said and done, SSL and S-HTTP are the closest to security standards that the Web has. There will be advances. I wouldn't be the least bit surprised, for instance, to see SSL and S-HTTP combined into one standard. What I would be shocked at, however, is seeing a completely new standard arise within the next two years.

Oh, and lest we forget, you must actually activate your Web server's security options. Having them in the server but not turning them on protects your server as well as having a car alarm system and then leaving the keys in your car. Use it or lose it.

The other security basics should be familiar to you from intro network security class. You were awake, weren't you? Right. Okay, here's a quick refresher. All public Web documents should be kept in a specific server directory that's guarded out to wazoo. In this directory and its subdirectories, and only there, is where you're going to be putting your public files. From the outside, this directory should be treated as the root for a separate directory tree. In Web language, this means that valid URLs for your site can only refer to paths and files in this directory tree.

If you must let the public see files that aren't in that directory, you do it by creating what Unix people call symbolic links to the external files. If you're a Mac maven, you know these as aliases, or in Win NT, shortcuts. No matter what you call them, the result is that only single files will be exposed to outsiders, and that indirectly.

Of course, there's much more to security than this. Still, even if you can't stand to wait one more minute before putting up a Web server, with this little bit of security you can move on to the grand setup.

## Setup & Management

Setup is another area where you'll be a better judge than I can be now because of the Web's ever-increasing change of pace. The Readers' Digest condensed version is that setting up a server should be as easy as installing as any other program. There's nothing complex about the basic job of a Web server. That should also be true of its installation routines. Of course, setup could involve a whole lot more, such as automatically translating files in the Web directory tree into HTML; but no one's made an installation program that's that bright...yet.

Management is another matter that I'll take up in a later chapter. What I can say now is that you'll want a management program that combines all functionality into a single interface. If there's one thing I hate about network management programs, it's that so many of them force you to use one program after another to keep the LAN working. It was stupid in the beginning, and it's even stupider now for maintaining Web sites.

Your management interface should also give you quick and easy access to your server's logs. If it does that, you've got a decent management front-end. In an ideal situation, what you really want is an interface that lets you sort and view data from the logs without having to program anything more complicated than a VCR controls. Yeah, I know, that's not easy; but, trust me, it's easier than writing out PERL code to see what happening with one site that keeps connecting and disconnecting with your server.

## Other Features

There are a few other features that you may want for your Web server. For example, starting with the Netscape servers, there's server push. This is when the server holds open an HTTP connection instead of closing it immediately and pushes data through this connection to a browser. While server push has in some ways been made obsolete by Java and ActiveX, it still serves a useful purpose by making it easy to update a browser display. Typically, server push is used for making simple animations using a series of still images. The effect is exactly the same as that used by the venerable flip-book. You can also use server push to update an information display, although here the newer technologies really have left server push behind.

Another feature set to look for are Web servers that also work as gopher or ftp servers. If you're like me, you'd like anything that will simplify your life; and having one server to do several jobs is my idea of a real win.

Your internal users will probably also be pleased if the server can work as a caching proxy server. A proxy server is yet another security measure in which all your company's outgoing Web requests are made as if they're all coming from the one server. This enables the system administrators to have more control over whether your company's users are pulling down the latest NetWare files from pdq.corporate.com or the latest, ahem, "wetware" files from xxx.xxx.xxx.

Okay, so that part isn't going to win the users' hearts; but that's business. What they will like is that a caching proxy server enables copies of frequently accessed pages, like the front-pages of the popular Web search engines, to be kept on the local server. The result? Much faster access to the most widely used sites. This, your people will appreciate.

# A Selection of Servers

In the PC world, Novell NetWare reigns supreme as the NOS of choice. Snapping at its heels is Microsoft with Windows NT. Now, both powerhouses have released Web servers—NetWare Web Server (NWS) and Microsoft Internet Information Server (IIS).

OS/2 Server is also worth considering for the PC market. IBM's Internet Connection Server (ICS) gives Warp users a decent server. Until recently, that was your only good choice. With the recent freeware release of Apache for OS/2, **http://www.slink.com/ApacheOS2/**, OS/2 administrators have another, and in my opinion, better option.

If you're already operating out of a Unix shop with mini-computers or workstations, there's no reason to switch. In fact, with such all-in-one solutions as Sun's Netra and Silicon Graphics WebForce, you may want to consider adding a Unix box to your LAN. If you don't have the money for a Netra or a WebForce, Apache is a freeware server that actually has the honor of running more Web sites than any other server.

Macintoshes are also capable of holding their own on the Web. As always, you'll want a fast machine. In addition, you'll want to be running System 7.5.3 or later. You can try running on 7.1, but you'll be asking for trouble. WebStar is the server of choice for Mac users.

Of course, no matter your operating system (save for OS/2 users), the Netscape servers demand your attention. Before going into further details on the big name servers, here are a list of servers that I've tested and have deemed intranet-ready. By the very nature of the business, I can't be comprehensive; but any of the listed servers should serve your intranet well.

### Table 13.1: Intranet-worthy Servers

<u>Macintosh</u>

·MacHTTP, `http://www.biap.com/`

·WebSTAR, `http://www.starnine.com/`

<u>OS/2</u>

·GoServe, `http://www2.hursley.ibm.com/goserve/`

·Internet Connection Server*#, `http://www.ibm.com`

<u>Unix</u>

· Apache%, `http://www.apache.org/`

·NCSA httpd%, `http://hoohoo.ncsa.uiuc.edu/docs/Overview.html`

·CERN httpd%, `http://www.w3.org/hypertext/WWW/Daemon/User/Guide.html`

·Gn HTTP%, `http://hopf.math.nwu.edu:70/`

·Spyglass Server, `http://www.spyglass.com`

·Internet Connection Server [AIX only], `http://www.ibm.com`

·Netscape Communication Server, `http://www.netscape.com`

·Netscape Commerce Server*, `http://www.netscape.com`

·Secure WebServer*#, `http://www.openmarket.com`

Windows/NT

·HTTPS for Win/NT$^{\%}$, `http://www.w3.org/hypertext/WWW/HTTPS/Status.html`

·Netscape Communication Server, `http://www.netscape.com`

·Netscape Commerce Server*, `http://www.netscape.com`

·Purveyor, `http://www.process.com`

·Spyglass Server, `http://www.spyglass.com`

·SuperWeb*[#], `http://www.frontiertech.com`

·WebSite[#], `http://www.ora.com`

\* Supports Secure Sockets Level (SSL) protocol

\# Supports Secure HTTP (S-HTTP) protocol

% Freeware

# Apache

You may not have heard of it before, but Apache is the most popular Web server on the Web. That's for three reasons: It's free; it now works on both Unix and OS/2 systems; and it's very, very fast.

Apache was built around the core of NCSA's httpd, but it has long since left its parent programming behind. While its cost and speed are the keys to Apache's popularity, it's also one seriously full-featured server.

For example, Apache supports both a cache proxy mode and, at this time uniquely, content negotiation. This feature gives the server the ability to poll browsers and automatically deliver the HTML version of a document that gives that browser the best possible view of the information. In the past, to do this, you had to write in a manual choice in your first Web page. This slowed things down for users, and was just a plain nuisance. With this new technology, while writing different versions of the same document to reach the widest possible audience is still a pain, it's a pain that your customers don't have to share.

Apache has the strength you need for even the biggest corporate intranet. It's the server that lies behind sites like HotWired, **http://www.hotwired.com/frontdoor/**, the MIT AI Lab, **http://www.ai.mit.edu/**, and the Internet Movie Database, **http://us.imdb.com/**. These average over a million hits on a good day. Clearly, Apache is one tough server.

Alas, Apache is also one tough server to install. While the OS/2 version is more manageable, the Unix version requires someone who knows Unix like the back of their hand, and a bit of C programming to boot.

Once in place, you're still going to be dealing with relatively primitive controls. The long and short of it is that to do any real management, you're going to have to hand-edit configuration files. With a Unix wizard on staff, that's not a problem—she'll be able to make Apache sing. If you don't have one, though, you might as well get ready to pay for a Netscape server or a Netra or WebForce box.

# Internet Connection Server

IBM's own server, ICS, isn't as fast as Apache's; but then it's a lot better integrated with OS/2, so you'll save time in installing and administering the program. In my experience, ICS is a resilient server that can handle the workload of all but the largest intranets.

Another ICS plus is that it supports SSL. In fact, it has its own internal certification authority for creating unique SSL keys for users—if, that is, they're using Web Explorer. These certificates won't work with other SSL-compliant servers or browsers. While this does make ICS useful for secure intranet communications, it also makes the server less useful than it could be for dealing with the big, bad Internet just on the other side of the firewall. Still, ICS also supports S-HTTP and caching proxy services, so it's not as if the server lacks for security. It's just that it could have been so much better so easily. Hopefully, by the time you read this, ICS will have full SSL support.

To manage all its features, ICS uses HTML forms. This makes remote administration simple; but the administration tools, while perfectly functional, aren't as complete as they could be.

In terms of performance, ICS runs in the middle of the pack. That should be more than sufficient for most intranets. If you require high-speed performance, however, Apache for OS/2 is the better choice.

# Microsoft IIS

Microsoft's IIS is a fast server despite its slow launch. You see, Microsoft didn't really want to be on the Internet. Yes, I know Bill Gates and friends now talk almost as if they invented it; but the truth is that Microsoft is playing catch-up. With The Microsoft Network (MSN), the company was all set to offer a proprietary way for Microsoft product users to connect with each other and with Microsoft. Then, the Internet revolution happened, followed by the Web revolution; and Microsoft saw Netscape riding that wave towards domination of the Web. Suddenly, the Web wasn't small ripples anymore. Instead of hurrying a product to market or playing the hype card, Microsoft did something rare: They actually took their time in bringing out IIS. In short, this time, Microsoft did it right.

IIS has less frills than the NetWare Web Server (NWS). You don't get an HTML editor with it, but you do get versions of Microsoft's Web browser, Internet Explorer, for all four main Windows variations. You also get some old-fashioned Internet basics. For instance, IIS supports both ftp and gopher with their own servers.

At Microsoft's Web site, Microsoft's Internet Assistant for Word is free for the downloading; but that's one of those products that Microsoft didn't take the time to do a proper job on. As HTML editors go, it's a pretty awful one that delivers—the ultimate no-no in Web editors—incorrect HTML code; so it's probably just as well that IIS doesn't come bundled with the program.

IIS is not just for x86 compatible processors. The program will run on any platform supported by NT 4.0. This means that you can also put your DEC Alpha AXP, MIPS, or PowerPC NT servers to work as Web servers.

Installation is as easy, and as hard, as installing IIS. If you already have a working NT 4.0 server, you'll only be a few minutes at setting the server up. If you don't, that's another story.

Where IIS begins to veer away from NWS, and competitors like Netscape's Netsite Commerce Server, is in its integration with the operating system. The Internet Service Manager, for example, uses NT's own administration tools for both users and file access. This has two benefits. The first is that if you know how to run NT, you already know the basics of administering the server. The second is that because it is so tightly tied to the operating system, it should run faster than other NT Web servers.

One place where IIS outdoes NWS is in reporting. Besides pouring out its information in standard ASCII Common Log File format, you can set it to feed information to any Object DataBase Connect (ODBC) compliant database. What IIS can report on, though, is little more than what NWS can report on. For overall performance, IIS can call upon NT's own Performance Monitor to pull ahead of NWS. However, Netscape's Enterprise Server, with its log analysis tool, pulls ahead of both servers in this area.

IIS shines brightest, though, with its ODBC database integration. With the use of an ODBC compliant engine, like Microsoft's own SQL Server, webweavers can make truly complex, interactive intranet and Internet applications. Of course, they'll have to write these with PERL and use CGI for the basis of their interface; but with capacities like ODBC connectivity to draw upon, developers will have far more reason to pick up PERL.

Microsoft wants more than that level of interactivity. IIS is meant to integrate the Internet with the Microsoft Back Office. To that end, IIS includes the Internet Server Applications Programming Interface (ISAPI), a Microsoft API that relies on dynamic link libraries (DLL) for applications that should be speedy, have a small RAM footprint, and will eventually lead to developers being able to directly connect end-user applications like Excel to net resources. This potential would be realized by using both ISAPI and Microsoft's ActiveX.

ISAPI seems guaranteed to play a role in the Web's future. Despite all the hype, I'm nowhere near as sure that ActiveX will overcome Java's lead. Unless your firm is working on developing ActiveX applets, I wouldn't worry about whether my server can support ActiveX—not yet, anyway.

Of course, you can see where all this is leading us to. In this brave new world, Microsoft would be defining the rules for application interoperability over the Internet. And, as we've seen, he who makes the standards wins.

# Netscape

What can one say about Netscape that hasn't been said? For commercial use, their servers are everywhere. The reasons for that are as clear as glass: The Netscape servers are fast, reliable, the features leaders of all servers, and save for OS/2, available on every important operating system in creation.

Netscape makes several editions of their servers. Each of them shares in the others' virtues. The real difference between the servers is their scale. Netscape changes the names often enough that I won't waste your time by telling you which one is for what level of performance. The best way to find out is to look to the Netscape Server Central page, `http://home.mcom.com/comprod/server_central/index.html`, and check the current listings.

From an intranet administrator's point of view, another good thing about Netscape is that you have more options to choose from with Netscape SuiteSpot and Netscape Open Network Environment (ONE). SuiteSpot lets you put together a complete intranet package with Netscape Web server, a proxy server, mail server, news server, and catalog-a server that automatically sets up and maintains distributed search and indexing databases of existing ASCII files and HTML documents.

ONE, while Netscape has been proclaiming its wonders, is little more than a statement of what standards Netscape currently supports. The good news here is that Netscape, while still inclined to shift HTML standard details, is committed to supporting existing open standards.

Netscape doesn't support all standards, but it does support the most important ones. While Java may be Sun's product, Netscape's wholehearted embrace of it is what's making Java the language of choice for interactive Web documents. Other standards, like ActiveX and WebNFS, have yet to prove themselves. Right now, for a standard to really be a standard on the Web, it really must have Netscape's blessing. Yes, Netscape is that important.

Let's make this short but sweet. Netscape servers are faster than anyone else's, they have more features than anyone else's, and while not as stable on operating systems as others, generally speaking, the Netscape servers are bedrock-steady under even the most demanding loads. Need I add that if I were tasked with building your intranet tomorrow, Netscape products would be my first choice? I thought not.

# Netra & WebForce

Do you want a Web solution that you can just unpack, plug in, hook up to the network wire and go? Well, there are two product lines you should consider: Sun's Netra server family, **http://www.sun.com/products-n-solutions/ hw/servers/netra.html**, and Silicon Graphics' WebForce, **http://www.sgi.com/Products/Web FORCE/**.

Both packages are complete high-end Unix systems with outstanding server software. The Netra uses, surprise, Netscape software, but it includes one potentially game-winning trick of its own: WebNFS.

Besides Web server software, the Netra also comes with Solstice FireWall-First! server security software, LiveWire Web site management software, Netscape Navigator Gold authoring software, the Java development kit, servers for every intranet service you could ever want to serve, and a DNS. If there's such a thing as a plug-and-play intranet server, this is it.

While Unix-based, this isn't your grandma's Unix. Everything is controlled from an easy-to-use, colorful GUI. I wouldn't feel completely comfortable about running it without a Unix maven on site for backup; but you could run this package even if you don't know your c-shell from a hole in the ground.

WebForce from Silicon Graphics takes a similar but less comprehensive approach. Here, you don't get as many software goodies, but you do get your hands on a Silicon Graphics workstation. If you're running a lightly utilized Web server, that means that with this package, you also get a top-of-the-line graphics workstation. Normally, running a Web server and graphics-intensive applications on the same machine is a recipe for disaster; but if you crank up your RAM to 64MB or more, this combo can do it.

Given a choice between the two, I'd go for a Netra setup if an intranet was my first priority. Still, I have to admit, the WebForce machines are the Rolls Royces of the computing world. If my company needed even a little of a Silicon Graphics system's glorious graphics, I'd be strongly tempted to go for a WebForce.

Of course, for all this power and ease of use, you're going to pay a hefty price tag. You know what, though? If you don't already have the necessary hardware for a Web server in-house, I think it's worth the cost.

## NetWare Web Server

NWS is a complete Web publication kit. Besides the server, the package includes the WordPerfect Internet Publisher (an HTML editor that works with WordPerfect for Windows) and a single user license copy of Netscape Navigator. You can, of course, opt to have your web-weavers use other HTML editors. NWS isn't picky about what flavor of HTML it's asked to serve out.

To use NWS, in addition to NetWare 4.1, you'll need the latest NetWare TCP/IP NetWare Loadable Module (NLM) and Network Directory Services (NDS) up and configured. The server hardware itself requires only 2 MB of disk space.

NWS takes little time to install and configure. Novell claims that it will take 10 minutes and, if you're an experienced NetWare administrator installing it to a preexisting NetWare 4.1 server, they're right. If you're also installing the bundled two-user license copy of NetWare 4.1 to a new machine, set aside several hours for your jaunt into LAN management.

Next comes setting up security. Besides using NDS to provide basic access and login control, NWS comes with its own security tools. Using this program, you can set security based on IP addresses, user name, hostname, directory, document, users, or group for fine-tuned security.

The graphical user interface makes most administration tasks simple for the webmaster. The webweavers, on the other hand, will need to learn how to use the Remote-Common Gateway Interface (R-CGI), BASIC, and PERL to produce sophisticated Web applications. Then again, sophisticated is as sophisticated does, as Forrest Gump the Web administrator might say. The server doesn't support either SSL or S-HTTP.

You also can't create documents that draw information from databases or dynamic documents or images, a process known as server push. So, if you had dreams of using CGI scripts and forms to pull data from Btrieve databases, you can forget about them for now.

NWS also lacks reporting capacities. While it will generate CSA standard logs, it won't automatically log comments. Neither does NWS enable performance logs or CGI scripts to produce their own logs. If you want to keep close tabs on what's going on in your server, you're going to need to add third-party tools. In other words, NWS is a fine setup, but it needs a little help to get the job done.

# WebStar

StarNine's WebStar gives the Mac OS a reasonable server with the ease of use that Mac users demand. The program also excels at turning unwanted intruders away from your site without any special help.

As you would expect from a Mac product, WebStar is the easiest server of all to install and to administer. Were you stuck in a position of having to get a server up in a hurry without anyone around who really knew what they were doing—a horrible thought, that—WebStar is the only server that I think you'd have a shot in hell of getting up before your deadline. Now, mind you, you never want to get stuck in that position; but if you do, go out and buy the faster PowerPC with an Ethernet card and 32MB of RAM, add WebStar, and pray. With WebStar, you have at least a chance of your prayers being answered.

Annoyingly, you can't remotely administer WebStar worth a damn. There is a very, let me say that again, very basic remote management program. For anything but the simplest jobs, you're going to want to be right there with the machine.

In terms of performance, WebStar won't have anyone doing cartwheels of joy. It consistently trailed behind the others in my tests. At times, the server also threw fits at Open Transport which resulted in server crashes. StarNine is well aware of these problems; and by the time you read this, the server should be faster and more stable.

All that said, I'd rather have Netscape as my Macintosh server. WebStar, while easier to install, just hasn't caught up with Netscape in terms of speed and administration tools.

# Closing Connection

Which one is right for your enterprise? Well, if you don't already have a commitment to any one NOS, one of the Netscape servers is your best bet. They just work better and on more operating systems than any other two servers put together. If you have a heterogeneous intranet, that's no small matter.

When it comes to simply getting the files out in a hurry, Netscape just inches ahead of the field. The real difference, however, lies in features—and there Netscape is miles ahead of its competitors.

Other products do have their place. Sun's Netra WebNFS support may prove to be a winner in the long run. You can't beat Apache's price with a stick, and it's certainly a decent system. For OS/2 users, Netscape isn't an option; and Apache for OS/2 runs pretty darn fast in its own right. Offices that have bought into the integrated NT Server/Microsoft Office plan will want to stick with IIS.

Before charging out and buying any product, though, remember that you can try out all of these programs before writing a check. Exercise that option. A little time spent now finding just the right server for your company's needs will save you a lot of time down the road if you had to back up and try another server.

# 14

## Putting the Best Face on Your Intranet

## Looking Good, Being Good

Before I delve into the question of how to get the most out of your Web server, I thought I'd examine a far more important issue: what your Web server should be presenting to the world.

Remember the early days of desktop publishing, when anyone with a laser printer and a copy of Ventura Publisher or Aldus PageMaker could, and did, produce their own 'publishable' documents? I do. They were some of the most bug-ugly documents that have ever disgraced a perfectly good blank sheet of paper. There were documents that had half-a-dozen different fonts per page, books with illustrations sprinkled over their pages with a salt shaker: The horror! The horror!

The same is frequently true of the Web today. Anyone can publish; but few know how to do it well. All too many companies have home pages that distract rather than engage the viewer, pages that annoy instead of inform. Your business doesn't have to be one of them.

I can't guarantee you perfect pages with the information below, but I can assure you that your pages will at least be useful and engaging. Compared to the Web site wasteland out there, that's saying a lot.

## The Wrong and Right Ways

Some of you may want to avoid the Web in favor of using mass e-mail mailings and Usenet newsgroups for advertising. One word: **Don't.** Companies who indiscriminately use e-mail and the Usenet this way are universally flamed—that is, attacked in mail and newsgroups messages—by tens of thousands of Internet users. Do you want to come into the office and find your intranet server dead in the water as a result of being swamped by a couple of hundred thousand nastygrams? I didn't think so.

If you set up your Web site so that people can join internal newsgroups or add themselves to your company's mailing list, that's another matter entirely. Better yet, have your webmaster set up these functions so that if users add themselves to either of the above, they get some kind of freebie—it can be as trivial as a cool graphic to download—as a reward for letting you send them mail. This is a far more effective technique. Instead of advertising offensively to everyone in the universe, you'll be talking only to those users who've already shown an interest in your company.

If you decide to use an internal newsgroup, or some other way of conferencing online, put someone in charge of maintaining an online presence for your company in these areas. People are a lot more likely to hang out on your site and ask questions if there's a real live person on the site who's paying attention to their comments and opinions. Finding the right person for this job can be a problem, since gifted sysops—shorthand for system operators, from the days when sysops were people who ran their own Bulletin Board Systems (BBSs)—are rare. They're well worth finding, since building an online community guarantees you a group of customers who will feel that they have some small stake in your company. Building community is the bread and drink of any good sysop.

## Organization, Organization, Organization

Would you send a disorganized sales brochure or a press release? Of course not. For each of these, you'd make sure your information was presented in an organized, attractive format. The same should be true of your Web site.

Why is it that so many sites lack organization, then? Damned if I know; but I've seen way too many sites that resemble those voice mail mazes where you can never find a living person—or, in terms of the Web, real information. Your rule for site design should be that old favorite of engineers everywhere: Keep it simple, stupid (KISS). If your customers wanted to wander through a maze, they'd be off playing Doom.

The Web does enable you to link information from anywhere to anywhere; but you need to use that freedom to create rather than to confuse. For example, ye olde Sears and Roebuck mail-order catalog makes a decent model for a sales Web site. Instead of paper text and illustrations, it has digital text and illustrations. Unlike mere paper and ink, a Web version lets users find out more about a product than they could ever learn from an ordinary catalog. Furthermore, it enables customers to post orders instantly via e-mail or forms.

At the same time, you don't want to just streamline the exisiting paper models. For example, if you sell widgets, include a link to a widgets FAQ file on a public site. You're a law firm, not a widget manufacturer? Include home pages for the various attorneys. When potential clients can see your employees as people rather than gray-suited demons waiting to vacuum out their checkbooks, they're a lot more likely to approach your firm. For that matter, include links to the amusing as well. There are lots of sites with lawyer jokes on them, for example. It never hurts to show that your business is not always staid and sober. People like to interact with people, not corporate clones.

Other companies offer support services over the Web. If you have any kind of customer help desk, you'd be well advised to move part of it onto the Web. The Web lends itself to this, since users can easily find their way to the solutions for their problems thanks to the Web's hypermedia format.

Hard to visualize? Let's look at a concrete example. Instead of just sticking in an e-mail link to customer assistance, you can have image maps of, say, your exercise bike. By clicking on various points on the picture of the bike, users could find identification numbers, assembly instructions, description of the tools they need, and so on. Your customers will be happy; your help desk can spend more time on real problems instead of tedious beginner's questions; and your overall quality of service should improve. Not a bad deal.

Other businesses are using the Web as a publishing venture. Their magazines and newspapers may even exist only as electronic text and graphics. While this format may not appeal to all readers, it does offer a way for both old and new publications to easily gain a worldwide online presence without substantial capital investment.

You may not be a publisher, but you can still use publishing principles to keep customers visiting your site. A Web-based newsletter updating your customers on new products, giving them tricks and tips on using your products—all these ideas and more can be used to keep your customers entertained.

A complementary idea is to keep changing the look of your site—a little. By adding new information and a somewhat new look on a monthly basis, you can keep your customers coming back for more. At the same time, though, you don't want to change your site too drastically, or worse yet, alter its underlying structure. When someone comes back looking for technical support or for the pricing details on the Whiz-Bang 5000, you want to make sure that they can still find it. If they don't find it where they expect it to be, you can be certain that your customer's blood pressure will rise, and that your sales numbers won't.

No matter how your site's looks may metamorphose, keep KISS in mind and in practice.

# Sites for Sore Eyes

Simply having an organized Web site is no panacea. I spend a lot of my time looking at commercial Web sites, and there are some sites out there that will turn your stomach. At least those sites are memorable. All too many sites look like paint-by-numbers with next to zero content within them.

The most common mistake is pointless graphics. If you have a large graphic, or lots of small ones, they should be more than just decorative. Pretty is all well and good; but everyone who visits your site has to sacrifice precious time for beauty. If I have to spend ten seconds waiting for your graphics, I'm going to expect some utilitarian purpose behind them.

For example, I've seen sites where, when you click on a product for marketing information, all you get is a GIF of the product box. To obtain any more information, you need to click again. Even if it's not a very big GIF, it's a waste of time. When I want product information, I want product information, not a look at the cover art.

Second biggest foul-up: "No there there" pages. You can't always tell a bad site at first glance. I found many sites that were truly attractive, with seemingly useful image maps. But when I looked past the surface, I found them to be as hollow as a rotted-out apple: No information, no substance, no nothing.

If you have a commercial Web site, make sure you have hard information behind the pretty pictures. Your audience already knows that you think your product is great. Your Web site's job is to provide enough information for everyone to come to the same conclusion. If all you do is tell us—via press releases and the like—that you're wonderful, no one is going to care a hoot about your products. You have to show us what makes you so special.

Next in my foul-up list is what I call "Fan-Dances with Webs." This flaw combines poor organization with lack of substance. Too many companies make you dig around in their pages for the information you need, bouncing you from table to chart to tech letter; and as often as not, what you're looking for never shows up except as a reference to an obscure paper manual.

Many so-called commercial sites don't quote prices at all. I've had some site managers tell me that's because they don't want to go online with prices. Nonsense. People have been quoting prices in print ads for centuries. If you're selling Webside instead of curbside, do your customers the courtesy of providing them with the information they need to make their buying decision then and there. If they have to get in touch with your sales office to get the goods, you've lost the momentum you gained from putting your information online in the first place. Besides, unlike static paper ads, you can update online price guides any time.

Our final specimen: Sales shyness. Some Web sites provide the necessary information, but fall down when it comes to using the Web to make the sale. If you're on the Web to sell something, give us a real sales pitch—don't get coy. Also, real security standards are out there: Use them. If, for some reason, you really don't want to trust the Internet with credit card numbers, at least have a hot button that users can push so that someone in sales will call the customer back to get the credit card number after they've sent in their order via a Web-based form. This requires no extraordinary technical prowess, and demands a relatively small amount of work on the part of your sales force.

Keep this simple, too; the user expects and deserves ease of use. Avoid doing what I've seen one company do. In lieu of using forms, this PC and PC component vendor requires customers to copy an order form into the customer's editor so that they can then use e-mail to send the completed form back to the company. Guess what? That company went bankrupt a few months ago. Big surprise. Don't follow them into Chapter 11.

Even that's better than the approach that another similar firm uses at their Web site. At first glance, the site will convince you that you can order online from it. Each item has a lovely linked highlight that reads: "Click ORDER to order this item." Sounds straightforward enough, doesn't it? In fact, this link is only a tease. Instead of popping into an online order form, you're presented with a form that needs—I kid you not—to be printed out, filled out with ball-point pen, and then faxed to the vendor. Troops, there is a better way!

What these vendors, and many others, are missing is that the Web is not paper and does not depend on salesmanship as we previously understood it. Graphics exist not only to draw the eye, but to invoke interaction. Information can be made complete enough for the most demanding customer, and potential buyers can make their deals at their own pace and in their own time.

# HTML Coding for the Masses

Wouldn't it be nice if your Web pages looked and acted the same with all browsers? Dream on. With HTML, you can't do it.

If you want your readers to see exactly what you produce, you need to go beyond HTML to SGML or PDF. Of course, if you do, you restrict your audience to people with SGML and PDF viewers. While those are growing both in sheer numbers and in percentage of your total audience, for today, you'll still be cutting out at least half of your potential buyers. Those, lads and lassies, are not the kind of numbers you want to build your enterprise on. For now, HTML must for now be at the heart of your Web pages.

What's a company to do? The obvious answer is to avoid the temptations offered by Netscape and Internet Explorer extensions. Yes, Netscape's many HTML extensions are particularly appealing; but succumb to their siren song, and you ensure that at least 30% of your audience won't see your pages the way you intended. At worst, your hours of work will melt into multicolored hash.

Netscape's extensions are hardly the only offenders. Some combinations of HTML tags and images will give any browser fits. There are two things you can do that will let all browsers get the essential information from your page: Provide text-only versions of your pages, and use the <ALT> attribute which provides text in place of images. This simple tool will make the essential information on your pages accessible to users of even text-based browsers, such as Lynx.

What if serving text to one group and graphics to another isn't an option, and you must show all things to all viewers? Can it be done? To some extent, yes, if you stick to the HTML 2.0 format. To do this, head straight for WebTechs' HTML 2.0 source, `http://www.webtechs.com/sgml/html-2.0/DTD-HOME.html`. If you want to live dangerously with the unfinished HTML 3.0 standard, you can also read through that at WebTechs, `http://www.webtechs.com/sgml/html-3.0/DTD-HOME.html`. However, these solutions will be useful only for people who live and die by HTML code.

For most average-Joe page authors, a tool that can report whether pages are readable by the masses is much more useful than digging through HTML specs. The brute-force method of testing is to round up the dozen or so most common browsers and view your page through each one. It's slow, tedious, and thankless, but it's actually worth doing once just to understand how different browsers interpret even simple HTML code.

A quicker tactic is to use an HTML editor that includes a built-in HTML verifier. Sure, you can write HTML code with Windows' notepad or Unix's vi text editor, but neither of those can check up on your work.

Some Web authoring programs, like SoftQuad Inc.'s HoTMetaL, `http://www.sq.com/`, and Cerebral Systems Development Corp.'s Webber, `http://www.csdcorp.com/webber.htm`, include complete code checkers. Other products, like Sausage Software's HotDog Pro, `http://www.sausage.com/`, and Brooklyn North Software Works, Inc.'s HTMLAssistant Pro, `http://fox.nstn.ns.ca/~harawitz/index.html`, have some error checking, but rely primarily on an outside browser for on-the-spot, realtime sighting of HTML bugs.

Of course, if you really can't figure something out, you can turn to the Web itself for page-checking resources. One of the best of these is Harbinger Net Services' HTML Validation, **http://www.harbinger.net/html-val-svc/**. Harbinger gives you the choice of either checking pages by their URLs or by copying and pasting choice problem bits of HTML code.

The Harbinger system can measure your HTML code against five different standards. The aptly named "strict" method checks not only for true HTML errors, but for common HTML mistakes that most browsers will let you get away with. For instance, strictly speaking, anchor statements should contain only inline markup commands, like <IMG> for image. The standard header tags <H1 to H6> shouldn't be within a header statement. Puzzled? Let's look at an example:

> **<A HREF="vna.html"><H1>Vaughan-Nichols & Associates</H1></A>**

displays my company name in large bold letters with Netscape 1.22, which is the idea; but to adhere to strict HTML rules, the line should read:

> **<H1><A HREF="vna.html">Vaughan-Nichols & Associates</A></H1>**

If your goal is a Web site composed of squeaky clean HTML code, you'll need to be very precise. There's only way to do that throughout a corporation: Set up an internal standard for HTML coding and stick to it.

Harbinger can help. With it, you can check a document according to HTML 2.0 standards, as well as the nascent HTML 3.0. The system also will check pages for HotJava and Netscape extension errors. Don't be too confident about Netscape, though—the site's authors aren't overly thrilled by its enhancements. The Harbinger program gives you three levels of reporting. You can choose to see just the mistakes, just the output of your code, or—if you're a real glutton for punishment—the output of your code with the trouble reports annotated directly into it. If you have a Unix system at hand, you don't even need to HTTP your way out of your own network. The programs Harbinger uses in its testing are available at WebTechs' site, **http://www.webtechs.com/**, along with a host of other Web authoring information.

Another useful program for finding your mistakes before the whole world does is htmlchek, **http://arirang. snu.ac.kr/www-archive/tools/htmlchek**. This "awkward" little program works with HTML 2.0 or 3.0 pages. I call it awkward not because the program is difficult to use per se, but because in order to use it, you must have access to either PERL or Unix's awk text-processing utilities.

As you pull out your virtual dishrag to clean up your code, you might want to consider for a moment just how badly the current browsers fare at reading HTML. For an eye-opening look at just how well, and how poorly, browsers read your HTML code, visit the BrowserCaps site, **http://ichiban.objarts.com/bc/**. You'll find an array of tests to put your browser through, along with the scores of others who tested their browsers there.

Another way to speed-check your browser is to head over to Hal Berghel's HTML Client Compliance and WWW Test Pattern site, **http://www.acm.org/~hlb/publica-tions/test-pat/test_pat.html**. Berghel's pages run your browser through a battery of HTML tests to probe its limits.

Would it surprise you to know that Netscape Navigator scored very well? Or that America Online's in-house browser didn't? Why write consistent, compliant code then, since it's really a browser problem? Because it's your best chance of ensuring that the majority of users can read your pages.

# Onward!

In case you haven't guessed by now, having a good web-weaver isn't just a good idea, it's a necessity. Without some seriously top-of-the-line people, you can't expect to have a platinum Web site.

Of course, in order for these people to do their job, they need the right equipment and software. I've already talked about Web servers in specific, but now it's time to start putting it all together; and that's exactly what I'll be doing in the next chapters. Buckle in, folks—here's where things get complicated.

# 15

## Are You Being Served?

## Web Server Requirements

By now you have a good idea of what an intranet needs. One thing I haven't done is gone over the generic requirements of a Web server. So, without any more delays, let's look at what all servers require.

In theory, Web servers can be run on almost any hardware platform. Then again, a bicycle **could** transport everything in your office from New York to Los Angeles; but several semi-trailers would do the job a lot more effectively.

Below, you'll find my rule-of-thumb table on what kind of system you'll need for the level of service, based on number of simultaneous connections you expect to provide.

**Table 15.1: Speed Needs**

| User Numbers | Processor Speed | RAM |
|---|---|---|
| 1-20 | 33/66Mhz | 24MB |
| 21-50 | 75/120Mhz | 32MB |
| 51-100 | 133/200MHz | 64MB |
| 101+ | 200MHz+ | 128MB* |

*At this point, you should look to putting together a cluster of Web servers (which, for practical purposes, means you should be using Unix for your operating system), instead of expecting one machine to do the job.

These numbers will, of course, vary depending on how you're using your server. If you expect to use the server for something else along with supplying Web pages, ramp up to the next level of processor speed and RAM.

Some processors are inherently faster than others. A 200 MHz Digital Equipment Corporation Alpha running Unix or NT will run rings around an Intel 200MHz Pentium Plus. To make the right processor decision is by no means a simple task. Unless you have more time on your hands than I suspect you will in putting up an intranet, just go with the processor family that you're already using within your company. Given a free choice, my own preference would be Alphas, followed in order of preference by MIPS, PowerPC, NexGen, and Intel.

Multiple processors in a system, an option which is supported by NetWare, NT, and Unix, can make things easier. To get any benefit from this, you must have a version of the operating system that supports a particular multiple processor architecture. While this will help, don't expect it to be an instant pick-me-up for your server. To my knowledge, no Web server software currently supports multiple processors. The result will be that your file throughput will increase, but you won't see a substantial boost in overall server performance.

RAM, as always, is the more important consideration. Additional RAM will solve more of your performance problems than a processor upgrade any day of the week.

Fast hard disks are also always a good idea. On any serious server, I want drives that start with random access times in the nine millisecond range. Since I also want to make sure that the server will keep serving no matter what, I'm also going to go with a system that includes Level 5 Redundant Arrays of Inexpensive Disks (RAID). A RAID disk system uses some disk space to make sure that even if one disk goes completely awry, you won't lose a bit of data. Properly tuned, a RAID disk can also give you higher output speeds. The real reason to have a RAID is data security, not speed; but the boost can be a nice added bennie.

Beyond the server itself, you're going to want to have the server hooked up to an uninterruptable power supply (UPS). If you can afford it, you'll really want to get the server, router, and other essential networking equipment a generator of their own. If you succeed in putting up an intranet, the main servers are quickly going to become the heart of your business, and you dare not let it stop beating.

## Software Requirements

Web servers require operating systems that are first, robust, and second, fast. As I've mentioned earlier, that means you're pretty much stuck with Mac OS, NT, OS/2 Server, and Unix. If I haven't thoroughly disabused you of the notion of using Windows95, AmigaDOS, or other operating systems for your server, let me do so now. These other operating systems simply don't have the stamina to compete in the demanding multitasking world of Web servers.

The ability to take really horrid errors and keep on ticking is essential for both intranet operating systems and programs. In terms of stability, I've found Unix to be the best operating system. For server programs, I've found Netscape's top of the line servers to be exemplary, with Microsoft's Internet Information Server following closely behind.

For other popular intranet services, I've discovered that Digital's AltaVista Mail Server <http://altavista.software.digital.com/products/mail/nfintro.htm> to be an outstanding mail server. I'm still looking for a Usenet news service I can recommend without hesitation. As for excellence at a variety of tasks, Netscape's still the best.

## Connection Requirements

Speed, speed, and more speed. Have I made myself clear?

What I haven't told you yet, however, is how to integrate all three components—hardware, software, and network connection—into one complete system. First, your intranet is only going to be as fast as your slowest component. For example, a Netscape Commerce Server running on Unix on a 200 MHz Digital Alpha with 128 MB of RAM is still going to seem slow as a slug with only a 56 Kbps frame-relay connection.

For top performance, you must divvy up your resources among the three subsystems to get just the right blend. My preferred order of importance starts with internal network speeds. If you're using anything less than 10 Mbps NICs, such as token-ring 4 MB cards, dump them now. Better yet, move to 100 Mbps Fast Ethernet or VGAnyLAN. After that, I want RAM, RAM, RAM.

Next on my list is the fastest possible outside connection to the Internet. Again, this depends on how much Web-based business you're going to be dealing with. If I have the funds, I'll always err on the side of more performance rather than less. Intranet sites have a way of getting far more traffic than one ever expects.

Finally, I want a fast processor. Here, I'm not willing to spend more money than I absolutely need to spend. A processor can suck up an awful lot of money if you're not careful (or even if you are).

There's nothing magical about my formula of internal network speed, RAM, external network speed, and processor; but if you stick with it, you'll have a fast intranet. And isn't that the name of the game?

## Putting It All Together

How much time and effort is going to take you to put this all together? The answer, as usual, is: It depends. If you already have an internal TCP/IP network, you're about 80% of the way there. If you're still carrying disks from machine to machine, it's going to take you a lot longer.

In general, it will take you at least an entire quarter to have your intranet up and functional. During the first month, you'll be deciding on which ISP to go with, how much to spend on hardware, and the like. After that, you'll need to order your lines and Internet service. Start getting ready to wait—it's going to be a long process. For even an ordinary T1 or Bonded ISDN line, you're looking at at least two months between ordering the line and finally getting the line— and the Internet facilities on the other side of them— in sync with your internal network.

While you're waiting, you shouldn't be nibbling on your nails and sending "hurry up!" notes to the ISP. It won't work. Besides, you've better things to do with your time. Such as? For starters, you may need to upgrade your entire network with new NICs. If that's not in your plans, move on to switching everyone to TCP/IP, starting with your intranet server. Just because you won't have a working Internet connection for months doesn't mean you can't get everything ready by creating your internal intranet in the meantime.

This can be done in several ways. My choice would be to bring up the intranet servers and then, starting with a small, select group of alpha users, bring them up on the new server and see what blows up. If you've been in the networking business for a while, you know what I mean.

Something always goes to hell. Once you've gotten past that point, you can start bringing other users on board.

Don't make the tempting mistake of trying to bring everyone up at the same time. It's an adventure, it's heroic, and it's also stupid. If I had a dollar for every time I've seen a "tiger team" attempt and fail to shift an entire enterprise's network over a weekend, I wouldn't need to write for a living.

While you're doing all this, you'll want to keep your old network and its servers running. Everyone hates that part, but it's the only safe thing to do. Network administrators who try to throw a switch and go directly from one network operating system to another have a common name—unemployed.

During this phase, you can test out all the servers and clients to your heart's content. At the same time, be certain to listen to the opinions of users and management. If your webmaster loves one program and everyone else hates it, you're going to have to drop that program. The intranet is here for the users, not for its administrators.

That doesn't mean that you have to stay stuck in the mud with older software or older ways of doing business because the employees prefer it that way. Bringing up an intranet means change, and some people will always hate change. You can't let these hidebound conservatives dictate the company's direction. Change and adaptability is the name of the winning business game. What you can do is try to make that change as smooth as possible.

By the time your Internet connection is finally up, everyone should have been shifted over to the final selection of intranet tools and be ready to go. You may not be ready yet, though. That's because aside from the hardware and all that jazz, you need information on that good old Web server to make your company more productive internally and more attractive externally. For that, during this same period, you'll need your webweavers to be creating successful Web pages. As it just so happens, that's the subject of the upcoming chapters.

# 16

## What's What on Web Servers

### The Care and Feeding of Servers

So the hardware lights are all blinking properly; everyone can find the intranet server's hard drive; and when you ping your domain's gateway from both within and without your intranet, the program answers properly. Now what?

Well, hopefully, by this time your administration and webweavers have gotten together and agreed on what should be presented on your server. This is no small matter. Too many corporate Web sites begin as informal efforts that grow and grow until a vice president or the like notices that, for potentially millions of outsiders and within the company itself, the company's image is being set by a brave but isolated crew of Internet power users. This often leads to a short, nasty turf battle, which results in the Internet supporters leaving, and management being stuck with a big black box of mysterious Web information.

Let's try to avoid this scenario, shall we? From management's point of view, if the people who put up the site did it right, you'll want to keep them. Replacing them will not be cheap. As for Web folks, remember that management may not always be right; but unless you prefer the unemployment line, try diplomacy first. You may well end up being able to run the Web site your way in the end, anyway.

After you've put this conflict behind you—ideally, with a peaceful solution—you need to figure out how you want to organize your site, what you want your site to say, and how it's going to say it. Organization is vital at this point. Anyone can create a Web site with just an HTML editor and a Web server. Putting together one that works requires knowing exactly what it is that you're trying to accomplish and what tools will enable you to achieve those goals.

## HTML & Beyond

The first of those tools is HTML. I'm not going to get down and dirty with HTML just now; I do some of that in the later chapters. Instead, we're just going to discuss the basics of how to produce attractive Web pages.

The best way to start this process is to study the information in sites that tell you, not how to use HTML, but what's what in a good-looking, hard-working Web page. The best of these are listed in Table 16.1.

## Table 16.1: Stylish Server Pages

Name
URL

Guide to Web Style
`http://www.sun.com/styleguide/`

Yale Web Style Manual
`http://info.med.yale.edu/caim/StyleManual_Top.HTML`

Netscape 3.0 Layout & Design
`http://home.netscape.com/comprod/products/navigator/version_3.0/layout/index.html`

Style Guide for Online Hypertext
`http://www.w3.org/pub/WWW/Provider/Style/`

Bandwidth Conservation Society
`http://www.infohiway.com/faster/`

Read these pages, then take the best of their ideas and make them your own. If lack of speed is a concern, the Bandwidth Conservation Society's pages are invaluable. For users who have decided to go with Netscape, Netscape's own design and layout page is a must for your hot list.

The most important information you'll find in these pages are the elements of good page design. Your site may be as ugly as a squashed skunk on the highway; but if it's well organized, it will still get some traffic from shrewd users.

You should also plan your site so that even users with bottom-line browsers, like the character-based browsers, can get some good from it. All too often, webweavers are so bedazzled by special effects that they forget to include simple alternative text links. When you make this mistake, you're cutting out a portion of your audience; and it isn't just the lower-echelon users, either. Remember that some users go with text-based browsers by choice. An ASCII browser is, after all, much faster than a browser that require you to sit and wait for graphics.

# Multimedia

Some use of images is a good thing. They'll brighten up your site and make it more appealing. To keep your use of graphics within reason, try to make sure that each image is useful as well as decorative. Your users will appreciate it.

For all practical purposes, you should only use GIF and JPEG images. While other image formats like PNG have been promoted for the Web, none of them have really gotten anywhere.

For the sake of speed, you'll also want to restrict your images to 256 colors or less. High-Color and True-Color graphic cards are still rare enough that you don't need to support graphics with more colors. Of course, if your site is all about great-looking presentations or the like, you'll want the high color resolutions. Just remember that the more colors you use, the bigger your images get, which in turn means the slower they'll go.

You may be tempted to snatch your graphics from anywhere you like around the Internet. Don't. Just because the net makes it easy to pick up and grab graphics it doesn't give you the right to use them on your Web site. There are many public domain icons and graphics out there—just make darn sure that these pretty pictures really are free and clear before you grab them. Otherwise, you may find yourself on the receiving end of an ugly lawsuit.

For creating your own graphics, there are several good programs to choose from. My own pick of the lot are in the following table. The first two programs are image processing tools which are best used for touching up scanned-in photographs. The others are drawing/painting programs.

**Table 16.2: Graphics Programs**

| Title<br>URL | Company | Operating System |
| --- | --- | --- |
| Picture Publisher<br>`http://www.micrografx.com/products/abcgs/abcgs-picpub.html` | Micrografx | Mac OS/Windows |
| Photoshop<br>`http://www.adobe.com/` | Adobe | Mac OS/Windows |
| CorelDRAW!<br>`http://www.corel.com/products/graphics&publishing/index.htm` | Corel | Mac OS/Unix/Windows |
| Freehand<br>`http://www.macromedia.com` | Macromedia | Mac OS |

Besides graphics, you can provide multimedia, audio, and/or video over the Internet. These technologies work better on an intranet than they do on the net at large. That's because on an intranet you're going to be looking at a minimum speed of 10 Mbps, while on the Internet, your customers may very well be viewing or listening to your spiel at the godawful rate of 14.4 Kbps.

There are three basic types of Web-based multimedia: animation, interactive, and streaming. For me, only streaming is mature, flexible, and powerful enough to be worth your consideration.

Animations can be done with any number of programs, including any advanced Web server if you know how to make CGI jump up and do tricks. They only have one problem, whether there's CGI or Java behind them: They're boring. There your viewers are, stuck with a few seconds of an endlessly looping splash display. It may look great in a demo; but on a Web site, it's dull as beans.

Interactive multimedia is still in the experimental stage. One day, and it won't be long, interactive multimedia will be big business on the net. Think about it: online, real-time action games. Need I say more? Some games, like id Software's Doom, already can do this in a limited fashion; but if anyone ever masters a universal solution for this kind of game, or any other sort of interactive video/audio environment, not only will a whole new industry spring up around the recreational possibilities, marketing will also undergo a sea-change.

But enough dreaming. Today, the only real, workable answers are streaming audio and video. The good news is that such answers exist; the bad news is that they're all incompatible with one another.

Before I go any deeper into this, yes, I know I've just slighted dozens of technologies that enable you to add sound and video clips to documents. I've done so deliberately. Those are all limited technologies that don't have the scope or possibilities of streaming technology. It may be nice to attach an AVI movie to a document, which Microsoft HTML extensions enables you to do, but it's also a dead-end. In this book, I'm trying to provide you with more long-term solutions.

The one exception to this is Apple's strongly-entrenched QuickTime, **http://www.quicktime.apple.com/>**, video format. QuickTime shows every sign of hanging on at least until the turn of the 21st century. Who knows; by then, Apple probably will have turned it into a streaming technology as well.

While even with these caveats, there are a host of audio and video formats to choose from, for practical purposes there are only a handful. These are:

### Table 16.3: Practical Multimedia on the Web

| Title<br>Type | Company<br>URL | Operating System |
|---|---|---|
| RealAudio Server<br>Audio | RealAudio<br>**http://www.realaudio.com/**<br>**products/server.html** | Mac OS/NT/Unix |
| Shockwave<br>Video/Audio | Macromedia<br>**http://www.macromedia.com/shock**<br>**wave/devtools.html** | Mac OS/Windows |
| StreamWorks Server<br>Video/Audio | Xing<br>**http://www.streamworks.com/**<br>**products/products.html** | NT/Unix |

| VDOLive | VDOnet | NT/Unix |
| Video/Audio | http://www.vdo.net/sales/ | |

So what do you need in order to add streaming audio or video to your site? It varies wildly, based on what you want to do. These services come at a cost. Except for Shockwave, which uses MIME to send its data, you'll need to get specialized server software, and that isn't cheap. You'll also need powerful servers and a minimum of a T1 connection to make your presentations presentable.

Another problem is that you must have at least decent audio and video equipment on site to produce anything that anyone wants to see or hear. Again, this is not cheap.

Is it worth it? If you want a Web site that will have people flocking to it like bees to honey, then yes, it is. Television is more popular than radio and radio is more popular than newspapers. It's really that simple: Add sound and motion and you attract more people's interest.

The trap, of course, with the Web versions of TV and radio is that your speed will be so pathetic that no one will stick around to see the show. Streaming technologies get around much of this, since these products store up information on the receiving end before playing it; but it's still a problem. For now, the solution is to have the biggest possible bandwidth on your server side and keep your video shows short and sweet. Audio has been perfected to the point that, while you sure wouldn't want to listen to music on it, you can do quite well with spoken news reports, product descriptions, and the like.

# Plain Old Text

Okay, so maybe it's about as exciting as reading yesterday's newspaper; but you can just drop ordinary text into a basic HTML format so that anyone with a Web browser can read it. Some programs will claim that they can painlessly turn your most sophisticated documents into Web documents. The hell they can. The most they can do is turn them into the HTML equivalent of plain ASCII text: Dull, dull, dull. But, it does beat not being able to give people the information they want when they want it.

Easily the most powerful program I've found to date for translating files from almost all popular word processing programs—and some that were never popular to begin with—is Adobe's Word for Word. It's not going to give you links; but it does make it possible to transfer old WordStar files into your choice of HTML 1.0, 2.0, or 3.0, including the Netscape-enhanced versions of each. There's nothing sorcerous about it, but it is impressive.

If you'll be working from paper documents, your first need is for a scanner. I've had good luck with the high-end, flatbed models from both Epson and Hewlett-Packard. For an additional cost, you can also get automatic paper feeders if you're working with loose pages. Whatever you do, don't get a hand scanner. Your company will thank you, because flatbed scanners are much faster, hence the price justifies itself in a hurry. Your graphics people will thank you, because your images won't wobble. Your hand will thank you, because scanning things properly manually means subjecting your hand and wrist to a lot of pain.

Of course, since a scanned page is just a big tagged image file format (TIFF) graphic, it's next to worthless for the

Web. You'll need optical character reading (OCR) software to turn page images into useful pages. The best tool for this, in my years of testing out OCR programs, has always been Xerox's TextBridge, `http://www.xerox.com/products/tbpro/`, family.

## Summing Up

With all this information on hand, you should have a good idea as to what you want to do with your Web site. Later on, I'll go into more detail on how to use HTML, still the premier language of the Web. When I get there, I'm not going to give you everything you need to become a master webweaver; for that you'll need other books, or, better still, access to some truly wonderful Web resources out there for aspiring Web authors.

Before I get there, though, we're going to take a longer look at how to make sure the information on your servers stays there. After all, you don't want your password, or (shudder) a customer's credit card number out wandering the Web all by itself, do you?

# 17

## Intranet Technical Management

## Intranet Nuts and Bolts

An intranet is not your plain old vanilla LAN. It incorporates features and problems unique unto itself. Some of these are Web-site specific; those I'll get to later in this chapter. Before I get that far, let's take a look at what the differences are between an intranet and a traditional LAN.

The biggest difference is that an intranet is always connected to a larger network—in this case, the Internet. A LAN might be connected to a Wide Area Network (WAN), but even if it is, its administrators don't really need to worry that much about what's going on in the wider network around them. That, my friend, is never an assumption you can make with an intranet. The entire online world is literally just outside your gateway, and there are things out there that you really, really don't want coming in. Thus even more so than on a LAN, security is a major intranet issue.

There are many programs out there that will help you manage your network. My particular favorites are Intel's LANDesk series, `http://www.intel.com/comm-net/sns/showcase/netmanag/index.htm`, and Symantec's Norton Administrator `http://www.syman-tec.com/lit/index_networkplatform.html`. None of these, however, are going to do much for keeping a firm hand on your intranet.

While there are tools that will help with Web administration and tracking Web usage, there aren't many that will help with the intranet as a whole. I'd love to be able to tell you that there's good software out there for figuring the who, what, when, where, how, and why of who's trying to crack your firewall; but I'd be lying if I did. There are ways to get all that information; but contrary to the movies, there's no cute program that will make this job anything more than a tedious examination of half a dozen different log records.

Normally, the way you'll find that someone has broken into your intranet is by seeing what they've screwed up inside your intranet—after the damage has been done. That's one reason that having strong intranet security is so important in the first place. If you can't stop them at the walls of your network, it's a hopeless job trying to pry them out once they're in. Your only choice will be to bring down the network and bring it up from the start, using backup tapes and the like, followed by immediately resetting your LAN's security parameters.

# Intranet Management

So what does an intranet administration program need? That's a good question; and I've asked it of Internet and intranet administrators at Digital Express, **http://www.digex.com**, a small national ISP; PSI, **http://www.psi.com**, and the Discovery Channel **http://www.discovery.com**.

First, such a program should integrate with existing network administration programs. Every administrator I spoke with agreed that they didn't want to learn yet another brand-new software package just to handle intranet specifics.

This program, or programs, should also run on a variety of platforms. No one wants to switch their network operating system simply because the intranet element runs only on a single operating system and it's not the system they're running. One way of blunting this problem is to use a package that relies upon open standards like Simple Network Management Protocol (SNMP). Netscape, for one, has seen the future, and plans on making all their servers SNMP compliant. Now, if only the SNMP programs were only ready to deal with intranet specific problems.

Another feature that any decent intranet management product should have is the ability to work with a wide arrange of routers, bridges, and firewalls. Centralized administration is the goal of intranet management. In short, an intranet must embrace interoperability.

# The Intranet Difference

But what specifically are the things that separate an intranet administration program from a LAN or Internet management package? According to my people, there are several important issues; but the main one is security.

Most network administration products concentrate on such important but everyday issues as tracking server load and distributing software. Some of these programs also have ways of tracking attempts to break into the network. Intranet administrators need the latter information too, but they need to know more. In particular, people want better ways of getting information from firewalls.

# Security

Most network administrators want more information from firewalls than the current generation of programs allow. Ideally, these people want firewalls that don't simply sit there and bar the way; they want active firewalls that can do reverse domain lookups and pursue an aggressive intruder back to their lair. This kind of "gray ice" is still more science fiction than reality.

In the meantime, many administrators don't want to rely too much on firewalls except for barring the way between Internet and intranet. Within the intranet itself, they want programs that can keep employees out of some areas while allowing access to others. This is, of course, a very old network problem. The problem is that using firewalls for this purpose is akin to using a flamethrower to light up the Yule log.

Instead, what intranet administrators want to see is a combination of traditional user access rights and passwords, and secure protocols like Netscape's Secure Socket Layers (SSL). And, of course, they want the tools to keep track of who's scratching away at doors that they shouldn't be anywhere near.

Another side of this is that intranet administrators need a way to make sure that someone within the network isn't using their PC as a sniffer to pull down passwords, and other material usually sent in cleartext, that then enables moles within a company to dig their way into sensitive information. This one is really hard to track down, because employees already have physical access to a given intranet segment.

The only ways to stop this one are to do periodic software auditing of all PCs, or to wait for someone to make a mistake. Again, security tools well beyond an ordinary network administration program are called for. In the latter situation, you want a program that will alert you to the fact that the company's CEO is roaming through the personnel files or such two hours after he logged off for the day. This kind of information is almost always in the logs somewhere; but unless you're Cliff Stoll, the astronomer turned famous Internet security guru, you're a lot more likely to find problems if you have a watchdog agent eyeing the logs for you.

# Workflow Administration

Another element that intranet managers will need to deal with on a regular basis is tracking workflow applications. For now, the intranet excels at static document transfer. By the time you read this, intranets will also be moving onto dynamic, DBMS-based document transfer as a mainstay. Lurking just around the corner from this is workflow software; but here, there are barely the beginnings of proper administration tools.

At this time, there are four workflow programs that will work adequately on an intranet. These are: ActionWorkflow's, **http://www.actiontech.com**, Metro; Netscape's, **http://www.collabra.com/products/**, Collabra; Open Text's, **www.opentext.com**, Livelink, and Ultimus', **http://www.ultimus1.com/index.htm**, WebFlow.

What's an administrator to do? Well, right now, the answer is: Not much. One of the products, Action Workflow, comes with tools that make it individually easy to administer from a network level. Alas, it doesn't work with SNMP, so you have to deal with the native interface. Others, like Collabra, should work well in a well-managed intranet; but at this time we're still months away from seeing an intranet version of the program.

With these products, the name of the game is going to be trying to manage a truly distributed system. By their very nature, that means information, servers, and clients will be scattered helter-skelter across your intranet. How are you going to manage them? That's a good question, and right now there are no good answers.

# Directory Services

Another frequently mentioned administration problem is directory services over an intranet. DNS serves well, although it's being overwhelmed by the sheer number of IP addresses; but LAN administrators coming to the intranet want more than just an addressing system. Novell network administrators in particular want directory services like those provided by Novell's NetWare 4.x's Network Directory Services (NDS).

In NDS, administrators work with a distributed, X.500-style directory system that tracks all users, servers, and resources, no matter where they are on the intranet. This provides centralized management of the network's entire resource and user base.

With NDS, everything is treated as an object. A user object contains everything from a user's name to their physical and IP addresses to their login scripts. While in some ways, NDS is similar to Sun's NFS Yellow Pages services and Apple's Name Binding Protocol, it goes far beyond either one.

Faced with the complexities of an intranet, you can see why someone accustomed to having vast information resources at their beck and call would want them even more in an intranet. Fortunately, they're about to get them in the first generation of true intranet administration tools.

The most noteworthy of these programs will come, as no surprise, from Netscape. Netscape is working on a Netscape Directory Service (ironically, also abbreviated NDS), based on the Lightweight Directory Access Protocol (LDAP) which incorporates aspects of RFC 1777. This NDS will provide an intranet global directory services for single-point network management. This server, like other SuiteSpot servers, will enable network administrator to manage the NDS using frame-compliant browsers.

Eventually, this system will evolve into tomorrow's integrated SuiteSpot. For now, this plan is little more than ideas, code-named Orion; but if there's one thing Netscape has shown during its short life, it's that it can transform ideas into products in a hurry (well, beta products, anyway).

Netscape's NDS will also provide standard replication and access methods for the database. If you're beginning to think that except for LDAP, this sounds a lot like NetWare's NDS, you're right. While the internals are quite different, both are based on the X.500 model; and an intranet manager will be able to get almost anything from NetWare's server that a NetWare 4.x administrator can get from Novell's NDS. With broad-based industry appeal—AT&T, Banyan, Novell, and Sun have all thrown in their support for at least LDAP—it seems likely that NetWare's NDS will be the basis of many intranet management programs of the future.

Need I add that Microsoft has its own plans? I didn't think so. Microsoft is working on an add-on for NT 4.0, the NT Directory Server (NTDS), that should provide an answer to NetWare's NDS. As is so often the case with Microsoft, plans are very fuzzy at the moment as to exactly what NTDS will be giving administrators.

## Administration Headaches

I remember reading an article by some less than with-it industry pundit that intranets would win the world because they were so much cheaper to run than networks. In some ways, he was right. But then he said they would also be inexpensive, because administration would be so much easier. I laughed until I cried.

Intranets, because they are so free-form, will take up a good deal more of your network administrators' time. Oh, some things will go easier. Installing a Web browser across your LAN is a whole lot easier than installing any other interactive, multimedia front-end that has ever existed. Similarly, switching everyone to a Post Office Protocol (POP) and Simple Mail Transfer Protocol (SMTP) mail client is a lot easier than working with the even the best of proprietary LAN mail programs like Lotus' cc:Mail.

That said, you're still stuck with the problem of managing nigh unheard-of amounts of information. With today's Web authoring tools, almost anything on your LAN can and will be made accessible. Trying to control that access is almost impossible. Throw in workflow programs and the current lack of any universal directory service, and let's face it: Intranet managers are hosed.

Right now everyone is still so enchanted by the glamor of the intranet that they're not seeing the administration problems underlying it. Unfortunately, that charm is going to wear off, which will leave administrators trying to explain to everyone why Sue's love letter was published on an accounts payable Web page; and by the way, what was accounts payable doing with a Web page in the first place?

This would be ugly enough even with proper administration tools. Without them...well, the best you can do is to create and enforce security and standard basics as best you can—through proclamation, leadership, and prayer. There's a rocky road ahead for intranet administrators. Let's make sure that neither you nor your company gets thrown off the road while waiting for tools that will make intranets truly manageable.

# Web Administration Tools

Intranet Web site management is one area where there are real tools available for today's webmasters. These tools are divided into two types. One is simply a Web site grooming tool. Programs of this sort go through looking through your Web site looking for broken links, list out all links, do global search-and-replaces, and check out overall site integrity. The other type of tool is much more active. These programs try to enable you to edit and manage the entire site from a single front-end.

# Keeping Your Site Tidy

Some cleanup programs are very narrow in focus. For example, Tetranet Software's Linkbot's, **http://www. tetranetsoftware.com/,** main job in life is to test out all the links in your Web site. Linkbot can also find such common mistakes as images without <ALT> tags label for people who aren't using graphical browsers.

A broader program with the same agenda is InContext's, **http://www.incontext.com,** WebAnalyzer, which creates a colorful map of your site's files and links. It also generates complete HTML reports on your files and incoming and outgoing links. WebAnalyzer's Achilles' heel is that while it can tell you about problems, it's up to you and your HTML editor to fix them.

MKS, `http://www.mks.com/`, offers a program called Source Integrity that allows you to maintain version control over your Web items. That may not sound like much; but having the ability to tell the difference between the latest version, an old version of the same page, and the version that's currently is on your site is absolutely invaluable.

Another useful program for making sure that out of date information gets tossed is Bungalow's Systems' Xpire Plus, `www.iquest.net/^lindell/bungalow/xpire.plus.html`. While Xpire can find outdated files in your program, you have to manually replace the offending files yourself.

This dichotomy between programs that report on problems and programs that both report and repair is one of the principal differences between the minor and major leagues of Web site management software. Don't turn up your nose at these more specialized tools. In the right situation, they can be more useful than the do-it-all programs.

# Heavy Duty Web Site Management

You probably haven't heard of it, but one of the most useful programs I've found for maintaining a Web site is GrayScale's `http://www.morning.asn.au/siteman/`, SiteMan. SiteMan does an excellent job of finding broken links, orphan files, and the like. Unlike the other programs I've already looked at, it then immediately enables you to fix the problems without having to head out to another utility.

Other programs, like Microsoft's FrontPage, offer you an all-encompassing solution, with everything from a Web server to a site manager and all the software in between.

Before you get too thrilled by the idea of an all-in-one answer for all your Web problems, you should know that FrontPage is slower than the post office on a snowy day, and that it hides everything from CGI to HTML from you. That's a charming idea, for some people. I think we're still a long way from the point where we can trust any single program with all the nitty-gritty details of running a Web page.

Another such program, and a superior one to my way of thinking, is Adobe's **http://www.adobe.com** SiteMill. This program works with Adobe's PageMill Web authoring package. This Macintosh product combines Web browsing with a global find and replace service that lets you drag and drop links from one document to another.

There are many other programs of this sort; and they come, go, and emerge in new versions faster than you can read this book. The best source for keeping track of what's what in the world of Web management is at the Site Development and Management pages of ServerWatch, **http://serverwatch.iworld.com/**, an online publication by Mecklermedia.

The key to all these programs is that you're looking for a program that will make your webmaster's life easier. If you find one that doesn't pass this test, pass that program by and look for another one. Another thing to keep in mind is that for a large site, you must have at least the equivalent of InContext's WebAnalyzer. Without tools that can show you what's what in your site, your Web presence will very quickly start to fall apart. A major Web site is too big a job for anyone to handle alone.

# Guest Book: Web Visitor Logging

Everyone knows how to record hits to their site. There's at least five different free or cheap counter programs (see table 17.1) for this purpose. What some people still don't realize is that merely counting raw hits to your site is next to meaningless. Quite frankly, hit counts alone are actually just fodder for drawing misleading conclusions about your site.

### Table 17.1: Counters Alone

| Title | Operating Systems |
| --- | --- |
| URL | |
| WWW Homepage Access<br>`http://warm.semcor.com/~muquit/Count.html` | NT, OS/2, & Unix |
| Counter for Win'95/NT<br>`http://geocities.com/SiliconValley/6742/` | 95 & NT |
| K Counter for the Mac<br>`http://diakonos.hum.utah.edu/kcounter` | Mac OS |
| Silicon Graphics WWW Counter<br>`http://www.sgi.com/counter.html` | IRIX |

Sure, they're cheap and amusing; but only use them on your home page. If you're using them on your corporate Web site, get rid of them, now.

So what do you really need? You need a program that collects all the information it can get from every visitor to your site. Once that information is in hand, the software must organize the information that's both immediately useful to both the Web administrator and to your company.

Statistics for one or the other is fine, but you really need both. For example, a Web administrator wants to know when the site is most active. Your marketing manager, on the other hand, wants to know who's spending the most time on a given page.

Delivering just statistics, however, isn't enough for a golden-gloves hit champion. Raw data isn't tasty at all. The information needs to be cooked by a proper analysis tool before its useful. A second-rank hit analysis tool will give you its own internal report and graph generator; but your company is already using a host of other database and report programs. Who wants to learn how to use another report software package, when your company has already standardized on Informix for its DBMS and Crystal Reports for reporting?

A first-rate Web traffic analysis program should be able to deliver reports to you, but it must deliver its data in a form that your other programs can use. The top programs will give you a way of setting up automated data massaging to get the data primped up for analysis, and then use open database connect (ODBC) or another realtime data transaction protocol to deliver the data transparently to your company's DBMS and report programs. Short of that, the program should be able to export its data to such popular DBMSs as dBase, FoxPro's DBF, Lotus' venerable wks, and non-proprietary formats like DIF.

Beyond that, you also want a program that will work with your existing log files. If you're like most of us, you want workable information now, and not in a month when you'll have a representative dataset to work with. In practice, you want a program that will work with both the Common Log Format (CLF) and Extended CLF (ECLF). That should take care of most modern Web servers.

You'll also need a program that won't choke at enormous log files. Lots of us have let our log files grow to jumbo proportions. A good program will at least let you access the entire log. A great one will let you extract only the sections of the logs that you want to examine. You'll also want software that's fully TCP/IP compatible to avoid operating system clashes.

Are there such paragons of Web counting virtue out there? Nope. Oh, with a crack team of C and PERL programmers, you could put together a home-brew that would do it all; but few of us can brag such astounding resources. Instead, let's take a look at what products are available.

## Table 17.2: Web Site Tracking Software

| Company URL | Product | Operating System |
|---|---|---|
| EG Software **http://www.egSoftware.com/** | WebTrends | Windows |
| Everywhere **http://www.everyware.com/Bolero/** | Bolero | Mac OS |
| Interse Corp. **http://www.interse.com/ourproducts/** | Market Focus | Windows |
| Marketwave **http://www.marketwave.com/** | Hit List Pro | Win95 |

net.Genesis            net.Analysis   Solaris & NT
`http://www.netgen.com/products/net.Analysis/1.0/`

net.Genesis            Desktop        Win95 & NT
`http://www.netgen.com/products/net.Analysis/1.1/`
`Desktop/`

Open Market            Web Reporter Unix
`http://www.openmarket.com/reporter/`

# Winners, Losers

At the end of the season, there's no clear-cut winner. The second-generation products listed above are better than the first generation, like the freeware VBStats; but there are no silver bats or classic hits yet. Those will only come as Web tools continue to evolve.

Perhaps the best thing I can say about this current collection is that all of them show at least some promise. With the ever-growing push for better products, some of these programs may actually have fulfilled that promise by the time you read this. Certainly, if you're in the market for a Web counter that really counts, these are the programs you should try first. Even if they haven't matured by the time you read this, give them time. By this time next year, I have no doubt that one of these products will have evolved into the real batting champion of Web hit programs.

# The Whole Shebang

There is no way of integrating it all. None. Zilch. In a few years, there will be. Today, though, an intranet administrator will need to carefully pick out and choose the tools she needs to manage her intranet.

This is not an easy time for intranet administrators. Between management's push for an intranet—right now!—and the lack of a complete set of tools, an administrator is going to spend a lot of time duct taping together solutions from several programs. You can do your best to make sure that it will all fit with your existing administration software; but you're still going to end up with some odds and ends that just don't fit into the pattern, but need to be there anyway to make the intranet work properly.

The job can be done. It's just not going to be easy. The only healthy way of looking at the intranet administration problem is to see it as a challenge. If you look at all the problems as a whole, you're likely to be overwhelmed. But if you take it one step at a time, and always keep security uppermost in your mind, chances are you're going to end up with a first-rate site despite everything. Still, I can't blame you if, like me, you want to shout: "I want integrated intranet administration tools and I want them now!" Since it is the net we're talking about, after all, odds are good that someone is going to hear us and deliver the goods before our hair turns completely white.

# 18

## Web Language Wars

## Writing and Winning the Web

Writing pages for the World Wide Web used to be relatively easy. The editing tools might have been primitive, but you were always using HTML. Although new editing tools have made writing Web documents easier than ever before, there are now several variants of HTML and a variety of document formats are being used in Web pages. For Web readers, this means the WWW is changing from a friendly place in which any Web browser can access virtually any document to a hostile world in which not all browsers work with all Web documents.

This has always been something of a problem for Web browsers-that's why there are viewers for different file formats. But in the future, the problem will only get worse. Pure HTML is no longer the only language of the land. Every day, more and more file formats are being used to carry the basic textual information of the Web. Let's take a look at the current main players in the Web language wars.

Now, I'm not going to tell you how to write HTML. That's a subject for a different book. Two titles I can recommend that do cover this area are: *Multimedia And Hypertext* by Nielsen (ISBN: 0-12-518408-5) and Bryan Pfaffenberger's *The Elements of Hypertext Style* (ISBN: 0-12-553142-7). As you'll see, though, there are plenty of online resources as well to convert you from neophyte to webweaving wizard.

# Once Upon a Time

SGML, the oldest one in the book, remains a possible HTML competitor. Programs like Electronic Book Technologies' **http://www.ebt.com** DynaWeb point the way to this future. DynaWeb is a Unix Web server that translates SGML documents into HTML on the fly for Web browsers' convenience.

Some SGML documents will prove too complex for timely translation. For these, manual translations into HTML will have to be performed. This tedious job can be semi-automated through the use of tools like Avalanche Development Company's (a subsidiary of Interleaf), **http://www.ileaf.com/avalanche_html.html**, SGML Hammer.

Other programs, like SoftQuad's, **http://www.sq.com/products/pst.htm**,   Author/Editor, provide an

SGML authoring tool. SoftQuad's RulesBuilder allows you to compile Document Type Definitions (DTDs) easily with the SGML declaration of your choice, turning special SGML features on and off and setting SGML quantities.

For those who are true believers in SGML, there's SoftQuad Sculptor. This program combines Author/Editor, SoftQuad's flagship authoring system, with an SGML-compliant scripting lanaguage. It's no Java or even ActiveX, but it does give SGML authors something stronger to work with than HTML webweavers' PERL and CGI.

Despite all these efforts, SGML seems condemned to playing second fiddle to HTML or some future language. Unless your company has a big investment in SGML documents, you don't need to look any further into this possibility.

# What the Future Holds

The Internet Engineering Task Force (IETF) in charge of HTML is trying to expand HTML into SGML territory by including the ability to create stylesheets and embedding presentation control into HTML. The IETF also hopes to moderate Netscape's and Microsoft's habits of making their own changes to the increasingly shaky standard. For presentations, the IETF hopes to add new elements and attributes to existing HTML tags or to use SGML-style processing instructions. Expanding the role of existing tags is the more popular approach.

Some webweavers wanting absolute control of document presentation are moving to Adobe PDF. PDF gives authors the ability to send documents with PostScript-like fidelity to the original, without PostScript's size and compatibility penalties. Although there had been some interest in using PDF as an HTML replacement, this idea has cooled off.

Instead, most webweavers are using HTML for their Web pages' front-ends and PDF for more complex documents. A very popular approach is to provide HTML menus to PDF manuals and white papers. This way, the user gets to read documents that require exact reproductions—say, a VCR manual—without having to wait for a larger, slower PDF menu.

Other companies, like Tumbleweed Software `http://www.tumbleweed.com/` with its Envoy program, are trying to carve out a niche for themselves on the business net with their own portable document format. With Adobe's dominance of this small marketplace, it seems unlikely to me that even a worthy product—which Envoy is—has a real chance of becoming an important Web standard. Of course, there is one blessing hidden away here for security-conscious Intranet administrators-an uncommon format would add another small measure of security for internal-use-only documents.

# The Font Thickens

Microsoft has created two Web products that don't look like much at all...at first glance. The first, Internet Assistant for Word for Windows, combines an HTML editor with a Web browser. What's not well known is that Internet Assistant can also generate Web documents in Word's native format. You can create these hypermedia documents with drag-and-drop techniques employing Microsoft's Active X protocol.

With ActiveX, Microsoft makes it theoretically easy to create Web documents that include its PowerPoint graphics, Excel spreadsheets, and Access reports. Sense a theme here? Despite Microsoft's support of the HTML open standard, the Redmond, Washington, giant is also pushing into the Internet with its proprietary file formats and interoperability protocol.

This is all part of Bill Gates's grand vision of a computing world united from the desktop to the Internet by Microsoft products. Windows95 is to be the summit of this effort, with its integration of networks, online service, and local desktop applications into a seamless whole.

That may be just your cup of tea—if you're a Windows user. You see, Microsoft's second Web program is Word Viewer. This is a program that enables users to view Microsoft's Web Word documents—if they're running Windows. If you're not running Windows, you're out in the cold. While there may eventually be a Macintosh version of Viewer, it's highly unlikely that Viewer will be ported to other operating systems.

Sad to say, all of this supports the theory that the Web is going to be divided into incompatible sections. If there is popular support for standard HTML and open systems, you'll still be able to roam over most of the Web freely. If not, then expect an end to the days when you could explore the Web from hither to yon without restriction.

# Getting to Work

Like the name says, HTML is a markup language. That is, instead of using codes like PostScript does, HTML's commands are in plain old English. You can utilize these commands to define display elements such as point size and page placement. More importantly, HTML enables you to create the hypermedia links between documents which make the Web the Web. You can produce all you need with any ASCII word processor, even Unix's vi or MS-DOS' EDIT. On the other hand, with today's HTML editors, who would want to?

Before going further, you'll doubtlessly be looking for an application that completely shields the user from HTML. Forget it—they're not here. Yes, Netscape Gold will let you create simple documents. Yes, Adobe's PageMill does a reasonable job of letting you create documents with moderate complexity. Even so, the truth is that none of these programs or their competitors are close to giving us a true "What You See Is What You Get" (WYSIWYG, pronounced wizzy-wig) Web page editor.

While intimate knowledge of HTML code is no longer required to write decent pages, your webweavers are going to need to know some HTML to be truly effective. By this time next year, that may no longer be the case; but it could take longer than that.

# Windows Editors

If you're a WinWord user, the first program you should look at is Microsoft's own freeware add-on to Word: Internet Assistant for Word (IAW). This turns WinWord into an okay HTML 1.0 editor and an incredibly slow Web browser.

IAW, which will only work with WinWord 6.0a and higher, makes it possible to use Word documents and dynamic data exchange (DDE) links on the Web. Using this proprietary functionality isn't the brightest idea in the world if your purpose is to reach the widest possible audience, which is the whole point of the Web. That aside, IAW is a decent tool for enabling expert WinWord users to start writing for the Web in a hurry. Unfortunately, IAW's code tends to be fairly awful, so for most users it's a stopgap solution for Web writing until they can pick up something better.

A better beginner's HTML editor is Netscape Navigator Gold 3.0, **http://home.netscape.com/**, This editor/browser sets the new standard by which other browsers will be judged. Gold's editing functions, though... Well, let's just say that there's some pyrite among those flecks of gold.

As a browser, Gold incorporates all the features of Netscape Navigator. Java, plug-ins, integrated e-mail, and news—it's all there. The editorial features vary depending on what operating system you are running. Usually, the Windows versions have fuller feature sets than the Macintosh and Unix editions. OS/2—as always, with its late start in the Netscape family—lags behind the rest.

To give Gold its due, it does have excellent WYSIWYG facilities—especially, no surprise, if you're using Netscape-compliant HTML. It also has all the basics a beginner might need. And, if you're a webweaver wannabe and don't know how to design a page, Netscape links you to a potpourri of ready-made Web pages suitable for homes, announcements, or businesses. Even if you don't know your HTML from a handsaw, Netscape's Page Wizard **http://home.netscape.com/assist/net_sites/ starter/wizard/index.html** will see you through. Gold's problem is that if you want to do anything fancy, you must use an external HTML editor. Nevertheless, for beginners, Gold is a 24-karat find.

Would-be webweavers looking for a more sophisticated Web authoring addition to WinWord should look to NICE Technologies' WebWizard, **http://www.nicetech. com/**.

At $79, it's no freeware program; but you get what you pay for. WebWizard enables you to write in HTML 1, 2, or 3. You can also use the program to generate SGML DTD files. With these, you can use Word to generate other flavors of HTML, like the Netscape variant. NICE Technologies will also be producing a Mac Word version shortly.

My favorite Windows HTML editor is the Sausage Software's oddly-named HotDog **http://www. sausage.com/**. This program comes in a shareware version that works for 30 days. From there, you can upgrade either to an inexpensive version for amateur webweavers or to a higher-quality professional version for serious Web work. With its point-and-click interface, it is perhaps the easiest HTML editor available at this time; and it can produce some yummy pages (no mustard necessary).

The granddaddy of Windows HTML programs is SoftQuad's HoTMetaL **http://www.sq.com/**. This program comes in two versions: HoTMetaL Free and HoTMetaL Pro. Either way, you get a good HTML generator. Some find the interface quirky; but you can decide that for yourself by giving the free version a test drive before paying the money to move up to its bigger, commercial brother. HoTMetaL Pro is also available in versions for Macintosh and Unix systems. Personally, I've found both versions difficult and counterintutive to work with. On the other hand, I know many people who swear by SoftQuad rather than at it; so you may find it to be just the editor you need.

Another interesting HTML editor, if you already know HTML, is Brooklyn North Software Works' HTML Assistant, **http://www.brooknorth.com**. This program also comes in both freeware and commercial versions.

# Macintosh and Unix

The best Macintosh HTML editor currently out and about is BBEdit, **http://www.barebones.com/bbedit. html**. It's quick, it has a first-rate spellchecker (something many editor programs lack), and I commend it highly for Mac-based intranet authors.

Another good one is Robert Best III's Web Weaver, **http://137.143.111.3/web.weaver/about.html**. This HTML 2.0 compatible editor looks and feels like an ordinary word processor, but with additional menu and toolbar commands for easier HTML editing. While the program isn't perfect—in this version, it only optimized for 68K Macs and had a document size limit of 32K—it does work well and quickly.

Unix users like getting their hands dirty with code, so there are comparatively few dedicated HTML editors for them. What Unix does have to offer, however, is the finest program for converting existing text to HTML: Interleaf's Cyberleaf, **http://www.interleaf.comip.html**. It can convert WordPerfect, FrameMaker, Rich Text Format (RTF), and the like into HTML without a hitch. At $795, though, Cyberleaf is for serious Web authors only. Cyberleaf also has extremely powerful Web managing tools. If I were in charge of a Web site, or if I were running a Web site business, Cyberleaf would be the first program I got after I put up my Web server.

No matter what program you end up using, it is only a tool—a means to an end. What will ultimately decide how successful your page will be is how well you use the programs.

# Beyond Editing

Having an HTML editor that's close to WYSIWYG is all well and good; but to produce good Web documents, you need to know what you're doing with it. Otherwise, you'll end up with the kind of brightly colored, meaningless page glop that so troubled our eyes a few years ago when DTP tools first appeared.

If you've never used HTML before, your first stop should be:

•A Beginner's Guide to HTML
`http://www.ncsa.uiuc.edu/General/Internet/`
`WWW/HTMLPrimer.html`

This will give you a solid grounding in HTML fundamentals. After that, you should read:

•Composing Good HTML
`http://www.cs.cmu.edu/~tilt/cgh/`

While it's no Strunk and White for the Web, it will steer you clear of common mistakes and show you some of the elements of good Web style.

One of the best ways to learn how to write decent HTML is to see how not to do it. You can find the "best" of the worst at the :

• Bad Style Page
**http://www.earth.com/bad-style/**

Another place to look for hints on how not to produce Web documents is Stovin Hayter's

• Why is the Web So Boring?
**http://www.demon.co.uk/eurojournalism/
stovin/design.html**

Another essential read, if you're going to be using the Netscape enhancements to HTML, is Netscape's own page on the subject:

• Netscape Extensions
**http://home.netscape.com/assist/net_sites/
html_extensions.html**

Regardless of the level of your webweaving abilities, a very useful site for finding further Web building information is:

• Web Developer's Virtual Library
**http://WWW.Stars.com/**

Another good general pointers for HTML education, though it breaks a lot of style rules in the process, is:

• D.J. Quad's Ultimate HTML Site
**http://www.quadzilla.com/**

Finally, I've always been pleased by the information in Hagan Heller's :

•Hagan's HTML Help Library
`http://www.netscape.com/people/hagan/html/`
`top.html`

Hagan pushes the envelope of HTML in creative and inter-esting ways. Most sites that try this end up showing how to abuse HTML in ways that your readers will hate. Not Hagan. Instead, he shows you how to stretch HTML in order to get the most from it.

# News & Views

For news and well thought-out information about the Web, a good site is:

•WebWeek
`http://www.webweek.com/`

This site features news from the WebWeek, the first news-paper devoted to the Web.

If you want insightful commentary on today's Web tools, both for webweavers and webmasters, the best spot on the Web is:

•WebDeveloper
`http://www.webdeveloper.com/`

This publication is a professional magazine done by people who really know their business. There are many other Web-oriented magazines online, but only WebDeveloper is con-sistently excellent.

Another useful source of information are the Usenet news-groups for Web writers. These include:

- `comp.infosystems.www.authoring.cgi`
- `comp.infosystems.www.authoring.html`
- `comp.infosystems.www.authoring.images`
- `comp.infosystems.www.authoring.misc`

You shouldn't expect miracles from these newsgroups; but you can find answers to common questions here quickly. You never know—sometimes, you'll get your tough questions answered quickly, too.

Speaking of tough questions, it's about time to look at at some of webweaving's trickier problems. Again, this won't be a substitute for works which directly address these issues; but with this in hand, you will know what the issues are and enough of the answers to know when you're getting the straight dope.

# 19

## The Writes and Wrongs of HTML

## Web Explanations and Explorations

There are many ways of transporting data across the Web. Everyone knows the most popular of these: HTTP. What's less well known is that virtually any Internet-borne information can be sent via the Web.

This is because the Web's addressing scheme, Uniform Resource Locators (URLs), can handle just about anything. A standard URL follows the structure:

```
scheme://host.domain[:port]/path/file-
name
```

HTTP is the most popular scheme, but it's hardly the only one. Other parts of an URL, like the port, are optional. The standard TCP ports are a convenience for users and programmers; but you don't have to use them. For example, unless you say otherwise, a Web server will make documents via HTTP on Port 80, and that's where browsers look for them. For security reasons, you can use eccentric port numbers to make it harder for crackers to penetrate your site. With schemes like this, you can stop someone dead in their tracks from seeing Web documents: Unless they know or can guess the right port number, they won't be able to dock to the Web document of their choice.

If you want to use ports, you should know the common port assignments.

**Table 19.1: Common TCP/IP Port Assignments**

| Port # | Keyword | Protocol |
|--------|---------|----------|
| 7 | ECHO | Echo |
| 11 | USERS | Active Users |
| 17 | QUOTE | Quote of the Day |
| 20 | FTP-DATA | FTP (Data) |
| 21 | FTP | FTP (Control) |
| 23 | TELNET | Telnet |
| 25 | SMTP | Simple Mail Transfer Protocol |
| 43 | NICNAME | Who Is |

| 53 | DOMAIN | Domain Name Server |
| 70 | GOPHER | gopher |
| 79 | FINGER | Finger |
| 80 | WEB | HTTP |
| 101 | HOSTNAME | Host Name Server |
| 119 | NNTP | Network News Transfer Protocol |

You can also use different schemes, sans port numbers, to supply information to the Web. The most popular of these are:

**Table 19.2: Beyond HTTP**

| Scheme | Explanation |
| --- | --- |
| file | Local system file |
| ftp | FTP server or server accessible file |
| gopher | Gopher server or server accessible file |
| http | Web server or server accessible file |
| mailto | E-mail address |
| news | Usenet newsgroup |
| nntp | Usenet newsgroup using NNTP |
| telnet | Telnet service connection |

WAIS               WAIS server

For most practical purposes, you'll want to use these rather than playing with port numbers. The exception, as I mentioned earlier, is when you want to add a smidgen more security to your site.

The relevance of all this to you is that both webmaster and webweaver have great power over what your company can and can't present over the Internet. Having a Web site doesn't simply mean that you can send out HTML documents. It also means you have the power to make inhouse newsgroups available for customer comments, for example, or enable employees to telnet to remote systems within the company.

# Tips Toward Safe Linking

You already know that one of the Web's great advantages over ordinary text is that you can jump both internally from place to place within a document, and link information thousands of mile away to your local Web document. What you probably don't know is how to do the latter without stepping on the toes of foreign site managers. Before diving into this discussion, let me give you a word of warning. I'm no lawyer; but as a journalist, I've been concerned with intellectual property issues for more than a decade. The thing to remember is that there are no hard and fast rules about what you can or can't do on the Web with other people's materials.

The problem, you see, is that neither copyright nor trademark law have caught up with the online world. This doesn't mean that the net is an anarchy where you can print what you please. It means that the rules aren't necessarily written down in stone, or even magnetic disk memory. To get information on these issues for your part of the world, the place to go is The Copyright Website **http://www.benedict.com/**. The Yahoo copyright section **http://www.yahoo.com/Government/Law/ Intellectual_Property/Copyrights/** is also a natural for any webweaver's link library. In the meantime, here are some general guidelines.

# Copyright

First, anything and everything on the Web is likely to be protected by copyright if it's an original expression of an idea. This can be words, an audio file, a graphics file, or what have you. The item in question does not need to have a copyright notice attached. This, thanks to the Berne convention on copyright, is pretty much true throughout the world.

A copyright notice will make the copyright's owner position stronger, but again, it's strictly optional. If you do bother with this, the proper form is: "Copyright dates by author/owner." The character "©" is often used in place of "Copyright," but it's never been recognized in law or in the courts. The phrase "All Rights Reserved" used to be mandatory, but it's obsolete now.

Even if you don't charge for access to the copyrighted material, putting it up on the Web can still land you in legal hot water. The key question is whether you've hurt the commercial value of the original material.

Copyright is also separate from both the ownership and the creation of a work. For example, if I write a story but grant the publisher all rights to the story, then the publisher, not me, owns the copyright to that story. It's also possible for someone to buy, say, a work of art, and not own the copyright to the item.

There are many things that people think that they can copyright which they really can't. Two of the more popular mistakes are names and ideas. While you can trademark a name—for example, Apple Computers owns the trademark "Apple" for computers, and Apple Records owns the trademark "Apple" for music—you can't copyright a name. Similarly, you can't copyright the idea of doing a book on intranets. The specific expression of that idea, such as the book you're holding in your hands, is a copyrighted item because of the investment of time, creativity, and expression that transformed a baldly stated notion into a specific copyrighted work. It doesn't have to be much, but there does need to be something more than an unadorned common idea there in order for a copyright to take hold.

If a story or the like isn't copyrighted, thus can be reprinted by anyone, it's public domain. You might assume that a posting in a Usenet newsgroup or a public mailing list is in the public domain: Wrong. The only contemporary things that are explicitly in public domain are those items that contain a statement like: "I grant X to the public domain." Without those words, any and all substantive works, even just three lines of a Usenet news message, are covered by copyright thus are not public domain. Of course, if the creator's been dead for 50 years, then it's public domain.

Sounds really restrictive, doesn't it? Actually, there are two ways out for Web authors that make getting around copyright fairly easy. The first is fair use. The "fair use" exemption to copyright law lets you use parts of a work for commentary, parody, reporting, reviewing, research, and education about copyrighted works without the permission of the author.

This isn't a license to steal. If you reproduce an entire article from the Byte site, you've both shown the intent to break copyright and you've damaged the article's commercial value. If you do something like this, you can eventually expect to find, at best, a cease and desist order. At worst, you'll get slapped with a lawsuit. In general, with fair use, you're dealing with a short part of the whole work, and you should attribute the work. Fair use is decided by courts on a case-by-case basis with little reliance on past case law. In short, don't push it: You don't need the headache. (Trust me—I'm a career journalist, remember?)

Just because someone doesn't immediately give you grief doesn't mean that you're safe. A copyright isn't a trademark. Trademarks must be defended or the courts will cease to recognize them. Copyrights last for your lifetime and years beyond.

# Implied Public Access (IPA)

The other way out for webweavers is an ill-defined concept called Implied Public Access (IPA). With IPA, the assumption is that since the Web is an open environment that encourages people to link to any other Web site by publishing on the Web, anyone who puts up a site has given implied permission to everyone else to link to their Web page and vice-versa. Neither copyright law nor the courts have to had to deal with this issue yet. For what it's worth, my opinion is that the IPA will hold.

While some sites plaster copyright clauses all over their pages, this doesn't make much difference. You already have copyright, and your site can still be sampled and analyzed in the news, educational institutions, and so on under fair use. With a public site, this can be taken as an attempt to slam the door on IPA.

My response to this is that if you really don't want people "borrowing" materials from your site, put it on an internal use only Web site. Materials that are always kept within the confines of your intranet are much more protected, both legally and practically, than anything you put on the Internet.

Your best move if you're going to link to another site is to follow netiquette, the etiquette code of the net. In this case, netiquette requires that you tell the webmaster at the other site that you'll be linking to them. If they object, remove the link from your site. It's as simple as that. Like a good deal of netiquette, it comes down to common courtesy.

If you put together what's called a composite site, one which is made up mostly of links and elements linked in from other sites, following this principle is even more important. Here, even one objection may be enough to knock your site for a loop. Even here, however, just like rap musicians, you should never oversample, with or without permission. Unless you're doing a parody of another site, if your site looks like little more than a mirror of another site, you're just begging to get socked by a suit.

In any case, an URL on your site is no more copyrightable than your phone number or street address. A list of links, however, if it uses originality in its creation, can be copyrighted. For example, the courts have ruled that a mere compilation of telephone numbers in alphabetical order is not a protectable document. If something cannot be copyright-protected, while it's not public domain, it might as well be for webweaving purposes. On the other hand, an annotated list, like Yahoo! Computing's `http://www.zdnet.com/yahoocomputing/` collection of computer sites or the I-way 500, `http://www.cciweb.com/iway.html` a listing of the top Web sites in a variety of categories, is covered by copyright.

# Making Effective Use of HTML and Beyond

For the most part, you shouldn't worry too much about the above. For a good site that will draw people back, you want to take your own unique approach to your company's ideas. All too many sites look just like every other site, especially in the corporate sector. Unless you want to be lost in an endless sea of boring copies, you need to have original content and art.

This means that your webweavers should be dedicated professionals from the fields of writing, editing, desktop publishing, and graphic art. If you're very lucky, you may even get people who already have experience with Web publishing; but don't count on it.

Once you have your crew together, you should allow them to do what they do best. Creative people may not work well in the normal 9 to 5 rut. While these folks do need to be in touch with the administrators in charge of your intranet's Web projects, lest they go far afield, they don't need anyone peering over their shoulders. Creativity doesn't always come when called. If you don't give these people space, their production quality is likely to drop like a stone—or, worse, they'll quit on you mid-project.

Publishers have had years to get used to this behavior; but for most companies, their Web site will be their first real voyage into publishing. The creative side of the Web is...different from the network administration side, and almost surely from any other division of your company. Like it or lump it, this is the way it works, so you'd best like it. Look at this way: If you give them what they want, creative freedom without micromanagement, you're much more likely to get a good original Web site than one that looks like it came out of a cookie-cutter.

As for the webweavers, creativity and originality must be the name of your game. When every significant company in the world is working towards having a Web presence, you must do things to stand out from the herd. You can't do it cheaply with bright, showy effects, like using ShockWave videos instead of GIFs, because the vast majority of your potential audience will be unable to view your site. Most of those who can are going to get tired of waiting for the video display to arrive, anyway.

Good webweaving means working within constraints to produce the best work possible with today's working technology, not tomorrow's bleeding edge. It also means relying on written words, short audio samples, and simple images as your building blocks. That doesn't mean that you shouldn't include StreamWorks films and the like; it means that, unless your company is in the video media market, one or two short films is probably more than enough for any site.

Doing the job right also means using bandwidth-intensive items with caution, even a big GIF. One fact to keep in mind is that users will soon be able to channel-surf the net as easily as they now do television. You need to make an impression, but you're not going to get much time to make that impression.

My own personal measure is that if the front page of a site takes more than 15 seconds to load on my 56 Kbps frame-relay line, it's too big. Think about it: If a site takes that long to load on my connection, it's going to take twice that long on most modem connections. Would you wait around for 30 seconds for an unknown Web site to show you its stuff? This is also a concern you should keep in mind as you develop your pages in-house. Within your intranet, where you're likely to be running at 10 Mbps or more, what looks adequately fast to you and your coworkers is going to look as slow as sludge to someone from the outside looking in.

There are many tricks on how to beat these performance problems. You'll find links to them in the documents I listed in the last chapter. For now, just remember that faster is better.

On your intranet, you're not limited to those bandwidth problems. It's on your intranet's internal Web sites that you'll want to use the fancy, time-intensive Web applications. This will not only make the internal sites more interesting to employees, it will give you the practice you need for the day when Internet bandwidth reaches a point where even a plumbing company may want to show videos of how their products send water racing around a building.

For plumbing diagrams, or corporate pie charts, current webweavers may want to look to Adobe's PDF. This format looks to be a stronger and stronger contender for Web design, especially for intranets. Want to know more? Read on.

## Total Control: Portable Document Format

## Alternative Future: PDF

Once upon a time, all Web graphics were GIFs, and all Web text was HTML. Today, the market requires that technology provide for high-caliber graphics and print-level typography and layout. Portable document viewers such as Adobe's Acrobat and Novell's Envoy enable Web users to view documents as God and the designer intended. In particular, Microsoft, Netscape, and Spyglass have all committed their product developers to incorporating Adobe's PDF viewers with their browsers.

Unlike HTML browsers, a document viewer gives designers absolute control over what the reader sees. In the past, Web creators making documents in anything other than HTML had to hope that each viewer would have a copy of the necessary reader linked into their browser to read the document. For instance, despite Adobe's aggressive efforts to promote PDF by making the reader freely available, PDF usage was only slowly penetrating the Web. Since Web authors couldn't be sure that their message would be received in PDF format, many opted to stay away from it in spite of its advantages.

No longer. Makers of portable document readers are forging ahead by going directly to the source: The browser creators. Spyglass was the first to make the Web safe for PDF. Starting with Enhanced Mosaic 2.0, Spyglass' browsers came with a software development interface (SDI) to enable other programs to work in harmony with Enhanced Mosaic. The first SDI-enabled applications are Adobe's Acrobat and SoftQuad's Panorama (an SGML reader). The SDI configures programs to work with Enhanced Mosaic directly, rather than as a user-configured helper application.

Spyglass may have gotten to the idea first, but Netscape is the company that made it famous. The idea has now been immortalized in Netscape Navigator as "plug-ins."

Netscape continues to move toward incorporating PDF into their browser. At first, both the Mac and Windows versions of the browser supported Weblink, a program that enables an Acrobat Exchange user to add HTML links to their PDF documents and launch Netscape or Enhanced Mosaic to view the HTML document. Since then, Netscape and Adobe have created a PDF plug-in that lets users seamlessly view PDF documents. Netscape and Adobe also plan on creating additions to Netscape servers, due out by the year's end, that will provide superior PDF document delivery.

The new server will deliver better throughput in two ways. First, the server will cache popular PDF documents. More importantly, the server will deliver what Adobe calls "browsable" PDF documents. With this technology, Navigator will be able to show PDF documents as they arrive rather than waiting for the entire document. This technology will also enable users to use links within a PDF document without waiting to download all the information in it. If successful, this will remove PDF's chief speed handicap.

Adobe is also building reader-level libraries. These will be bundled with the Acrobat software developer's kit (SDK). Since Adobe is not asking for a per copy royalty on the use of these libraries, it seems almost inevitable that all major browsers will include native PDF support within a year.

What this means is that, like it or lump it, PDF is going to become an increasingly important Web format. While PDF remains proprietary, its faithfulness to the author's intent, its future browser integration, and its increasing speed guarantee it a place on the Web.

# What PDF Means for You

For most of the Web's brief life, almost all of its documents have been written in HTML. All things change. Today, Adobe's Portable Document Format (PDF) is well on its way to becoming part of the warp and woof of the Web. By tomorrow, even casual Web explorers will find that they need to deal with PDF.

You may ask: What's the big news here? The Web has always been full of formats. Yes, it has; but unlike Postscript, SGML, or even that most painstaking of page description languages, TeX, PDF is swiftly becoming a rival to HTML, the Web's main language.

Many corporations and government agencies, especially those who were early adopters of Adobe's PostScript printing language, want to extend their investment to the Internet. PDF gives users the PostScript advantages of enables authors to create documents to retain their look and feel across different platforms.

Like HTML, PDF is a hypermedia language that can link to other parts of the same documents or to remote documents. Unlike HTML, PDF is a proprietary format. HTML is free; and its fate is in the hands of the IETF and the W3C. While Adobe has made PDF freely available, PDF is Adobe's property.

PDF challenges HTML on the home pages of the Web for one vital reason: PDF gives its author precise and absolute control of what the reader sees. With HTML, a Web author can only create works that approximate what you'll actually see on your display. Even aside from non-standard HTML additions like Netscape's, with HTML you see the author's creation the way your viewer wants you to. The once-popular Cello browser, for example, presents links by default as text enclosed in boxes, whereas most browsers display them as underlined colored text. The author has no control over HTML text's color and only limited direction over its font and point-size. PDF, on the other hand, enables authors to create works that will look precisely the same to all users-within the limits of their hardware capacities—regardless of the browser.

This is no small matter. The inability to describe exact visual representations is heresy to graphic and page designers. They believe that a given page should look always look exactly the same way, and that a particular expression of a page exists for a reason. These designers make the excellent point that people respond to things in different ways based on the way they look. Because it enables designers to keep such firm control over that look, some go so far as to say that PDF is the only sane choice for electronic publishing.

PDF, however, gives you more than just complete control over the look and feel of the document. It, like HTML, is a hypermedia format. You can navigate through PDF documents in exactly the same point-and-click way you do in an HTML document. Of course, PostScript always gave authors this power, but at the cost of huge files.

In the past, for some technical documents, authors and readers have been willing to make this compromise. Long before HTML, PostScript was the first hypermedia Internet format. HTML, with its small size, is what made the Web feasible. PostScript continues to dominate high-end screen resolution and printing, but it will never control the Web desktop. Web denizens agree that the time cost of shipping massive PostScript documents across the Web is too high to make it practical for most Web publishing purposes.

So why hasn't PDF conquered the World Wide Web? Until recently, the answer has been a simple lack of support. To read PDF documents, you need a copy of Adobe Acrobat Reader set up as a viewer. Adobe has pushed for PDF acceptance by making DOS, Macintosh, OS/2, Windows, and Unix versions of its Reader freely available; but this has had only limited success. It's only been in the last few months that browsers began to directly support PDF.

Now, we're going through a strange time, with PDF gaining fans and webweavers either incorporating PDF into their pages or avoiding it completely. Some webweavers feel very strongly that the Web's primary language should be free and open—in short, HTML—rather than the proprietary PDF.

This resistance to PDF is understandable. HTML's biggest advantage is accessibility. It is the current broad standard; it's not going to go away overnight. For beginners, HTML is also much easier. All you need is a navigator and a text editor, and you can start learning and producing HTML documents. For PDF, you must have Adobe Acrobat in order to do any Web publishing.

For amateurs who do not require complex layouts, sticking with the HTML they know makes sense. For an intranet webweaver, the stakes of avoiding PDF are much higher. As HTML fragments into mutually incompatible dialects, a new, stronger standard will be needed; and that standard is more likely to be PDF than any other format.

Some authors are concerned about Adobe gaining a chokehold on the Web as a result of its control of PDF. For example, you currently must have Adobe Exchange to generate PDF documents, although other authoring tools eventually will show up. Adobe, which acquired Aldus last year, has incorporated PDF into Aldus FreeHand as a graphics exchange format. Adobe recently bought Frame Technology, and announced that a PDF-based publishing program would be forthcoming. But for the time being, Adobe's Exchange is your only choice.

Furthermore, Adobe Acrobat Pro, the master PDF creation program, has a hefty price of admission to Web publishing. This looks especially bad when HTML allows you to get in for free. The network version, Acrobat for Workgroups, costs a fair chunk of change even by corporate standards.

PDF does not have the field to itself. Corell is pushing Envoy, a page description language and viewer created by Tumbleweed Technologies, which the two companies are jointly marketing. Still, how many standards can one environment support? Especially when one of the Web's chief selling points is that it provides a universal interface to all forms of data.

PDF currently has the most momentum as a contender to HTML. Will PDF drive HTML off of the Web? Nah, I don't see PDF killing HTML. Each language has its place on the Web of the future. While PDF gives designers the artistic control they want, almost anyone can be a Web publisher with good, old-fashioned HTML. From where I sit, the Web is big enough for both of them.

# A PDF Primer

Want to see what all the excitement is about? The first thing you'll need to do is to get an appropriate version of the Adobe Acrobat Reader. These are available at many sites; but you can always count on finding one from Adobe, **http://www.adobe.com/**.

Ready to go? Here are some of the best places to find top-quality PDF publications:

**Table 20.1: PDF Pride**

Title
URL

Acropolis, the magazine of Acrobat Publishing
`http://www.acropolis.com/acropolis`

New York TimesFax Internet Edition
`http://nytimesfax.com>`

US IRS Tax Forms
`http://www.irs.ustreas.gov/basic/forms_pubs/index.`
`html>`

Wharton Business School
`http://www.wharton.upenn.edu/`

After glancing over these sites, I think you'll agree that PDF should be part of your intranet Web plans. Most of these sites use HTML pages as a wrapper around the more important PDF documents. It's exactly this role that I foresee for PDF on the mainstream Internet.

While PDF is unlikely to become the dominant language of the Web, it will almost certainly become the language of choice for documents that require exact reproduction. Also, since intranets are much faster than the Internet, I can see companies with strong internal graphics and publishing departments turning entirely to PDF-based Web sites.

Whichever format you end up using, the one thing I know neither of us wants is your company's secure information escaping from your Web site, in any format. In the next chapter, we'll look at ways you can plug up any holes that would let information seep out of your intranet.

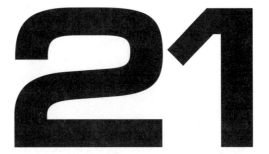

## Securing Your Intranet

## Safe Intranetting

An intranet looks a lot like a LAN—too much so. If you're hooked onto the Internet, you're facing a whole new level of security problems which you may not see at first. It's all too easy a mistake to make, because you can run an intranet without any trouble for years. Until, that is, someone walks right into your intranet and sucks down all your critical information with a virtual vacuum cleaner.

This is not a matter of, "if" it will happen. Like death and taxes, intranet break-in attempts are inevitable. If you do things right, chances are these assaults won't be successful. Without the proper protection, however, why not just throw your accounts receivable down in front of your chief competitor and have done with it?

Actually, it's unlikely to be a competitor prying away at the locks on your virtual door. A much more likely candidate is a disgruntled employee. Most break-ins aren't really break-ins at all. They're done by people who are fed up with the company and want to hit the business where it hurts. After that, the next most likely candidates to go poking their nose around where they're not welcome are crackers.

Crackers? Yes, crackers. Contrary to popular belief, **hackers** are often interested in finding out about systems for information's sake alone, or just for the fun of figuring out the elaborate puzzle of a well-designed security system. **Crackers**, on the other hand, try to break into your site either to do malicious mischef or to actually score money off of you. They may pretend otherwise, with phrases like "information should be free;" so they copy out one of your programs to be distributed to friends—or paying friends, anyway. However they disguise it, though, a cracker is just a crook who wants to do you and your enterprise harm.

Between peeved employees and crackers, the ticked-off employee is the one who's much more likely to get you. After all, an employee already has a good idea where valuable information can be found. A cracker may have a good idea, since businesses tend to store vital data in the same places; but he doesn't know where to pinpoint the files that are the most vulnerable to significant damage.

Think of it as the difference between the sort of random bombing done during World War II and the kind of laser-guided bombing down air-conditioning shafts that we saw during the Gulf War. A cracker can blast things almost at random. An unhappy employee, on the other hand, can wreck your company with pinpoint accuracy; and you may not even know that a particular data vault has been blown to smithereens until you look inside it. If they're very good, you won't even see the harm that's been done until it's too late. The secret to avoiding the former situation is to always give employees a fair shake. (How to do that, alas, is far beyond the scope of this book!)

There are, however, seven ways to barricade your internal network from the Internet which I can discuss. Not every company will need to use each of them; but if you don't want your profit and lost statements to end up at www.joes.info.on.a.byte.com, you must use at least some of these measures.

# Packets of Protection

The first is that old standby—insisting that access to vital systems or information is protected with a user password system. You will want to put in additional passwords for mission-critical resources. The problem here is in making sure that people use passwords properly. Strict protection and use of passwords will also make it much harder for unhappy employees to do widespread damage. In any case, more data is lost every year because of lazy password practices than from any team of crackers.

There's an old but true joke in computer security circles that the easiest way to break into any system is to make friends with the office manager. He'll know all the passwords for the people who can never remember them, and he probably has them written down for easy reference on his desk. Everyone knows the old password-in-the-top-desk-drawer trick. The best way to shore up security is to make certain that everyone obeys the password rules—and that no one leaves their password lying around.

The next step, and a necessity from where I stand, is packet and route filtering. With packet filtering, your gateway to the Internet only allows access, in and/or out, by certain TCP/IP protocols. When you use route filtering, your router only allows network connections in or out from pre-specified IP addresses. For example, you can set your system so that people can only come into your network from systems with IP addresses belonging to your corporation. This enables you to create a clean break between your intranet and the Internet. This can be further restricted by allowing limited access to all users, say by only allowing in HTTP requests and denying all others. This way, you can still let people into your public dataspace without hassling them; but your private data remains private.

Of course, these methods can be combined. While tricky to manage, I believe route- and packet-filtering provides the best balance of security and access for both public and remote company users.

Next up are firewalls. If you're serious about connectivity between your LAN and the outside world, firewalls aren't just a good idea—they're a requirement. In this security scheme, one router exclusively handles contact with the outside world and talks only to one system in your department. That system, in turn, connects to your network through a different router. Essentially, a cracker not only has to make it through the filtering, they then must work their way through the external router, the system in the middle, and the internal router to get into your network.

You can create firewalls with software alone, but it's not as safe as shelling out the extra cash to buy a standalone system to man the barricade between networks. A plain old PC with the proper routing and firewall programs will do the job just as well as a more expensive dedicated system.

From the inside looking out, these systems are often used as proxies. With a proxy, you can control what kind of data requests a user makes to the Internet, or restrict them to visiting only particular sites. Before putting up the walls, however, check to see if your software is up to the job and that your network administrators can handle putting the proxies into place and then making all the necessary changes to the applications, so that your users won't find themselves locked into your intranet.

If you want to get really serious about protection, you may want to consider Application Layer Gateways (ALGs). ALGs require that all outside connections are run from a single designated ALG machine which attempts to duplicate firewall protection in one machine and enforces strict packet filtering by application type. In essence, ALGs can be thought of as stronger firewalls, with a correspondingly higher maintenance cost.

For the paranoid administrators who believe in completely sterile computing, there are specialized encryption gateways (SEGs). An SEG encrypts and decrypts all Internet traffic. This gives you a way of transferring low-security materials over the Internet via another SEG. Of course, if you're using a purely SEG setup, it also means that your site can't be visited by Internet people in general, and your people can't visit the Internet. SEGs are best kept around to be used on an ad hoc basis for those days when you want to use the Internet infrastructure, but you don't want to use any of the Internet's resources.

You can also give LAN encryption a try. Here, all of your intranet's data packets are encrypted. While it's guaranteed to slow your network to a crawl, it's also almost a sure bet to keep outsiders from sticking their noses in where they don't belong.

Finally, there are unique approaches to building the wall between Internet and intranet. One that has caught my fancy is Artisoft's LANtastic 7.0 and LANtastic'95, **http://www.artisoft.com**. Artisoft enables you to have one system serve as the Internet gateway, while all the other systems can access the Internet using the NetBIOS network protocol instead of TCP/IP. Without any obvious protection at all, I can guarantee you that trying to jump over the TCP/IP to the NetBIOS network segments will give even the most wily cracker fits.

Intranet programs are changing faster than anyone can keep up with. Still, if you stick to mainstream servers and clients, you're unlikely to run into a situation where your security system becomes the problem instead of the solution. For more information about Internet security measures, you'll want to check Security FAQs, **http://iss.net/sec_info/faq.html**, National Computer Security Association, **http://www.ncsa.com/ncsamain.html**, and Packet Filtering in Internet Firewalls, **http://www.willamette.edu/~dlabar/firewall.html**. The Internet security companies to seriously consider are: BBN Planet, **http://www.bbn-planet.com /doc/spatrol/spatrol.html**, for a cradle-to-grave solution; Cisco Systems, **http://cio.cisco.com/ warp/public/778/security.html**, as many administrators happily live and die by Cisco's top of the line intranet, Internet, and security software and hardware; Ingress, **http://www.nohackers.com/**, whose "no-hackers" URL says it all; Livingston Enterprises,

**http://www.livingston.com/**, for hardware security and router solutions; and Raptor Systems, **http://www.raptor.com/**, makers of some of the best security software around. You can also put together a decent secure intranet with freeware, shareware, a little hand-coding and a lot of time. The vast majority of us will be better off buying at least part of our solution commercially.

# Security, Sales, SSL, and S-HTTP

It's so close you can almost taste it. Waiting right outside your virtual door are literally millions of potential customers; but you can't sell them a thing, because you can't safely take their credit card number. It's hopeless...or is it?

Don't despair. Hundreds of businesses are successfully selling products and services over the Web. The low-low-tech way of doing this, of course, is to include a phone number and/or fax number, just as you would in a paper advertisement.

Fear not—there are more sophisticated ways of handling financial transactions over the Web. Two that are already in place and working are CyberCash, **http://www.cyber-cash.com**, and First Virtual, **http://www.fv.com/html/fv_main.html**.

With CyberCash, instead of your site handling the customer's credit card number, the software encrypts the transaction and sends it via the Well Fargo & Co. or Checkfree financial transaction lines to the customer's bank. You never see the credit card number at all—you just see the placed order, an authorization from CyberCash, and the funds for the transaction in your account. First Virtual uses a similar approach.

Another company, NetCash, **http://www.teleport .com/~netcash**, takes an entirely different route. NetCash takes deposits from customers and gives the customer e-mail netcoupons in varying denominations, each with a unique serial number. When you accept NetCash for a transaction, your customer pays for your service by sending you e-mail with the amount in NetCash coupons and the serial number of the virtual cash. You, in return, send NetCash back their coupons; and for a transaction fee, it's turned into real cash for your real accounts.

The best and brightest hope of commerce on the Internet rests on the success of two security protocols: Secure Socket Layer (SSL) and Secure Hyptertext Transfer Protocol (S-HTTP). In the past, holes have been poked through SSL; but its sponsoring company, Netscape, has fixed them all. Another company, Terisa Systems, **http://www.ter-isa.com/**, is working on combining SSL and S-HTTP into one universal security solution.

No matter's who working on it—and essentially, every company in the Internet business has their hand in—the goal is the same: to make a thief-proof way of sending credit card numbers over the Internet. The solution isn't quite here yet, but it should be soon. When that day comes, you'll be able to let your Web server take credit card numbers for purchases instead of operators. When that day comes, the Web will truly burst forth in full commercial mode.

# Secure Electronic Transaction

That time is almost here. MasterCard and Visa, along with Microsoft, Netscape, and a host of smaller financial transaction and computing companies, have agreed on a universal electronic buying protocol: Secure Electronic Transaction (SET). Sitting above SSL and S-HTTP, SET enables buyers and sellers to use a credit card, a digitized version of the customer's signature, and a password to make buying and selling over the Web as easy as—and probably safer than—signing a credit card form at your local department store.

SET has the key to becoming wildly successful because it's almost universally accepted, in principle, by businesses and computing companies. After long delays, the final standard was laid to rest in June 1996. By late '96, you'll be seeing ads from amber vendors to zebra wranglers proclaiming that they support SET. If you haven't talked to one of the two major credit card companies yet, do so now. Short of a security hole the size of Lake Erie, SET will be the standard that everyone will be using. If you're interesting in buying or selling on the Internet and you miss this train, it's going to run you down.

# Ready, SET, Go!

You might think that the digitized signature is the key to this security scheme. You couldn't be more wrong. The signature function is really just there to make managers and customers feel warm fuzzies. The real key to identifying a customer is a SET-encrypted ID number, called a digital certificate.

To get this certificate, you'll need to sign up online for a SET ID. From a customer's viewpoint, it will look a lot like an online version of a credit card applications from any bank or store. The credit card issuer will physically mail out the SET registration program. Next, the customer will fill out the application and send it back via surface mail. Finally, the customer will get the actual SET software and digital certificate via snail mail for installation to their computer. If a user has a SET-enabled credit card, she will be able to get a SET account. There will doubtlessly be a few who are turned down; but their numbers should be tiny.

To use a SET account, the customer must have a SET-enabled browser. Microsoft and Netscape are already planning on including these in their next browsers. The same is true on your intranet's side: You must have SET-capable servers. This shouldn't be a problem. It's expected that most server companies will offer it as a free upgrade to existing servers.

One reason this will be so easy to implement on the server side is that your company never actually decrypts the number. All a SET-enhanced server will do is forward the SET information to the credit card's issuing bank. The bank, in turn, sends the information to MasterCard or Visa via these companies' own highly secured intranets. These systems will be set so that only participating banks, credit unions, and savings & loans can access these intranets. To make the actual payment, the credit card company approves or disapproves the sale, and the whole process starts up again in reverse.

One problem with this system has probably already occurred to you: It can be painfully slow. There's no answer for that. At a storefront, a credit card transaction takes about 20 seconds. Using SET, the same transaction will probably take about a minute. The companies behind SET expect that customers won't have a problem with that delay. I'm not so sure of that myself. If I were you, I'd have at least a support page on site that explains why such transactions can drag out.

From my point of view, this is a long, awkward, and frankly stupid process. It's based on the premise that users are frightened to death of sending financial information over the net even once. That's purely a matter of a bad rep, not technology. S-HTTP or SSL could handle the job nicely today. It's also a matter of the dinosaurs of finance not trusting online financial transactions. One reason we have the SET protocol is that deep in their hearts, all too many managers don't understand or accept that secure transaction protocols are already in place.

Technical excellence has nothing to do with marketplace success. In this case, it's taken this very slow, roundabout process of establishing SET to convince the financial giants to support online transactions. Because of this, we're all going to be using SET, when we could have been using Digital Cash, SSL, or several other methods more than a year ago.

If you want to know more about how SET works—and if I were you, I certainly would—the site to go to is Visa's SET page, `http://www.visa.com/cgi-bin/vee/sf/set /intro.html?2+0`. This page likes to wander about, so you may need to search for it. If that turns out to be the case, start with `http://www.visa.com` and move out from there.

The one thing that may slow SET down is acceptance by banks. It's not that banks don't want to take their percentage of an online sale. They're worried about competition— from Microsoft. Banks see a real possibility that software companies, especially the ever-grabby Microsoft, will move on to control the entire financial pipeline, leaving banks on the outside. Customer demand—not to mention the way that Microsoft has been rebuffed from such deals as trying to buy out Intuit, the makers of Quicken, today's most popular home finance package—should ease bankers' fears and SET's broad acceptance.

# Toward a Secure Future

What will this new wave of transactions mean for your company? Your intranet's connection to the Internet will become even more important. It's one thing to have your main means of getting advertising and support out to customers go down for a few hours a month. It's another thing entirely when the Web site itself becomes a major cash cow for the company.

Security, reliability, and speed are all going to become increasingly more important for your intranet's window on the world. This is even more of a reason to integrate Web and intranet projects into the company's mainstream. Even a year ago, many managers might have thought that both technological spinoffs from the Internet would play little part in their company. Your business can't afford to wear such blinders anymore.

With secure transactions almost in place, the intranet goes from being more than a LAN, more than a way of getting some information to customers, toward becoming the functional center of many businesses. Even companies that never thought they had anything to do with the Web will have to confront this business model transformation. This entire book revolves around the theme that intranets are going to make powerful and profound changes to your business. If you haven't been convinced yet, one look at SET should make you a believer.

## Creating the Interactive Web

## Lights, Servers, Action!

Once the Web was a relatively passive medium. When all was said and done, all you used to do on the Web was send and receive ASCII or binary files. Yes, CGI made it possible to fill in form information and do a little bit of animation; but while this was a step forward, it wasn't a big enough step to substantially change the Web.

It took the advent of Sun Microsystems' Java to make that step. Suddenly, developers could use this interpreted, object-oriented language to deliver actual working programs, or applets, over the Internet and your intranet. Java, although still wet behind the ears, became all the rage among Web publishers.

Microsoft, despite their recent ads, was slow to recognize the importance of the Internet. Eventually, Gates et. al. got a clue about the Internet and intranet's potential and popularity and announced the release of their ActiveX application programming interface—a product that simultaneously both competes with, and conceivably complements, Java.

HTML and PDF are all fine and dandy in their place; but when it comes to making interactive applications on the Web, they really can't cope. To make the Web really come alive and respond with more than just canned responses, you need to use one of the Web's leading interactive languages: Common Gateway Interface (CGI), Microsoft's ActiveX, or Sun's Java.

Each comes with its own advantages and disadvantages. There is no one-size-fits-all application language for the Web. That's a pity, because interactive applications are vital to making the Web more responsive both to intranet and Internet users. Worse still, interactivity is proving, unsurprisingly, to be very hard to manage.

Problems and all, your Web site needs to be responsive to user's demands. Users expect this from Web sites. If you fail to deliver this, your visitors won't be back again.

Unlike static Web sites, however, making interactive sites is a lot of work. Even with the best tools on the market, you'll need to hire actual programmers to create your pages, not just webmasters or weavers. There are a few simple things you can do with prebuilt code; and a webweaver with a knack for programming should be able to build a few simple CGI or JavaScript applications. Still, for seriously interactive Web sites, you're going to need serious programmers.

If you don't have this kind of talent onboard, you should consider outsourcing it to an ActiveX, CGI, or Java developer. It takes months for even good programmers to learn to produce high-quality interactive Web sites. Once they reach that skill level, though, unless you have lots of work for them to do, chances are they're going to walk with their extremely marketable skills. So it is that for most business intranets, finding someone outside the company to do the work for you is likely to be your best course of action.

What do I mean when I say interactivity, anyway? For all the buzz, it's really a very simple concept: An interactive Web application lets users input information and run a program. That's it.

# CGI

CGI is the oldest way of creating interactive applications. If you've used the Web at all, you've seen CGI in operation. CGI lies behind most user interactivity interfaces as data entry forms and image-maps.

With CGI, your server takes the information, whether it's a name and address or a coordinate on a map, and sends it along to a program either on your server or another network server. When the remote program produces the information, it delivers the appropriate information to the user. In CGI, this reply is almost in the form of a few statement within an HTML page.

Since CGI rides on top of HTTP and HTML, it is, to be honest, a kludge. CGI programs are usually kept in a special directory, normally called CGI-BIN. Servers recognize that the information kept in this directory are not documents, a Web server's usual fare, but are programs and must be treated differently.

CGI programs can be written in almost any computer language. Script languages, which work with the operating system itself rather than at a lower level of the computer, are especially popular for writing CGI. Everyone's favorite language for this task is the Unix-based, but long since ported to almost every operating system in existence, PERL.

Unfortunately, using CGI is slow and using a script language, like PERL or VisualBasic, is slower. Since you can use faster, better languages like C for CGI work, or just link in an already assembled program to be faster still, CGI is an old mule trying to compete with thoroughbreds. While CGI-based programs do have a role to play on the Web, they're really too slow for all but the simplest tasks on a major Web site.

To make sure that your CGI programs work as efficiently as they can, I suggest that you visit the following sites. Some of them have ready-to-go CGI programs for some of the more common Web jobs, while others will teach you the ins and outs of CGI. Enjoy.

**Table 22.1: CGI Essentials**

Name                                  Area Covered
URL

The cgi-lib.pl Home Page          Guide to popular PERL library-
**http://www.bio.cam.ac.uk/cgi-lib/**

CGI Programmer's Reference     CGI FAQ and link list
**http://www.best.com/~hedlund/cgi-faq/**

CGI Scripting in C                    Beginner's guide
**http://www.he.net/~searsbe/ScriptingInC.html**

CGIWrap                                 Guide to a secure version of CGI
**http://wwwcgi.umr.edu/~cgiwrap/**

Common Gateway Interface      CGI Programming
**http://hoohoo.ncsa.uiuc.edu/cgi/**

Matt's Script Archive               Useful set of CGI/PERL scripts
**http://worldwidemart.com/scripts/**

Selena Sol's CGI Archive          Best CGI collection
**http://www.eff.org/~erict/Scripts/**

Web Engineer's Toolbox            Canned CGI PERL scripts
**http://www59.metronet.com/cgi/**

# ActiveX

ActiveX may hold the future of the net. Today, ActiveX is little more than "veneerware"—software that looks good in demos but has little substance behind it. Nonetheless, ActiveX must be taken seriously. ActiveX began life as object linking and embedding (OLE) custom controls, or OCXs. Now, Microsoft has rechristened them as a standard for linking Component Object Model (COM) objects across the Internet. So far, despite the hype, it's just a repackaging of what the product already was.

Beginning with Internet Explorer 3.0, Microsoft's Web browser, and Internet Information Server 2.0, Microsoft's Web server, ActiveX will be used to provide a common, distributed object-oriented way of transferring active data from one site to another. ActiveX's API will, of course, also be used to make other BackOffice products capable of running data updates and programs across the Internet.

ActiveX, although it's being bundled with software programs, isn't designed to be an application add-on. Its real purpose is to exist within the operating system and to arrange things such that, for all intents and purposes, both remote and local programs appear as if they're local within your system. That dream, however, is far away. At the earliest, ActiveX won't be appearing in operating systems until the Cairo version of NT appears, and that's at least one generation away from today's NT 4.0.

When it does reach that advanced form, one of ActiveX's problems is that it will be, at least to start with, specific to the Microsoft operating system. Even then, to get an ActiveX application to work, you'll need different ActiveX controls for each Microsoft operating system.

**Table 22.2: Getting Active with ActiveX**

| Name | Note |
| --- | --- |
| URL | |
| | |
| ActiveX Developer Support | It's in Japan, but it's worth the trip |
| **http://activex.adsp.or.jp/** | |
| | |
| Microsoft Site Builder | Microsoft's ActiveX information |
| **http://www.microsoft.com/activex/** | |
| | |
| ZD Net's ActiveXfiles | Best collection of ActiveX files |
| **http://www.zdnet.com/activexfiles/** | |

These days, ActiveX is nowhere near as universal a solution for Web interactivity as CGI or Java. If you want to reach the widest array of people with your interactive programs, which you should, ActiveX is not the software for you. With these problems, even an intranet based entirely on Microsoft products might want to take their time about using ActiveX for interactive applications.

If you take out the word "Internet," all of this will sound very familiar to the object-oriented community. As Chris Stone, president of the Object Management Group (OMG) (Framingham, MA) put it: "With ActiveX, nothing has changed except the name: It's still COM and OLE." OMG's own Common Object Request Broker Architecture (CORBA) and its Object Request Brokers (ORBs) are the multi-platform equivalent of Microsoft's COM and ActiveX. Unlike ActiveX, however, ORBs are already alive and well in such systems as DEC's ObjectBroker, Hewlett-

Packard's ORB+, and IBM's System Object Model (SOM). Beyond this are such open desktop information systems as Apple and IBM's OpenDoc. Stone sees ActiveX integrating with CORBA, but he shrugs: "OMG's job is to create fully distributed, platform-independent objects. Microsoft's ActiveX will do neither."

CORBA standard applications will soon be appearing on the Internet. SunSoft and OMG have come up with a standard for Java applets to connect with CORBA applications: Java Objects Everywhere (JOE). Java applets that can work with a CORBA object request broker, called ORBlets, will be compiled with the OMG's Interface Definition Language compiler. SunSoft, Postmodern Computing, and Iona Technologies are all working on such compilers.

# Java

With CORBA, the support of many companies, and a host of developers frantically working on it, Java is moving from being an overly complex toy language to becoming a major tool in the Web page developers' toolbox. But when I say complex, I do mean complex. As Ryan Scott, Web developer for NetCreations (Brooklyn, NY), says, with tongue only slightly in cheek, "Until recently, Java's learning curve was not for humans."

That's not far from the truth. Java looks more like C++, an extremely powerful but obtuse language, than such user-friendly languages as Pascal or VisualBasic. However, products like Symantec's Café, **http://cafe.syman-tec.com/**, Borland's Delphi for the Internet **http://www.borland.com/internet/**, and JavaScript **http://home.netscape.com/eng/mozilla/2.0/hand-**

**book/javascript/index.html** are making Java much more accessible. JavaScript, for instance, is a simple programming language that writes real Java code.

Still, no matter how well you program in Java, the language is slug-slow due to its interpreted nature. The very nature of the language requires that you send broad definitions for each object, Java's classes, for each Java application. This makes sending and receiving Java applets a major network load. The up side of this is that it also makes it possible to run any Java applets on any platform. If you want to reach the broadest possible audience, and you want to break the chains of CGI, Java's your only decent choice.

**Table 22.3: Java Helper**

| Title URL | Note |
| --- | --- |
| Digital Espresso<br>**http://www.io.org/~mentor/jnIndex.html** | Excellent Java newsletter |
| Gamelan<br>**http://www-b.gamelan.com/index.shtml** | The be-all and end-all of Java links |
| JavaScript Authoring Guide<br>**http://home.netscape.com/eng/mozilla/2.0/handbook/javascript/index.html** | JavaScript's essential guide |
| JavaScript FAQ<br>**http://www.freqgrafx.com/411/jsfaq.html** | The title says it all |
| JavaWorld<br>**http://www.javaworld.com** | The Java pros' brewing magazine |

Java has other problems. Besides its speed troubles, many Internet security authorities have become very wary of Java's security holes. In fact, one group, the NASA Automated System Incident Response team (NASRIC) <http://nasirc.nasa.gov/NASIRC_home.html>, has stated that by its very nature, Java is insecure. NASRIC has a point. Every time you run a Java or ActiveX program off of a foreign Web site, you have no idea what you may be letting loose in your system. There may be a cure for this one day, but that day isn't today.

# Interactive Futures

In the long run, Java supporters believe that CORBA's use of proxies and other security features will make JOE applets safe. Microsoft, of course, believes that its security measures will also make ActiveX safe for all users. In any case, for now, Java and JOE are the only real interactive, distributed object Web languages, security risks and all. ActiveX will soon be catching up with them; but it's an open question as to whether ActiveX, despite Microsoft's backing, has a chance of making any real impact on the Web.

# Two Generations Short of a Revolution: Web DBMSs

## Commander Data

Information is the new gold standard. Precious metals and gems are all well and good; but true wealth and power belongs to those who control information access.

At first glance, the Web appears to be a field of informational diamonds ready to be grabbed up. Until recently, though, most people who dug in just wound up with a handful of dirt. Finding information on the Web was a nasty, brutish, and never short job. Putting information on the Web was just as obnoxious a task.

Today, though, we're in an information revolution. Thanks to the amazing jump in database management system (DBMS) and Web server interoperability, placing and finding information gems online is easier than ever.

Don't believe me? Visit Alta Vista `http://www.altavista.digital.com/` or Open Text `http://www.opentext.com/omw/fomw.html` to see how home-brewed DBMS systems have made the Web's wealth usable. And, if you want to see the unmanageable managed, look at what DejaNews `http://dejanews.dejanews.com/` or Excite Netsearch `http://www.excite.com/query.html` does with the no-man's-land of Usenet newsgroups.

If want more than information about the net from the net, there are programs for you, too. Want to find your customer's new phone number? Try Switchboard `http://www.switchboard.com/`, a searchable database of more than 90 million Americans, both individuals and businesses. Got his number? Good; now make sure that your Federal Express `http://www.fedex.com` package is scheduled to arrive there at the right time. Need a place to stay in the next town on your itinerary? Check in at HotelChoice 2001 `http://www.hotelchoice.com/`. While you're away, you can keep track of your investments with Lombard Institutional Brokerage's real-time trading and research programs `http://www.lombard.com`.

Things are only getting better. Any day now—probably by the time you're reading this— you'll be able to get your Social Security, `http://www.ssa.gov` Personal Earnings and Benefit Estimate Statement (PEBES) online. Fannie Mae, `http://www.fanniemae.com/`, the US' largest home mortgage service, is working on a service that will let you submit a mortgage application online and get a loan approval in—believe it or not—an hour. This isn't science fiction, folks; these are plans for fiscal year 1996.

## DBMSs With Web Solutions

— askSam 3.0, which claims to offer the largest variety of searches of any database program, is a frontrunner in the DBMS-to-the-Web race. AskSam has long had a reputation as being among the best freetext database search engines in the DOS/Windows world. You can see how it rates in the Web world by downloading a free demo copy at askSam Systems' home page: `http://www.askSam.com/`.

— Shhh... It's a secret, but not much of one, that Borland, `http://www.borland.com/Product/Lang`, will soon be enabling their Delphi visual programming environment for making the DBMS to Web connection. Delphi's a pleasure to work with; and with tens of thousands of Delphi programmers out there, this release should kick the DBMS migration to the Web into high gear.

— Claris Corporation's classic FileMaker Pro 3.0, `http://www.claris.com`,—soon available for Windows 3.1 in addition to its current Win95, Windows NT, and Macintosh versions—can now be put on the Web with AppleScript. In other words, it's only a Web solution for Macintosh houses.

— Informix Software, Inc., `http://www.informix.com/ informix/dweb/grail/solution.htm,` provides links not only to its own free interface kits for current customers, but also to such commercial solutions as Silicon Graphics' WebFORCE product family, Netscape's Netscape Application Platform, `http://home.netscape.com/comprod/netscape_products.html`, and freeware products for SQL, CISAM, and PERL developers. It's no wonder that the URL of this wealth of solutions contains the word "grail"!

— Microrim, Inc. rises to the challenge with R:WEB 1.0. You can learn all about it at the product's information page: **http://www.microrim.com/RBASE_Products/Software/RWe b_Features.html**. Want to know more? Then trek boldly back to the company's home page http://www.microrim.com/ for more data.

— Oracle7 database management system meets the Web in Oracle System's Oracle WebServer 2.0, **http://www.oracle.com/prod-ucts/**. Details about the company's latest release, the Oracle Universal Server, were not available when this book went to press; but the details should be there by now. The system is said to use Oracle7 release 7.3 and will support nearly a dozen platforms from RS/6000s running AIX to SPARCstations with Solaris.

— Powersoft's, **http://www.powersoft.com/**, Powerbuilder is an application-building program for the '90s. Powerbuilder 5.0 is one of the first applications that makes it possible to use Microsoft's ActiveX in Internet-to-DBMS applications. Is that a good idea? Well, if you have Microsoft pro programmers, yes, it is.

— To check out Sybase's web.works, head over to **http://www. sybase.com/Offerings/webworks.html**. If you like what you read, you can download the beta3 version for Solaris 2.4/2.5 and Silicon Graphics IRIX 5.3. Windows NT users and others will have to wait for a later release.

Now, some of you may be thinking that this is old-hat. In a way, you're right: Most of the above tasks have been accomplished with online systems before. What's new and different is that these tasks are now done by automatic DBMS systems that require thousands of man-hours less per year to maintain than larger human sales staffs do.

Still not impressed? Consider that we're only seeing the tip of the iceberg. Soon, you'll be able to make Web pages that provide each customer who comes into your Web shop with their own custom-tailored view of your company. Within the year, you'll be able to make your legacy database available to anyone in the company with a Web browser.

# DBMS + Web = Success

Let's examine exactly why connecting your business' data to the Web makes sense. Until now, most companies scrambling onto the Web have seen it as just a hot new advertising platform. Some of the more daring have also added sales and technical support to their Web sites. Those uses are fine; but with DBMS integration, your enterprise's horizons really begin to open up.

Whenever a customer—or one of your own people—needs to track an invoice, an up-to-the-minute price quote, or an item's availability, they can access this information much quicker with the Web. In the past, every DBMS came with its own front-end or with a crowd of third-party front-ends. Even within your own firm, supporting these could be a real headache; and you certainly couldn't expect customers to have the software and networking required to get to your DBMS. The Internet and the Web have trashed this old model. Now, anyone who you want to access your data can do so with a Web browser.

The raw advantages for any company are clear. You can cut costs by reducing support staffs. After all, if your customer can see that her order is now in shipping, she doesn't need to talk to someone on an 800 line to get the same information.

From a strategic point of view, adding DBMS access to your Web site gives you a major sales point over your competition. Companies that rush to make detailed information available to the public will gain customers sooner than companies whose sites offer only advertising.

DBMSs also enable you to create Web pages on the fly for individual users. A properly programmed combination of DBMS and Web server can use the information it has about any particular caller to generate individualized Web pages. Say, for example, you have a customer who uses only one of your products. If you've got the right setup, every time he accesses your site, he'll find all the latest and greatest on his product right away. This is the kind of personal service that keeps customers coming back for more, and more, and more.

Another plus is that the user training curve is lowered. Once someone has learned to use a Web browser, they're at least three-quarters of the way to knowing how to access your data. From the development side, you're likely to spend as much money as ever on connecting your databases to the Web as you do hooking them up with a proprietary front-end; but the other advantages more than make up for this.

## Making the Connection

When you decide to link the Web and corporate DBMSs, you're immediately faced with several choices. The first of these is which approach you're going to use. At this time, there are four main ways to make the connection: Rollyour-own coding; a Web server that supports a major DBMS or DBMS data transfer protocol; a DBMS with Web support; or a middleware program that stands as translator between the Web server and the DBMS server.

To date, the most popular and successful approach has been coded from the ground up. Well-known search engines like Alta Vista, which uses the C programming language, and Lycos, **http://www.lycos.com** which is written in PERL and C, were programmed the old-fashioned way—by hand. While the resulting DBMSs are very fast, they were also very labor-intensive to build.

These solutions also must use a scripting language, like PERL, to enable the Web's programming interface—the Common Gateway Interface (CGI)—to communicate with the DBMS servers. This bridging stage is inherently slower than either of the servers, and can be a real performance bottleneck.

Finally, if past DBMS programming experience holds true, such DBMSs will be very time-consuming and expensive to maintain. Unless your company is already in the programming business, steer clear of this path.

All the server businesses that dream of ruling the Web are investing in servers that also directly support DBMSs. The big names here are familiar to anyone who uses the Internet: IBM's Internet Connection Secure Server (ICSS) **http://www.raleigh.ibm.com/iss/iss over.html**; Microsoft's **http://www.microsoft .com/INFOSERV/** Internet Information Server (IIS); and Netscape's **http://home.netscape.com/comprod/ server_central/product/livewire/index.html** LiveWire Pro. Respectively, these servers support IBM's DB2, Microsoft's SQL Server, and Informix Software's `http://www. informix.com` DBMS line. LiveWire Pro, which is actually an add-on product to Netscape's servers, also comes with native support for Oracle, Sybase, Illustra, and DBMSs that support the Open Database Connectivity (ODBC) protocol.

With the IBM and Microsoft server solutions, you're committing yourself to each company's proprietary operating systems—AIX and OS/2 for IBM, and NT for Microsoft—as well as to a particular DBMS. While both products also support database standards—IBM supports the Object Management Group's `http://www.omg.org` Common Object Request Broker Architecture (CORBA) and Microsoft stands behind ODBC—each company would prefer that you use their DBMS.

Netscape, while it has the fullest support for Informix, offers a more flexible approach. If you're not ready to commit to one set of systems, or you have legacy systems in one of the Netscape-supported DBMSs, a Netscape server might be just what the CEO ordered.

## DBMS With a Web Punch

Many of the most popular DBMSs that run best on minicomputers or mainframes, such as Oracle, Sybase, and Informix, are now supplying their own answers to Web connectivity. No matter the product, the answer almost always takes two forms.

The first, which I'll call type 1, is simply an additional product or DBMS enhancement that enables DBMS programmers to connect the DBMS to the Web by entering Structured Query Language (SQL)—or another DBMS query language—and PERL statements in HTML code. A good example of this kind of program is Sybase's web.sql **http://www.newmedia.sybase.com/Offerings/Websql/regi.html.**

These programs are stopgap packages that make it easier to build CGI DBMS applications. As such, they'll be useful if you already have a team of good DBMS programmers and HTML webweavers. This kind of solution doesn't take up time and resources the way programming from scratch does, but it's not easy, either.

All the major DBMS companies are also working on programs or enhancements to their existing DBMSs that will enable DBMS programmers to use either the DBMS' native language or Microsoft's ActiveX and/or Sun's Java to make applications that both are easy to program and run quickly. Some of these development tools even go so far that they instantly generate HTML pages from DBMS programs. For simplicity's sake, let's call these type 2 programs.

By the time you read this, any DBMS company worth its salt will have at least one type 1 product on the market. The biggest names will have type 2 products as well. As time goes on, most big-time DBMS vendors will move on to exclusively type 2 solutions.

Some smaller firms, more nimble than their larger cousins, have already released type 2 products. O2 Technology **http://www.o2tech.com/,** for example, has a complete set of Web-oriented, Object Database Management Group (ODMG) **http://www.odmg.org/** compliant DBMS and development tools.

Web-enabled DBMSs that are more suited to a workgroup or a single, tightly focused application are also currently available. Some of the more notable include askSam's

Systems' askSam 3.0, Claris Corporation's FileMaker Pro 3.0, Microrim's R:WEB 1.0, and Microsoft Access.

Like their bigger brothers, these companies are, for the most part, shipping type 1 products. Microsoft, for instance, with its Internet Assistant for Microsoft Access for Windows95 **http://www.microsoft.com/msaccess /it_acc.htm**, enables Access programmers to create HTML documents that link to Access DBMSs. In the future, these DBMS products will also come with type 2 Web enhancements.

Some companies, such as Microrim **http://www. microrim.com/RBASE_Products/Software/index. html** with R:WEB, are already there. R:WEB runs on any Windows NT compatible Web server and automatically converts R:BASE forms into Web pages without any CGI, HTML, or PERL programming. Besides R:BASE, you can use R:WEB with any other ODBC-complaint DBMS. Solutions like these are ideal for companies that have plenty of DBMS programmers and a paucity of web-weavers.

## DBMSs for the Web Generation

A few companies are now creating DBMSs that are born to Web. Whether these DBMSs will ever overcome the inertia of the terabytes of data already locked in older DBMSs is an open question. What is clear, though, is that if you don't already have a lot invested in another DBMS technology, and making your data Web accessible is a primary concern, then you should check these DBMSs out first.

Behind Illustria's dashingly named Web DataBlade **http://www.illustra.com** lies an interesting combination of object-oriented and relational DBMS (RDBMS), the Illustria Server. Since this DBMS will in theory be able to handle the graphics and audio so near and dear to Web lovers' hearts with the meticulousness of RDBMSs, this is a DBMS that deserves attention from anyone who wants a Web-oriented DBMS solution.

By itself, Illustria Server can't do the job; but when you add the Web DataBlade module, things get interesting. DataBlade dynamically creates HTML pages from preset SQL modules. Combine this with the ability of programmers to do global search and replace across both your Web site and your databases, and you get one really fast and flexible Web page generator.

Purity Software's, `http://www.purity.com/`, SuperNova DBMS is built from the ground up for online users. Unfortunately, while SuperNova will be very useful for Mac-based intranet creators, it won't be that useful to Internet developers. This is because SuperNova relies on Apple Events for its communications model. This is great when you can count on your people working with AppleTalk, but it makes the product less than useful for dealing with the wild and woolly Internet.

# Middle Ground: Middleware

DBMS developers have long known about middleware software. These are programs that help create attractive front-ends or more effective search engines for often recalcitrant DBMS engines. The Web's advent has opened up new opportunities for middleware vendors. Some of the most advanced tools for connecting Web pages and DBMSs are coming from these companies. Yes, you'll have to pay for these programs in addition to your DBMS; but if your DBMS makes connecting to the Web a chore, they'll more than pay for themselves with improved programmer performance. Let's look at some of the best of these packages.

Allaire's **http://www.allaire.com/** Cold Fusion is a Windows NT and '95 program that enables developers to build applications by combining HTML with templates of stored SQL commands. Cold Fusion allows you to quickly create data entry forms and dynamic Web pages. Maximizing Cold Fusion's power output, however, requires that your developers know their way around both HTML and SQL.

Besides SuperNova, Purity Software has a product, WebSiphon, for helping Macintosh developers working with untamed DBMSs. WebSiphon consists of a CGI application that lets you create dynamic CGI programs from templates for any ASCII-command addressable DBMS. As such, WebSiphon doesn't aspire to much; but if you need its services, you'll really need a copy badly.

Nomad Development's, **http://www.ndev.com**, WebDBC is much more ambitious. WebDBC does essentially the same job as WebSiphon but it uses wizards, automated production routines, to produce SQL-enabled CGI programs. Where Nomad parts company with WebSiphon is that instead of just producing generic CGI code, WebDBC can be set to produce Microsoft/Process' ISAPI, Netscape's NSAPI, or Spry's BGI code. What that means is that if you're using a server that's compatible with one of those standards, like Microsoft's IIS or Netscape's FastTrack server, you'll see DBMS additions and inquiries handled at least twice as fast as they would be on another platform. In a word, vroommm!

Fast as WebDBC is, it can't compete with Corel's **http://www.corel.ca/webdata/** CorelWeb.Data in features. This Windows NT/'95 product also generates CGI code. While its code can't take advantage of the faster APIs, it can work with far more databases. Besides working with ODBC-compliant DBMSs, Web.Data cam use data held in Microsoft Excel spreadsheets and FoxPro databases, Borland's dBase and Paradox DBMSs, fixed length ASCII files, and even Lotus 1-2-3 spreadsheets.

Web.Data can also be set to display its information using Netscape, Internet Explorer, or HTML 3.0 extensions to make the most attractive possible presentations of your data. Web.Data can also work as a CGI server application which gives it a real kick in the pants when it comes to speed. It's still not in WebDBC's class, but its additional options will make it a more attractive option to many webmasters.

The most fascinating add-on technology to the Web-DBMS connection comes from NeXT Computing **http://www.next.com/WebObjects/** with its WebObjects. WebObjects uses NeXT's tried and true object model to bridge the gap between almost any DBMS and any Web server. WebObjects isn't so much of a tool, or even toolset, as much as a development environment. In this environment, you can create or use NeXT-supplied objects that come ready to work with your legacy data.

Unfortunately, WebObjects manages its connection to the Web via CGI; so WebObject applets aren't going to be the fastest data spiders in the Web. On the other hand, this disadvantage may not be that sticky when you consider that WebObjects are extraordinarily easy for programmers to work with. If I had to get a Web DBMS project up and running tomorrow, WebObjects would be my first middleware choice.

# The Care and Feeding of Web DBMSs

Any DBMS attached to the Web will require the usual upkeep that any DBMS needs. You really shouldn't see any increase in your DBMS maintenance costs. That is, if you take the sensible step of making sure that any publicly available DBMS is accessible only on a firewalled system. Putting your firm's DBMS onto the net without this elementary security precaution is just begging to get burned by some bored cracker.

How should you handle your data, then? Well, it depends on your requirements. If you need visitors to get absolutely current data, you can simply set the firewall (easier said than done) to have them pass only authorized information requests through the firewall to the DBMS. The minor problem with this is that there's still a chance that a very clever cracker could slide into your data. The major problem is that your network traffic will increase, your DBMS server load will go up, and you may end up in a situation where your own internal DBMS performance goes to the dogs. This is, shall we say, not an ideal situation.

A path that's safer in every way, but is likely to cost you in response time to the outside world, is to enable your DBMS' real-time data replication to keep copies of the databases on the firewall system. You'll again see an increase in network traffic and server load, but it shouldn't be anything like the increase you'd see with a direct DBMS connection to the Web.

If keeping your data up to the moment isn't an issue, you can always fall back on that old database standby of refreshing the Web site's data on a periodic basis. This way, your data is safe, and no one inside your LAN is going to be complaining that they've come back from their coffee break and they still haven't gotten their report.

Somewhere in the middle? Well, to get seriously technical for a moment, the Web's HTT is a stateless protocol. No, that doesn't mean it's from Canada; it means that except for the moment the data transfer is occurring, there's no connection between a Web browser and server. What that means in English is that when data changes on your server, there's no way within HTTP of letting the browser know that it's working with out-of-date information.

There are ways around this. For example, any competently constructed online Web sales system won't let you sell an out-of-stock item. For the most part, though, your users aren't always going to get your most current information, anyway. Just include this fact in your plans, and you can live very happily with a Web DBMS that doesn't wear your system down and still gets reasonably timely information into everyone's hands.

# Where Are We Going To?

I have looked into the future of the Web, and lo, I have seen DBMSs. Last year, the question—which wasn't much of a question—was whether your business should be on the Web. The answer was yes. This year, it's, should I use my DBMS on the Web? Again, the answer is an unqualified yes. Yesterday's Web sites were static; tomorrow's sites will be dynamic.

The tools are still being made, and there aren't any Web DBMS experts yet; but even so, the advantages of being able to put fresh, customized Web pages in front of every user are crystal clear. The future of the Web belongs to those who most quickly and successfully integrate DBMSs into their plans. It's that simple.

## 10 Top Database Web Sites

Tomorrow is already here on some sites. Here's what some people have already done with the tools that are already available.

1. The Open Text Index, `http://www.opentext.com/omw/f_omw.html`, can search its vast database at top speeds, handling both HTML and SGML. While its database is not as large as Alta Vista's DBMS, it's expected to grow enormously. Open Text's software is also used by Yahoo!, internetMCI, and IBM's infoMarket Search Service.

2. The Alta Vista, `http://www.altavista.digital.com/`, search engine is the result of a research project at Digital, Inc.'s Research Laboratories in Palo Alto, California. The software, written in C under Digital Unix, is combined with databases on machines ranging from a DEC 3000/900 Alpha Workstation to an Alpha Server with 6 gigabytes of memory to provide the most up-to-date and fastest Web search engine around.

3. InfoSeek, `http://www2.infoseek.com/Query`, was developed using the Python DBMS. This hunter provides access to a number of news and business databases which can't be reached by other Web search engines. Users can get even further access to these databases by subscribing to InfoSeek on a monthly basis.

4. DejaNews, `http://www.dejanews.com/`, another special-interest search engine, is the Usenet news finder par excellence. Its database connects to over 50 gigabytes of searchable data, now including

the alt.*, soc.*, and talk.* newsgroups, excluding binaries. If it's on Usenet, you can find it with DejaNews.

5. Delivering over 11 million packages a day, the United Parcel Service, `http://www.ups.com`, relies heavily upon its database to keep track of everything—some 9800 gigabytes of storage. Users can schedule and track deliveries through the company's Web site.

6. At Coldwell Banker Online, `http://www.coldwellbanker.com/`, you can click your way to your new home on an ever-more-detailed image map, from the whole United States to individual counties. Buying, selling, and financing advice are also available at the site, as is a yearly comparison guide for home prices across the country.

7. AskERIC, `http://ericir.syr.edu/About/`, acts as a front-end to both the federally-funded Education Resources Information Center database and the SunSITE, or Sun Information and Technology Exchange. Like an online librarian, AskERIC sifts through the vast amounts of data to help you find the papers you need...and there's always the AskERIC Cow Gallery to keep things mooving.

8. Among the various options offered at Microsoft Support Online, `http://198.105.232.6:80/support/`, unquestionably the best one is the Microsoft Knowledge Base. This search engine enables you to access Microsoft's vast database on the spot instead of waiting in virtual queues.

9. Coordinate.com's Switchboard, `http://www.switchboard.com`, has gleaned the phone numbers of over 90 million individuals and 10 million businesses nationwide from phone books and other publicly available sources. Expansion of the listings to include Canada is under consideration.

10. At HiltonNet, `http://www.hilton.com`, you can expect a response to your e-mailed reservation request within two hours. A smiling concierge is on hand to guide you on a full-text search through

the subtly stylish pages of Hilton resorts, travel packages, bonus offers, and special attractions around the world.

# 24

# Getting It Together

## Groupware

Years after its creation, groupware continues to be misunderstood. Up until recently, the theory of computer supported cooperative work which was embodied in groupware remained unfamiliar to almost everyone. At long last, groupware's practical benefits are finally starting to gain recognition and support.

## Groupware's Point

So what is groupware for? Simply put, it enables many people to work together in groups on a given project. Making groupware work requires more than just buying and installing the software. It takes more than simply setting up your intranet to encourage interactivity. It requires a dedication to changing how your company works from the top down.

Groupware makes group work possible, but it's up to administration to support it—and I don't mean sending out a mission statement. Support means teaching everyone not only how to use the new tools, but how to make the new tools work for them. Intranets encourage this approach; but without the proper training, an intranet is no magic solution to your business woes.

You may not want to take the groupware approach. Groupware empowers workers; it moves a certain amount of decision-making power from the top of the hierarchy down to the workgroup level. Many companies are either too frozen in structure or too overwhelmed by the press of immediate work to make the changes needed to get the most out of groupware.

For businesses that are willing to take the plunge, though, groupware can mean a renaissance that leads to greater productivity both within and without the company. By choosing to go with an intranet, you've made this path easier. It's up to you and your executives to decide whether the cost in training and transformation is worth the potential benefits. I think it is, but it's your call. Remember, though, even if you decide to try another path, using an intranet means that the door remains open for groupware. If not today, then maybe tomorrow you'll find that groupware is right for you.

At the same time, many of the concepts originally included in groupware, such as e-mail, joint work projects, and easier access to data, are already part of the intranet model.

In 1991, Eric Sall, then director of product management for Lotus' Lotus Notes, **http://www.lotus.com/notes/**, the premier groupware product, said that groupware gives you "connectivity with not just everyone in your company, but also with vendors and customers. By working with teams that are blind to organizational boundaries and technology differences," there is a chance for greatly increased productivity—all true—and also all part of the intranet model.

Now, an intranet doesn't have to adopt any but the most basic groupware ideas. For example, everyone in the company should have e-mail. An intranet just makes the idea of cooperative work much more accessible without the use of expensive groupware programs.

Dedicated groupware software like Notes has always had inherent problems. Empowering workers requires more than software. It also requires that users have greater access to corporate data. Unfortunately, that information may be impossible to reach through incompatible hardware, network operating systems, or data formats. Of course, as we've seen in the last few chapters, one of an intranet's main selling points is overcoming these very problems.

For years, groupware developers have worked on integrating programs and data with custom code. The company intranet, by using established open standards, offers the promise of seamlessly uniting corporate data and software. Traditional groupware, on the other hand, has always had problems working and playing well with other products.

In the early days of groupware, most experts predicted that the winner of the groupware derby would be the product which was most successful at integrating with existing databases and e-mail systems. By that standard, the winner is already here. Its name is the Internet, along with the business intranets threaded along its length like pearls on a necklace.

## Table 23.1: Intranet Groupware

| Name<br>**URL** | Notes |
| --- | --- |
| Collabra Share<br>**http://www.collabra.com/** | Message-based and realtime conferencing |
| Internet Conference Pro<br>**http://www.vocaltec.com/conference/iconf_pro.htm** | Group work, whiteboard |
| WebBoard<br>**http://webboard.ora.com/** | Message-based conferencing |
| Proxima Podium<br>**http://xenon.proxima.com:80/podium/** | Whiteboard |
| Web Notes<br>**http://www.spyglass.com/products/webnotes/index.html** | Message-based conferencing |

So what can groupware programs do for you that normal intranet programs can't? There are basically two things. One is to enable numerous employees to work on a single project across the network. This one is slowly but surely being subsumed by application software. High-end word processors and desktop publishers, for example, make it possible for many people to write changes to a single document and simultaneously make it clear who's done what to the manuscript.

The other groupware function, which is not neatly duplicated by the mainstream of intranet computing, is meeting support software. However, this need is being addressed by a new generation of intranet-based programs.

Even if your company is married to Notes or Novell's GroupWise, `http://corp.novell.com/market/apr 96/mm000077.htm`, that doesn't mean that you need to choose either intranet or proprietary groupware tools. Slowly but surely, all the groupware vendors are redesigning their programs to work with an intranet. By the time you read this, there will be very few programs indeed that won't work with intranet-based LANs.

## Meet Me On The Net

Meetings—you can't live with 'em; you can't eat doughnuts without 'em. It might be easier to live with them using software that changes the way face-to-face and virtual meetings are conducted. Dubbed collaboration software, these packages—Collabra Software and WebGenesis—are designed to overcome the logistical and interpersonal hurdles that often get in the way of productive meetings.

The next big question is: Do you need to meet online? If your meetings are trouble-free and cost-free, the answer is no. If, on the other hand, you've found that face-to-face meetings are unproductive at best and dysfunctional at worst, or if it's impossible to get people together at the same place and time, then collaboration software can help.

And if record keeping is essential, these programs can also generate meeting minutes, putting an end to the constant questions of who said what or exactly what decision was reached.

Of course, much of what these programs do can be duplicated by online services and groupware products, such as Lotus Notes. For example, like Notes, the three meeting software packages here provide front ends to client/server database engines. Unlike such groupware or whiteboard programs, the focus of meeting support is not workflow and document management. Although it has some of these capabilities, this type of tool is meant for realtime, structured group discussions on specific topics. These programs introduce some unique features: realtime, organized message conferencing; the ability to take votes; an electronic facilitator who controls the agenda and the decision-making (or voting) process; and brainstorming tools that let all users post ideas to a shared display or window on the desktop. For example, Insitu's Internet Conference, `http://www.vocaltec.com/conference/iconf_per.htm`, enables groups to share electronic whiteboards and to surf the Web together.

Let's say you and a few colleagues are using Notes to debate the merit of a prospective employee. This "conversation" will appear as a document, with various responses embedded. What you can't do, and what meeting software allows you to do, is hold this conversation in real time, and then solicit votes on whether or not to hire the candidate. These programs provide a variety of voting tools. For example, you can rate ideas or goals on a 1-to-10 scale, a 1-to-5 scale, or by a simple yes or no.

In addition, groupware and other packages usually don't employ a formal facilitator. Without one, discussions tend to drift from the topic at hand; thus was coined the term, "topic drift." True, a Notes participant can send a message saying, "Hey, we're straying from the point here." But with meeting support software, an appointed facilitator can back up these words with actions. Collabra Share, for example, lets the moderator change a discussion category's name, description, and keywords to better reflect the thread's contents. All participants are notified of this via an onscreen message. Moderators have other powers, too. They can preset an alarm that will let all users know when it's time to wrap up, a feature that helps prevent meetings from running into overtime.

Other benefits to meeting software—in theory, at least—are that it allows attendees to think out loud together, and it encourages users to express opinions more freely because participants can remain anonymous. Of course, this has its pros and cons. On the positive side, it creates a forum in which an idea tends to be taken on its own merit, and its acceptance is not influenced by the status or presentation style of its proponent. Also, formerly reticent attendees may be less intimidated and more inclined to share their thoughts. But anonymity has its down side, too. It can open the door to inappropriate comments, as some users become emboldened by being faceless (check out the conferences on most any online forum if you doubt this). Furthermore, it's highly likely that users' identities will be conveyed by the messages they enter, as individual communications styles are not always easily suppressed.

Meeting programs are no panacea. Making the best use of these tools typically requires training and an all-the-way commitment. When you buy an electronic meeting program, you're not just buying software, you're buying a new way to do business.

Cost is also a major concern. Intranet or no, these programs usually come with hefty price tags. Still, if you're already spending thousands on bringing employees to meetings, the cost of meeting software doesn't look so bad. Of course, if you're willing to work with more primitive tools that were never meant for meeting support but can be faked into it, then you won't have to spend much money at all.

## Meeting Online Without Meeting Software

Before meeting software was a gleam in some business management professor's eye, the Internet, online services, and bulletin board services (BBSs) were making it possible to exchange messages on subjects near and dear to their hearts. Indeed, if it wasn't for their example of how easy it can be to carry on virtual conversations, meeting software might never have been developed. In fact, all three long ago conquered the toughest part of the equation. First, messages must be bundled together in response order rather than chronological order. Message threads presented only by time of entry tend to confuse an issue rather than shedding light on it.

A few programs still opt for the machine-easy, user-hard approach of using only chronological order within topic folders. For reasons beyond my comprehension, *The Washington Post*, **http://www.washingtonpost.com**, uses such a system. Avoid these interfaces: They never had much charm to begin with; and there's no reason to put up with them now that you have more choices. Other programs, even old, purely character-based interfaces like Unix's rn and trn, thread messages on the fly when you open a newsgroup.

Why not use such services for meetings, then? Well, some companies do. Many businesses maintain customer support and feedback facilities via Usenet newsgroups. While public newsgroups quickly become unmanageable, a closed newsgroup—one that only your customers or employees may join—is a great method for not only distributing technical support but making decisions as well. Realtime chat, using protocols like Internet Relay Chat (IRC), can also be used for realtime conferencing.

When you get right down to it, there's not much technological difference between Usenet newsgroups, IRC, and conferencing software. Of course, with the older alternatives, you don't get any of the extras and chrome; but for the basic job of trading information, it's hard to beat newsgroups or IRC.

Of course, IRC-type models are harder to manage than newsgroups. While IRC lets everyone talk, there's little structure to IRC conversations. Although you can dedicate an individual "channel" to a particular topic, with no way of formatting everyone's messages, online meetings rapidly disintegrate into chaos.

Meeting software avoids this by providing very rigid strictures for realtime messages. For example, when you're brainstorming, your ideas will appear to others as either a single line or a subject heading in a list of new ideas. Responses to your idea will be posted beneath it so that everyone can follow the train of thoughts attached to a particular idea.

# Meeting Adjourned

Why spend so much time on conferencing software? Take some time to think it over. I believe that if you do, you'll realize that while some aspects of groupware may be over-rated—group writing, for example, is something I've seen work smoothly about once a year—group conferencing is another matter entirely.

By freeing workers to stay at their desks and work, most people will be more productive. Message-based systems let you respond to non-critical items when you have the time to answer issues intelligently. Realtime systems enable you to address the Cambridge office's issues in minutes from your San Jose office instead of spending three days on a needless and costly transcontinental jaunt.

By using the intranet to replace not just paper mail and faxes but meetings as well, I truly believe we can revolu-tionize and revitalize the workplace. Even if this approach only works half as well as I think it can, it will save your company both time and money by cutting down on travel. For that reason alone, if nothing else, consider the group-ware intranet path. Both you and your corporation's bank account will be glad you did.

# 25

## 2000 and Beyond

### Looking Ahead

So where do we go from here? Pragmatically speaking, you're going to assemble a team to put your intranet together. What I'm doing in this chapter is looking down the road to see what's coming next.

First, let's forget about the nifty new programs and all that jazz and talk about real business issues. Once in place, your intranet is going to be more expensive to run than your old LAN. You can count on budgeting in a minimum of two new employees during its first year of operations: a webmaster and a webweaver.

Later on, finances will depend on how your system grows. If your public Web site is a great success, you may find yourself needing to rebuild the entire company around its Internet connectivity.

That's not likely, but it can happen. So keep your eyes open. For instance, if you find that your sales are beginning to jump from Web sales while telephone sales are remaining stable or even declining, you may want to think about shifting your emphasis to a Web sales orientation.

You also need to think about hiring specialists. Right now, if you want to use Java and the like, you're going to be paying big bucks for someone who understands Java, frames, and the art of getting DBMSs to talk to Web servers. Tomorrow, though, people with these skills are going to be a lot more common; and tools to make interesting, interactive Web pages are going to be widely available and much easier to use. In other words, right now it's a Web developer's market. It isn't going to stay that way for more than more than two years, tops.

For real talent, of course, you will always need to pay real money. Anyone can use a hammer, but only a master carpenter can use it to make a house that's also a work of art. Right now, though, we're all having to pay extra for anyone who knows which end of a hammer to hold. By 1999 at the latest, it will be a buyer's market; and run-of-the-mill webweavers will be a dime a dozen. Shortly after that, they'll be out of the job market, and the webweaving job scene will look a lot like today's desktop publishing market. That is to say, you'll be able to find decent talent at a decent price; while top-notch talent will get what they ask for, because they're worth it.

Webmasters, however, while they'll become far more common, will always cost your firm a pretty penny. I don't see any sign that networking is going to be settling down any time soon. Frame-Relay, Asynchronous Transfer (ATM), Asymmetric Digital Subscriber Line (ADSL), ISDN—who knows which will eventually win out as **the** way to connect your intranet to the Internet? And that's just the tip of the technology iceberg. No, webmasters and network administrators may become more common; but their jobs are going to be secure until well into the next century.

Enough of generalities. Let me focus my crystal ball in on the specifics and see what there is to see.

# The Future of the Web

The Web will continue to grow, and grow, and...well, you get the idea. For a time, the Web will grow so fast that it's going to outstrip the ability of the Internet to carry it. Within your intranet, data will still flow quickly, but data is going to flow as fast as a sludge in a sewer on the net at large for a while.

A large part of that problem will come from bandwidth intensive applications. Videoconferencing programs, fat Java applications—all of these are going to block the information flow. The ever-growing horde of new users will also play their role in slowing the system down.

The Web is also going to fragment. Now, with an advanced browser, you can go almost anywhere and make some sense of the site you arrive at. For a time, though, many sites will be completely unavailable due to their wholehearted embrace of non-standard technologies.

This period of diversity to the point of anarchy won't last for long. One way or another, standards will be established in hypertext, graphics, audio, and video. If I had to put money down, I'd say that Netscape HTML, GIF and JPEG, RealAudio and ShockWave will become the dominant technologies in their respective fields.

For interactive technologies, I can find enough good and bad in both Java and ActiveX to say that I don't know who the winner will be in the long run. In the short run, I know it's going to be Java. The question in my mind is whether Java will survive the security storms that lie in its future. As for databases, ODBC and SQL will rule. Both work well, both are close enough to being open standards as to make no never mind, and most DBMS already support them to one degree or another.

As for data transfer protocols, I think that HTTP and WebNFS will both survive. This is going to make creating servers and browsers that must support both a real pain for developers; but each has its own unique advantages. HTTP is clearly the best for true hypermedia; but when it comes to just shifting large amounts of data around in a hurry, WebNFS is already present on most TCP/IP networks, and it will be a force to be reckoned with on the Web.

You'll also see a Web with too many sites to even begin to track. Because of this, some truisms about the Web are going to be stood on their head. For example, anyone can indeed be on the Web, but the big companies who know how to work the Web are going to dominate Web popularity the same way they do in other media fields. Right now, and for the next year or two, small traditional businesses have a golden chance to catch up with their multi-million-dollar competitors by getting out there and getting known.

If you're a small business, though, you must seize the day. That means more than just putting up a site, it means maintaining a Web site that will constantly inform and entertain the buying public. If you wait a year or two before doing this, you'll have blown your chance. When Web sites number in the megamillions, no one is going to notice your site unless it's truly extraordinary (and you convince Web reviewers at major Web cataloging sites of this fact). It won't be easy.

Another problem that the Web, and any enterprise on the Web, is already facing is that the sheer size of the Web makes it difficult to search. You only think it's bad now. It's going to get worse, a lot worse. The Web search engines, like AltaVista, and catalogs like Yahoo, are getting better; but the catalogs are being completely overwhelmed. In the future, even the fast search engines are going to fall behind.

I'm not sure what the answer will be here. Part of the answer will be catalog sites that devote themselves to specific topics. Yahoo Computing!, **http://www.zdnet. com/yahoocomputing/**, for computing sites and AT&T Business Network, **http://www.bnet.att.com/**, for business sites already exist and they'll be followed up by others. Many companies are working on business yellow pages, but with the Web's growth, I don't see these sites being especially useful. In particular, I can't see them being useful for businesses. On paper, yellow pages work for businesses because you can place large, eye-catching ads. Yeah, you can do that on a Web-based yellow pages site; but who's going to stick around for your ad to download? Something will need to take the place of yellow pages, but the only thing I'm sure of is it that it won't be today's attempts to duplicate paper on bits and bytes.

Why bother, then? That's an easy one: The Web's audience is going to continue to grow. I'm no believer in Internet box computers that let people surf the Web for cheap. The problem with this technology is that a decent Internet device will cost almost as much as a real computer. Why get an Internet device when for two hundred dollars more you can get a real computer? What is going to happen, however, is that WebTV devices will make the family TV a source for Web viewing as well as TV viewing. Need I point out what this is going to do for the demographics of Web users? Didn't think so! The Web is where the buyers will be, and that's why you must be there as well.

## The Future of Browsers

For the next few years, browsers will continue to exist as increasingly feature-laden programs. Then, browsers will be completely absorbed by operating systems. In 2001, you won't buy Netscape Navigator or Internet Explorer, you'll buy SunOSNavigator or Windows Explorer 2000 to run your computer and browse the Web. Experts will be able to tell where the operating system ends and the browser begins, but users sure won't.

In short, Sun's old dream of the network becoming the computer will finally come true. Our operating systems, the networking operating system, and the common interface that binds them together will be merged together into a hybrid of operating system and Web browser. By 2005, when people talk about standalone browsers, it will be with the same nostalgia of talking about Apple IIs today.

# The Future of the Internet

The Internet will be the tie that binds the world together into one community. I'm not talking about warm feelings and the brotherhood of man, I'm talking about a fundamental shift in the way business transactions occur. Some businesses will move lock, stock, and barrel onto the Web. Today, we only talk about having a global economy. The Internet is going to accelerate that trend.

Most companies still have one central geographical location or headquarters. For businesses that buy in to the groupware paradigm, that won't be true any longer. Your firm may be incorporated in the Caymans, your products made in China and Mexico, your sales force at home with their own net connections, Marketing may be centered around San Francisco, but their "company" meeting office will be a nice little Chinese restaurant where they get together once a week. And your executives? Well, I've always liked the Virgin Islands myself.

That scenario won't happen everywhere, but there will be a tendency to decentralize and internationalize. That will put countries with high labor costs, like the United States, into even more hot water, because the Internet will encourage manufacturers to move to places with low labor costs. After all, with the Internet, your communication costs are going to plummet. In a world where doing business with Taipei doesn't have appreciably greater travel costs than working with Des Moines, global enterprise will bloom as never before.

Even for smaller businesses, breaking international business barriers will become more attractive. With the Web, you can find markets for your widgets in places you would never have dreamed of doing business.

Of course, it won't all be sweetness and roses. The net, as mentioned earlier, is going to have terrible cases of the slows at times. There are many who pooh-pooh these nightmare scenarios, claiming—accurately—that all the major Internet providers are increasing their bandwidth at an exponential rate. Why, yes, they are; but I predict that between demand and bandwidth-munching applications like videoconferencing and multimedia, we're going to need all that new bandwidth and more. Don't think so? Well, back in the early '80s, Bill Gates thought that no PC user would ever need more than 640K in their computer. Bill weathered that failure of imagination; but it took Microsoft more than 15 years to build an operating system that could deal properly with all those applications that required megabytes of memory.

There will also be some massive system failures on the Internet. Some of you are old enough to remember the great Northeast power outages of the early '60s. Others can remember when AT&T long distance service went haywire briefly in the '80s. The Internet also got bludgeoned one in the great Internet Worm caper, in which Robert Morris, Jr. managed to create a program that brought almost every SunOS-based server on the Internet—which was most Internet servers—to a grinding halt. It will happen again. Things fail. It's just that as we grow more dependent on the Internet, these failures are going to affect more and more of us in increasingly painful ways.

# The Future of the Intranet

That's one reason why you want your own secure intranet rather than a system that's connected transparently to the Internet. With security measures in effect, your public Web server may go down in an Internet systemwide failure; but internally, your company can keep humming right along.

By the year 2000, most businesses will have intranets up and running, and some proof against failures by the greater Internet. Most of your users will be working with a universal interface that makes reading the boss' memo on their machine, using the company DBMS to check the facts for their response to the boss, and then sending a reply to the quality assurance group, all part of a seamless whole. Besides making work faster, since you won't need to walk from one application to another, training costs will go down. Today, an office worker needs to know half-a-dozen applications to be the office computing wizard. Tomorrow, since everyone will need to know two or three applications, more people will be using their computers more efficiently and taking less time to reach that level of proficiency.

The tools will all have become fine-tuned to the point that, within the intranet, doing such things as videoconferencing group meetings will be as simple as writing e-mail is today. Companies that maximize the benefits of such tools will be quicker, more responsive to this brave new world than any business is today to the fluid business dynamic.

This may have two effects in your company. Some businesses will work at about the same rate due to what I call the dither factor. For example, word processing now makes creating documents faster than we could every make them with typewriters. However, are most companies actually more productive now? Not really. The reason is that now that we have the tools, many companies aren't using them to increase bottom-line productivity. Instead, they're using them to smooth their documents to near perfection. While you certainly don't want a misspelled word in your document, laying out a standard report in three columns with a color photo on each page doesn't really help your business worth a damn. It does mean that your people are still producing the same volume of work they were back when IBM Selectrics ruled the company. The better change is to take advantage of these tools to increase real productivity instead of encouraging pseudo-productivity. The intranet can bring a revolution to your workplace, if you have the courage to change the way your company does business. Just do it.

Another, similar change is that even now, the white-collar elite refuses to work with computers. The day for that sort of outlook is long since gone; and anyone who thinks like that is already holding your company back. Tomorrow, they won't simply be burdening your business, they'll be an anchor around your company's neck dragging it to its doom. Tomorrow, real business power will belong to those who can use the unparalleled communication and information abilities of the intranet. It's time to stop putting up with featherbedding executives and get rid of them. They've got their golden parachutes; so I wouldn't shed any tears for the executive who insists that a Web is just something a spider makes.

You may not, of course, be in a position to make those kind of changes. In that case, it's time to move on to a company where those changes can, or already have, taken effect. I can't predict what the business model of the Internet-connected world of the 21st century will look like. I do know that the 19th century bureaucracy that's already creaking its way to collapse is not going to survive in a world where speed and information rule. Sound unlikely? Take a long hard look at some of our older companies—even the ones that are doing well right now, like AT&T and IBM. Look at their business plans; look at how the right hand of most of the corporate giants often have no idea what the left hand is doing.

As a case in point, look at how IBM handles their OS/2 operating system for PCs. You can buy OS/2, but you can't buy an IBM PC with OS/2 on it. Instead these machines carry the operating system of their competitor, Microsoft. Sheer inertia keeps companies like IBM going, but the pace of business in the day of the intranet is going to start tearing them apart unless they can shift their business methods to address a changing world.

# To Tomorrow

Transformation, metamorphosis, evolution in action—the rise of the intranet is all this and more. You know the issues now; you know enough of the technical details to make informed decisions. Now, it's up to you. The new day is what you will make of it. Ignore the changes, and you'll have cause to regret it. Ride the winds of change, though, and you can take your business to new heights. Enjoy the trip. It will be a hell of a ride, but the rewards at the end will make the voyage more than worth the effort.

# Index

## Extensions

.arc, 195
.arj, 195
.com, 158
.gz, 195
.gzip, 195
.hqx, 195
.shar*, 195
.sit, 196
.tar, 196
.tar.Z, 196
.tar-z, 196
.taz, 196
.Z, 196
.zip, 196

## Numbers

10 top database Web sites, 396-398
100BaseT, 45
100BaseT4, 45
100BaseVG, 45
10Base2, 44
10Base5, 44
10BaseF, 44
10BaseT, 44
10Broad36, 45

2000 and beyond, 409-419
8-bit color, 68

## A

Acceptable Use Policies (AUPs), xviii
access rights, 311
across the gread divide: LAN to the Internet, 94-97
ActionWorkflow (http://www.actiontech.com), 312
active solutions, 55-58
ActiveX, 55-58, 259, 329, 373, 376-378
  sites list, 377
Adams' Scott, 113
adding TCP/IP, 30-31
address format (online services - table), 169
addresses
  domain, 158
  mixed-case, 158
addressing (RFC822 examples), 158-159
administration,
  headaches, 314-316
  network level, 312
administrator network tools, 137
Adobe Acrobat, 12
  Pro, 356-357

## O

## P